From GRANDMA'S KITCHEN

From GRANDMA'S KITCHEN

MORE THAN **100** YEARS OF HEIRLOOM COOKING AND BAKING RECIPES

Marilynn Brass & Sheila Brass

RODALE.

This exclusive direct mail edition, published by Rodale Inc. in 2014 with permission from Black Dog & Leventhal Publishers, New York, NY, includes text and photos from *Heirloom Baking with the Brass Sisters* and *Heirloom Cooking with the Brass Sisters*.

Text copyright © 2006 and 2008 by Marilynn Brass and Sheila Brass

Photographs © 2006 and 2008 by Andy Ryan

Printed in the United States of America

Rodale Inc. makes every effort to use acid-free ♾, recycled paper ♻.

Library of Congress Cataloging-in-Publication Data are on file with the publisher.

ISBN 978–1–62336–494–6

4   6   8   10   9   7   5   hardcover

We inspire and enable people to improve their lives and the world around them.
For more of our products, visit rodalestore.com or call 800–848–4735.

Contents

CHAPTER 5

Soup of the Day

CHAPTER 4

Side Dishes

CHAPTER 6

Staff of Life

CHAPTER 7

Home Plates

Preface

We are two roundish bespectacled women who have a combined total of 126 years of home cooking experience. We have always felt comfortable in the kitchen because we learned to cook at a very early age. Our mother, Dorothy, was an inspired home cook, and the meals she produced when we lived on Sea Foam Avenue, in Winthrop, Massachusetts, more than 60 years ago are still memorable.

When we could barely reach the kitchen table, we were already turning scraps of dough into miniature braided challah loaves and turnovers, lovingly brushed with an egg glaze to make them shiny. Working at the black cast-iron stove with its green enamel trim, we learned to ignore its idiosyncrasies to produce the soups and stews of our childhood, recipes we still make with pride today. We believe that there is nothing more comforting than the smell of a thick vegetable soup simmering on a back burner, a glistening brisket braising in the oven, or a dish of macaroni and cheese with its golden crust of buttery crumbs. We still relive the glories of the appetizers, vegetables, salads, and main dishes that came out of that sunny kitchen to become satisfying home-cooked meals. And we cherish the good times we had with our mother when she

Sheila, third grade, 1943; Marilynn, first grade, 1948

patiently instructed us, transferring her love of family and the art of baking to her two young daughters.

When we want to replicate these precious family recipes, we go to Mama's first cookbook, *All about Home Baking*, fragile now but priceless, with her handwritten recipes on the front and back pages. We couldn't have written *From Grandma's Kitchen* without consulting our manuscript cookbooks, those treasured notebooks of personal recipes compiled by home cooks. It is these living recipes, these notes handwritten on crumbling scraps of paper or the pages of old, well-worn cookbooks, that inspire us to interpret the lost recipes and family stories of others. We continue to find these recipe collections, gathered together in bundles or in small boxes at yard sales, in used bookstores, or on the pantry shelves of friends.

Our personal collection of manuscript cookbooks has grown to more than 150 over the years. Inheriting heirloom recipes is what we enjoy most—next to eating what we prepare. It is the excitement of the search and the thrill of discovering these treasures. It is the talking about, the chewing over, the digesting of an old recipe, whether it is passed down to us in oral or written form. It is the art of interpreting the recipe; preparing it; observing how it looks, tastes, and smells; and finally serving it that gives us such joy.

In this book, we give you the choice of planning and serving an entire heirloom meal or preparing a special heirloom dish or dessert from primary sources, the recipes handwritten by home cooks from all over the United States and Canada. You may recognize some of these recipes as similar to ones prepared by your own mothers, grandmothers, and aunts. The recipes we present are culturally diverse and tempting, from a German sauerbraten recipe from Ohio to a sophisticated liver paté from New York City. Discover Arline Ryan's Swedish Meatballs with Sour Cream Sauce from Indiana, Sweet Potato Pudding from North Carolina, Elinor's Shrimp Creole from Florida, and Danish Roast Goose Stuffed with Apples and Prunes and served with Red Cabbage and Caramelized Potatoes from Minnesota. Scottish baps appear as well as sweet-and-sour cabbage rolls and French-Canadian tortière. Mrs. Fredman's Coleslaw, from our childhood, is represented right along with Southern Icebox Pickles. For dessert we present a colorful choice of Red Velvet Cake, Green Tomato Pie, or a New England Blueberry Buckle, as well as other classic home-baked desserts.

We also pay tribute to the inexpensive vegetarian meals that utilized and celebrated the bounty of backyard gardens—those dumplings, frittatas, and pancakes that often served as main dishes in families that had more love in their kitchens than money in their purses.

From Grandma's Kitchen contains chapters on appetizers, soups, salads, vegetables, breads, and main dishes, as well as a multitude of pies, cakes, and cookies. We have interpreted these handwritten recipes so that you can reproduce them in your own home kitchen, and we've tried to simplify the ones that once took hours or days to put together. To do this, we've turned to the culinary tools of 21st-century America—the mixer, the food processor, and, occasionally, the microwave oven. Some recipes, such as those for bagels, have been scaled down and reinterpreted so that you will be able to prepare a home version of something that was usually produced in large quantities commercially. Not only have we kept it simple, we've also given you the freedom to adjust the seasonings, the size of the portions, and the cooking times. Please remember that the more exotic dishes, such as curries and patés, are interpretations of how an heirloom cook would have prepared these dishes in her own home kitchen. The recipes for roast goose and sauerbraten require more time to prepare and would have been served on special occasions.

What has influenced our appreciation of heirloom cooking the most has been the culinary journey we've taken across America. We've traveled through the South, the Midwest, and New England, meeting old friends and making new ones. It was a sentimental journey because these visits with home cooks all over America have reinforced our belief that every family has a story and a recipe to document its own personal history. Sometimes the stories are sad, sometimes they are funny, but all are touching.

For us, traveling across America was a movable feast. We shared chicken pot pie in St. Louis, and we ate pierogi and stuffed cabbage in Ann Arbor. We learned about a Danish-American boy from Minneapolis who, upon losing his mother when he was

Sheila and Marilynn, Winthrop Beach, 1944, and today

Handwritten recipe for Maple Syrup Cookies, 1930s, and Peach Bavarian, 1920s

15 years old, learned to cook the substantial meals needed to sustain his construction worker father. We were told of a young girl who, married at age 14 to a Russian Orthodox priest, fed her five children her delicious cheese and farina dumplings between entertaining the bishop and ironing the church linen. There was the sprightly white-haired woman in Philadelphia, with a no-nonsense haircut and merry blue eyes, who advised us to add brewed coffee to our soups and gravies to give them a richer color. Later, we found the same advice in a Southern cookbook from the 1870s.

These encounters were precious, but the message was always the same. Cooking is the way we show our love for others. It's the way we nurture and support our family and friends. We do confess that working on this book brought back some very pleasurable family memories. Writing it has been a labor of love. We are dedicated to recovering, updating, and—above all—enjoying the best home recipes from America's past. By presenting these recipes simply and with a contemporary flair, we are hoping to help a new generation of cooks (and their families) discover and enjoy the special tastes of the culturally diverse American kitchen. We hope *From Grandma's Kitchen* will encourage you to explore and celebrate the culinary legacy of your family and friends. We have provided you with a special chapter of blank lined pages at the back of this book on which to transcribe the stories and recipes of your own family. We encourage you to listen to each story, write down the recipe, and make the book your own.

MARILYNN AND SHEILA BRASS

How to Use This Book

We hope you will enjoy using this book. We have tried to make the recipes easy to understand and the ingredients easy to find. We'd like you to be so inspired by the recipes that you go into your own kitchen and start cooking.

Nearly all of the ingredients for the recipes in *From Grandma's Kitchen* are those found in most home pantries. You probably won't have to make a stop at your local gourmet shop to stock up on special spices, herbs, flours, or extracts. If you do find that some ingredients prove to be elusive, we have included a short list of suppliers (see Sources on page 379). Most of the savory recipes will make four to six servings; several of them can be successfully halved or doubled. Some of the soup recipes make more than 4 to 6 servings. We suggest freezing leftover soup. What constitutes a serving size is often subjective and open to interpretation, so for some recipes, we have tried to give you measurements in cups or slices for each serving. Decreasing or increasing the recipes may result in adjustments to cooking times.

➤➤ SOME SUGGESTIONS ◄◄

BEFORE YOU BEGIN

- Read each recipe several times. Make sure you understand the directions, know what ingredients are needed, and note how many servings the recipe will yield.

- Adjust oven racks before turning on the oven.

- Have all ingredients at room temperature, unless otherwise stated.

- Prepare pots and pans, and set out racks for cooling.

- Assemble your ingredients and utensils.

COOKING AND BAKING TIPS

- Combine ingredients in the order they are listed.

- Set a timer when a dish is in the oven or special timed directions are given, such as "boil for 2 minutes."

- Allow completed dishes and baked goods to cool completely, unless otherwise noted.

- Store cooked dishes in appropriate containers and refrigerate.

Ingredients

BRANDY, SHERRY, AND WHISKEY

We bought small amounts of good-quality brandy, sherry, and whiskey to have on hand when making heirloom recipes. We use them to flavor recipes, plump raisins, and season fruitcakes.

BUTTER

For the recipes in this book, we use unsalted or sweet butter, softened at room temperature. Some recipes call for butter that is refrigerator-firm or melted before it is combined with other ingredients. We used generic store-brand butters and found them to perform as well as commercial brands. If you do not have unsalted butter on hand, you can use salted butter for cooking, but do not use salted butter when baking because its moisture content can affect your results. We suggest that you reduce the amount of salt when cooking if you use salted butter. Do not use whipped butter in any of the recipes.

CHOCOLATE AND COCOA

Chocolate was often a luxury ingredient in the kitchens of the women whose recipes we tested. Occasionally, we introduced a gourmet chocolate when testing a recipe and noted a subtle enhancement of flavor, but we also found that familiar commercial brands of chocolate and cocoa produced good results. We discovered that by judiciously adding small amounts of bitter or baking chocolate to semisweet chocolate, we could achieve the complexity of flavor we were seeking. When a recipe requires baking chocolate, we use bitter chocolate. We were vigilant about using the correct cocoa,

Tin advertising displays for candy bars, 1920s–1930s

either American-style or Dutch, depending on the rising agents used in the recipe. Store chocolate and cocoa in a cool, dry, dark place. Milk chocolate candy bars can be used for Milk Chocolate Pound Cake (page 267).

DAIRY PRODUCTS

The recipes in this book use homogenized milk, not skim milk, and cultured low-fat buttermilk. We used whole-milk ricotta. We do not use reduced-fat cream cheese or sour cream. For cream, we use heavy cream, whipping cream, or, in cooking, half-and-half. We use canned sweetened condensed milk and canned evaporated milk. We use farmer's cheese or pot cheese instead of dry-curd cottage cheese. We do not use reduced-fat cheese or products referred to as cheese food.

EGGS

For consistency, we used only U.S. graded large eggs. Unless otherwise noted, the eggs should be at room temperature. Some recipes call for beating the eggs before adding them to the other ingredients. Egg whites should be at room temperature before being beaten. Eggs added directly to a warm or hot mixture run the risk of cooking too rapidly. To temper the eggs, stir a small amount of the hot mixture into the eggs before adding the eggs to the recipe.

Toy milk jugs, 1930s

EXTRACTS AND PURE FLAVORED OILS

Vanilla is the most popular flavor in the recipes we tested. We use only pure vanilla, lemon, and almond extracts. Pure citrus oils, when substituted for extracts, resulted in some very true flavors, and we provide a source for ordering them (see Sources on page 379).

FLOUR AND GRAINS

Use all-purpose bleached or unbleached flour unless the recipe calls for a specific type, such as bread flour, cake flour, or pastry flour. Some recipes require graham flour, rye flour, or bran. We also use yellow and white cornmeal interchangeably. Even though most large grocery chains carry specialty flours, you can easily order these items (see Sources on page 379). For smooth gravies, we suggest that you use quick-mixing flour, which is finer than regular flour. It is available in grocery stores under the brand name Wondra. We tested several recipes with well-known commercial brands of flour, but we found that using store brands produced the same satisfactory results.

Measure flour by scooping a cup of flour and leveling it with a knife. If a recipe calls for "1 cup sifted flour," sift the flour and then measure it. If a recipe calls for "1 cup flour, sifted" measure the flour first and then sift it.

Measuring spoon, 1930s; bowl, American, 1930s

Roseville Pottery bowl, American, 20th century

FRUIT—FRESH, DRIED, AND CANNED

We use the fruit called for in the original recipe whenever possible. Most of the manuscript cookbooks call for raisins, currants, prunes, cherries, dates, figs, and candied peels such as orange, lemon, or citron. When we did make substitutions, such as dried fruit for fresh or fresh for dried, we noted it. We use fresh fruit when it is in season and buy dried fruit in small quantities. Often, we found that plumping dried fruit in orange juice, tea, or brandy before using added another level of flavor.

We used canned fruit when it was appropriate to the recipe, such as canned pineapple and mandarin orange sections for Dot Luke's Hawaiian Jellied Salad (page 96) or the cranberry sauce for Aunt Ida's Apple Cranberry Noodle Pudding (page 255).

LARD AND SALT PORK

We buy only commercial brand lard for use in recipes that call for lard. Old pastry recipes often call for a combination of lard and butter. We found that some cookies and pie crusts were particularly flaky and tender when made from lard or a combination of lard and butter. We also found that using lard gave an old-world flavor and texture to finished dishes. We use commercial brand salt pork to add flavor to heirloom dishes. Salt pork is remarkably salty. Since it might be necessary to remove the tough skin and blanch the salt pork, we suggest that you substitute bacon or pancetta (Italian bacon), when appropriate.

LEMON, ORANGE, AND LIME JUICE AND ZEST

We use medium-sized lemons and oranges, as well as regular-sized Persian limes, with firm, unblemished skins. Use a Microplane zester/grater or a traditional grater to remove the zest, or colored part, of the rind, leaving behind the bitter white pith. Roll the fruit on a flat surface to break up the juice pockets first. Then cut the fruit in half and juice it on a reamer; strain the juice to remove any seeds. A lemon weighing $4\frac{1}{2}$ ounces yields approximately 2 teaspoons grated zest and 3 tablespoons lemon juice. An orange weighing $6\frac{1}{4}$ ounces yields approximately 2 tablespoons grated zest and 4 tablespoons orange juice. A $3\frac{1}{2}$-ounce lime yields approximately 2 teaspoons grated zest and approximately 5 teaspoons lime juice.

NUTS

Our choice of nuts depended on the original recipe. Walnuts, pecans, peanuts, and almonds were typically found in the larders and pantries of the women whose recipes we tested. We introduced pistachios and pepitas, but only where we felt they would not greatly affect the original results of the recipe. Buy nuts in small quantities and store them in sealed and dated plastic bags or covered plastic containers in the freezer to preserve their freshness.

SALT AND PEPPER

We generally use freshly ground black pepper in our heirloom recipes because its flavor is more assertive than white pepper. However, white pepper has the added advantage of not being visible in white foods. We use table salt as well as kosher salt in our recipes. Kosher salt has larger crystals, and it draws more fluid out of protein when sprinkled on its surface. This is part of the koshering process. Because table salt has finer crystals, 1 teaspoon of table salt contains more than 1 teaspoon of kosher salt. Specialty salts sold in gourmet shops should be sprinkled on top of dishes to add a burst of saltiness and to enhance the flavor of the dish. We've adjusted the salt and pepper in recipes according to our own taste, but we suggest that you taste and adjust seasonings to your taste.

SPICES AND HERBS

Cinnamon is the most popular spice in our recipes, followed by nutmeg, ginger, cloves, and allspice. For those who wrote these living recipes, spices were not easily accessible and were often expensive. Some cooks were creative and mixed small amounts of different spices or herbs to achieve multiple levels of flavor. Buy spices in small quantities and store them in a cool, dark place.

Early heirloom recipes called for herbs that were readily available, such as parsley, sage, thyme, and rosemary. Basil, oregano, dill, summer savory, and saffron were introduced with the arrival of immigrants from the Mediterranean, Eastern Europe, and India. Spice blends such as curry powder, garam masala, and red curry powder have gained in popularity as America's cuisine becomes more diverse.

Vintage spice tins, American and English

SUGAR

Use white granulated sugar unless a recipe calls for a specific type, such as light brown sugar, confectioners' sugar, or sanding sugar. We generally do not use dark brown sugar because we think the flavor is too assertive for most of the recipes, but you may prefer it. If you use dark brown sugar, use the same amount as light brown sugar. Brown sugars should always be firmly packed in a measuring cup. Store in a tightly closed plastic bag to prevent it from hardening. We tried store-brand and commercial-brand sugars and found that both provided successful results. Sweeteners with additional flavors include maple syrup, molasses, honey, and light and dark corn syrup. Store confectioners' sugar in a sealed plastic bag so that it is easier to measure. Sift it after measuring to remove any lumps. Sanding sugar, also known as decorating or sparkling sugar, is coarser than table sugar and is found in the baking sections of grocery stores.

VEGETABLE OIL AND OLIVE OIL

We use a pure, unflavored vegetable oil such as corn oil or canola oil for deep-frying and baking. We always use fresh oil when we deep-fry. We use extra-virgin olive oil for pan-frying and for some of the salad dressings. It's worth the extra cost because of the superior flavor it adds to finished dishes.

VEGETABLE SHORTENING

Solid vegetable shortening can be used for some of the recipes. We buy it in small containers to ensure its freshness and store it according to the manufacturer's instructions. Whenever we had a choice, we used butter instead of shortening.

VEGETABLES—FRESH, CANNED, AND FROZEN

We used fresh vegetables when they were in season. We used canned vegetables only when we wanted to replicate the flavor and appearance of an heirloom recipe because most cooks used their own home-canned vegetables. We also substituted frozen vegetables, when available, for out-of-season fresh vegetables or canned vegetables.

YEAST

We used active dry yeast in baking the recipes that called for a raised dough. We used a quick-rising yeast only when we found the recipe benefited from its use. We did not use cake yeast. We proofed our yeast in water that had been heated to 115°F.

Utensils, Stoves, and Appliances

BAKING PANS

We are specific about noting the size, weight, and material of cooking and baking ware and always try to use standard sizes. We use only 9-inch ovenproof glass pie plates, not the ones with handles or ruffles. Manufacturers of glass baking products often suggest lowering the baking temperature when using their products. We suggest that you follow the instructions that come with any product you use. However, the temperatures we state for ovenproof pans are the ones we used for these recipes. No one knows your stove and baking equipment better than you do. Many of our baking pans and utensils are more than 35 years old. We are used to working with them. Several were purchased at yard sales for a few dollars. If you need to buy kitchenware, we suggest that you explore all the options, buy brand names, and keep instructions on how to use them in a file folder in a handy place.

MIXERS AND FOOD PROCESSORS

We used a KitchenAid standing mixer for most of the recipes because one of our goals was to save home bakers as much time as possible. We used the dough hook for easy kneading. A handheld mixer will also work for many of these recipes, as will a wooden spoon or a whisk, but it will take more time and effort, and the texture and result may vary. We are careful to note that certain recipes such as those for muffins and quick breads benefit from gentle hand mixing.

We use a 7-cup Cuisinart food processor, usually with the metal blade attachment. Using a food processor for mixing pastry or cookie dough and switching to alternate blades for grating or shredding saves time and provides uniform results. For many recipes, a blender can be used in place of a food processor, and we've noted where that substitution is applicable.

Toy steamer and pots, 1890s–1900s

➤➤ POTS AND PANS WE FIND USEFUL ◄◄

- 9-inch by 13-inch by 1-inch jelly roll or half-sheet pan
- 14-inch by 16-inch metal baking sheets
- 17-inch by 11-inch by 1-inch metal jelly roll pan
- 8-cup and 10-cup Bundt pans
- Metal springform pan
- Round cake pans
- 9-inch by 5-inch by 3-inch metal loaf pan
- 10-inch by 4 $\frac{1}{4}$-inch angel food cake or tube pan
- 8-cup tube pan
- 8-inch by 8-inch by 2-inch pan for bar cookies and brownies
- 9-inch by 9-inch by 2-inch pan
- Muffin tins
- Round jelly mold
- 9-inch by 13-inch by 2-inch metal or glass pan
- 9-inch ovenproof glass pie plate
- 9-inch, 10-inch, and 12-inch quiche dishes
- 1 $\frac{1}{2}$-quart ovenproof glass or ceramic baking dish
- 2-quart ovenproof rectangular glass dish
- 8-inch and 9-inch round tart pans
- Metal pudding molds
- Large metal roasting pan for water bath
- 8-inch and 10-inch nonreactive stainless steel heavy-bottomed frying pans
- 5-quart nonreactive stainless steel heavy-bottomed saucepan
- Cast-iron and enamel Dutch oven
- 8-quart nonreactive stainless steel stockpot
- 12-quart nonreactive stainless steel stockpot
- Ovenproof custard cups
- Set of nonreactive glass or stainless steel mixing bowls
- Double boiler
- 8-inch round soufflé/casserole dish

STOVES AND OVENS

We used a gas stove to test the recipes. Since every stove is different, we suggest that you honor the idiosyncrasies of your own stove and use an oven thermometer. Turn cookie sheets halfway through baking if you have any hot spots in your oven. We usually bake one sheet of cookies at a time, but if you do multiples, be sure to switch them from rack to rack and front to back halfway through baking. A microwave oven is also helpful to melt butter and chocolate; be sure to use the lowest setting.

Miniature molds, American and English, 1870s–1920s

COOKING AND BAKING AIDS
WE CAN'T LIVE WITHOUT

- Standing mixer with paddle, whisk, and dough-hook attachments
- Food processor with metal blade and grating and shredding blades
- Microplane zester/grater (to grate zests)
- Offset spatulas (to smooth batters and frost cakes and cookies)
- Tongs
- Turkey lifters
- Turkey baster
- Potato ricer
- Thermometer to check oven temperature
- Candy thermometer to test sugar syrup and oil temperature
- Instant-read thermometer to test water temperature when proofing yeast or checking temperature of roasts
- Scale (for weighing ingredients)

- Disposable gloves
- Disposable piping bags
- Strainers (for sifting, removing seeds from juice, and dusting with confectioners' sugar)
- Cooling racks in a variety of sizes
- Parchment paper
- Wax paper
- Silicone baking liners
- Set of stainless steel measuring cups for measuring dry ingredients: $\frac{1}{8}$ cup, $\frac{1}{4}$ cup, $\frac{1}{3}$ cup, $\frac{1}{2}$ cup, $\frac{2}{3}$ cup, $\frac{3}{4}$ cup, 1 cup
- Set of stainless steel measuring spoons for measuring dry and liquid ingredients: $\frac{1}{8}$ teaspoon, $\frac{1}{4}$ teaspoon, $\frac{1}{2}$ teaspoon, 1 teaspoon, 1 tablespoon. Spoons with a rectangular bowl are easier to dip into narrow-necked spice jars.
- Measuring cups for measuring liquid ingredients: 1 cup, 2 cups

Cooking pamphlets, American, 1950s

Meals and Memories from Grandma's Kitchen

There is nothing that tastes as good as something cooked by someone who loves us. It is the memory of these comforting meals and treats that sustains us in a world that constantly changes. People need a place where they feel safe, even if it is constructed from the ephemeral aromas and tastes created in the kitchens of their past.

As we look through our collections of manuscript cookbooks, we realize that everything old is new again. In the 21st century, we see a return to cooking with local seasonal ingredients and an interest in taking from the earth the best it has to offer. We also find a continuing commitment to maintaining the earth as a healthy and bountiful resource.

It is important to celebrate the heirloom kitchen in our own home kitchens by re-creating those meals and memories and honoring that commitment. We want to preserve the flavor, taste, and value of heirloom recipes, but we must listen to the stories of the people who created them. We have to understand their daily obligations to provide and maintain a home. We have to learn about the types of foods they raised or bought and the amount of time it took to harvest or secure those foods and prepare them for their family's meals. People have always had to confront the challenges of hard times when just surviving was a victory, but to survive while making a family feel loved and protected was heroic.

We are fortunate that handwritten recipes still exist. They may be fragile and crumble as we touch them, but they are, nevertheless, living recipes. They will never be lost if we assume their stewardship by cooking them in our own kitchens. We are grateful that our grandmothers, mothers, aunts, and friends had the foresight to jot down their personal recipes in old notebooks, sometimes attaching fragments of even older recipes to the pages with safety pins or bent nails. Through these, often-multigenerational, documents, they have bequeathed to us what they valued most—their own personal histories illustrated by the meals they cooked every day. They have taught us that we have much to learn about food and how it's prepared to appreciate its value. We must never forget that these women were not just home cooks, they were "homemakers," a title that was hard-won and worn with pride.

Because women came together socially at church or temple gatherings, at holiday celebrations, or through something as universal as sharing a cup of tea or coffee, they were able to exchange recipes and advise each other on how to make the best corned beef hash or bake the best refrigerator rolls. These formal and informal get-togethers provided an opportunity to educate each other on how to run a household, feed a family, and, more importantly, how to create a home. They also provided a universal meeting place for women to support and celebrate one another when they talked about their fears and joys. Not to be forgotten are the men who found themselves maintaining their homes by going into the kitchen to cook family meals.

Developing a self-image has always been important to women. Except for the years that America took part in World War II, when women's skills and labor were needed in manufacturing, most women did not work outside the home after marriage until just after the middle of the 20th century. One of the few ways a woman could individualize herself, whether she was formally educated or not, was by creating and personalizing a recipe admired by others. More than one husband urged his wife to ask for the recipe for brisket or macaroni and cheese or carrot cake served by their hostess so that it could be prepared in their own kitchen.

Because so many women were honorable in crediting the creator of a recipe, more than 50 years later, we are able to acknowledge a recipe for Lemon Chicken, authored by Anna Morse. This was one of the recipes she shared with the members of "The Railroad Club," a group of women who met morning and evening when commuting from the North Shore of Massachusetts to Boston. The women loved to exchange

Cast-iron baking pan, American, early 1900s

recipes and discuss the stock market on their commute, eventually forming an investment club.

We found that heirloom cooks were clever at substituting ingredients and judging how much was needed from large ingredients such as heads of cabbage or sweet potatoes. The guidelines for recipes were more permissive, and with the introduction of standardized measurements by The Boston Cooking School and its zealous director, Fannie Merritt Farmer, the burden of replicating the amounts of ingredients was lessened. No longer was a teacup, a tumbler, a gill, or butter the size of an egg a mystery. Yet women did not hesitate to jot down notes in a printed cookbook, using the endpapers for recipes gathered by word-of-mouth. A woman could personalize her book with handwritten notes on how to improve upon her neighbor's gingersnaps or a cousin's banana bread.

In comparing heirloom recipes, we found that a woman established her own guidelines for selecting and purchasing the major ingredients for the meals she cooked in her kitchen. When buying fish, she would often ask, "What's fresh today?" If it didn't pass her scrutiny, she turned to canned tuna and canned salmon with very good results. Women were comfortable cooking with commercially canned foods because most women had learned to preserve foods at home to feed the family when times were lean or when food was out of season. However, home-canned food was only as good as the skill of the person who canned it. In a farm society with no refrigeration, heirloom cooks kept food in cold places such as icehouses or cellars. Sausage meat was highly salted and kept in crocks and covered with a layer of lard. This sometimes led

Cooking pamphlets, American, 1920s–1950s

to spoilage. Most home cooks eventually switched to commercially canned foods because it was convenient and more dependable.

With refrigeration came the choice of frozen foods, and women who were now working outside the home in increasing numbers took advantage of this new way to reduce time-consuming repetitive chores like washing and cutting up vegetables and fruit. Women still buy canned tomato sauce and cream soups because their mothers used them or because they enable the modern home cook to quickly prepare casseroles and meatloaves with a traditional taste.

The campaign slogan of Herbert Hoover in 1928 promised a chicken in every pot, but during the Great Depression, the home cook sometimes found herself struggling to pay dearly for that chicken and searched for ways to make it go further. Chicken soup and chicken pot pie were two good ways to stretch a poultry purchase. If a woman lived on a farm and raised chickens herself, she served them only for special occasions because she needed the chickens to provide the eggs she sold. It was traditionally accepted that women could keep for themselves the money they made by selling eggs. Often, Mother's egg money became a nest egg for emergencies or special treats for the children.

During the 19th and early 20th centuries, veal was described as a budget meat. It was less expensive than chicken. Veal was particularly favored for Italian dishes, but it also found its way into recipes such as Mock Chicken Salad and Swedish Meatballs. Veal was a lean meat and responded well to periods of long, moist cooking, making it an economical choice to feed the family.

Beef was the standby of the home kitchen. Even the more challenging cuts of beef could be transformed into appealing home plates such as sauerbraten, meatloaf, and corned beef. These culinary challenges resulted in leftover favorites such as corned beef hash and meatloaf sandwiches. The creative heirloom cook could use her skills in braising, stewing, and roasting to tenderize the less expensive choices, and there was always ground beef, a versatile ingredient that found its way into soups, sauces, and casseroles.

Pork has always been the salvation of the kitchen budget, whether utilized for stuffing cabbage leaves, making a ham loaf, or baking beans. Hearty and satisfying, pork dishes fed many for very little. Most American women lived on farms during the 19th century, and some still did up until the middle of the 20th century. Most farm families raised their own pigs and learned to utilize them "from tail to snout."

Heirloom cooking often used generous amounts of cheese and eggs. Although dishes such as frittatas and macaroni and cheese may not have met all of the requirements of vegetarianism, they were still able to satisfy the culinary needs of those who refused to eat meat, fish, or poultry. An added bonus for the home cook was that eggs and cheese were both available and inexpensive.

Living recipes made use of familiar spices—cinnamon, nutmeg, cloves, and ginger—for savory dishes as well as sweet. As transportation improved, the price of spices declined, and it was often worth spending money for small amounts of spice to enhance the flavor of home cooking. Women sought to prevent their cooking from becoming repetitive or dull. Two recipes—our mother's Romanian Stuffed Cabbage made with tomato sauce and Bunny Slobodzinski's Polish Stuffed Cabbage with Salt Pork Gravy—taught us that two home cooks could prepare a recipe using the same primary ingredients but still end up with two very different dishes, each reflecting her ingenuity and her cultural heritage.

With the coming of immigrants from the Mediterranean and Eastern Europe, herbs such as thyme, oregano, dill, and basil were put to good use as homemakers duplicated the dishes they had first learned to make in their homelands. The home cook could grow herbs on a kitchen windowsill. Because living recipes continuously used the same ingredients—cabbage, cheese, eggs, ground meat, macaroni, potatoes—home cooks found it necessary to personalize them with their own combinations of spices and herbs. A few adventurous women learned to cook with the exotic spices of India, and curries of chicken, lamb, and shrimp were included in their repertoire.

In baking from these handwritten recipes, we've gained an education in kitchen chemistry. We learned early on how different flour was 150 years ago—its texture and flavor often depended on the location of the mill where it was processed.

Understanding a recipe from the 1950s, for example, often hinged upon finding flour similar to the brand a woman used then. Sugar was different, too, until processing and shipping led to standardization early in the 20th century—from hard cones of loaf sugar, which had to be broken and pulverized, to the joys of confectioners' and superfine sugars today.

Oven temperatures and baking times were not given in many of these heirloom recipes because each wood- or coal-burning stove was consistent in its own special way. A woman had an intimate relationship with her stove. She cleaned it, she polished it, and she stoked it. A hot oven meant one thing to one woman; a quick oven meant something entirely different to another.

Heirloom recipes provide us with valuable information about who these home cooks were, how they lived, and what they prepared in their kitchens. Because they belong to the past, they can teach us so much about what life was like then and what they hoped life would be like for those who came after them. We cannot go into our kitchens without thinking of these generations of women who honored their responsibility to feed their families and preserve their homes. These are the women who knew how to banish tears with a slice of homemade bread and butter or calm fears with a bowl of hot soup and a hug. When we reproduce their recipes, which have lain forgotten on shelves or in boxes, in our own kitchens, we are filled with expectation, remembrance, and joy.

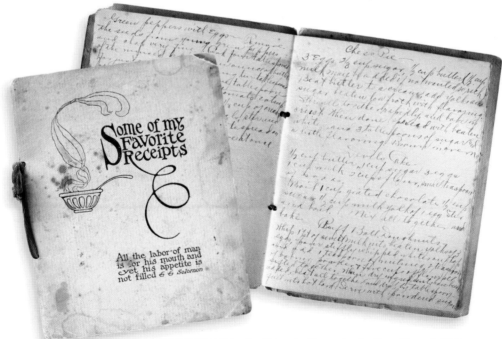

Manuscript cookbook with handwritten recipe for Chess Pie, early 1900s

CHAPTER 1

WAKING UP TO BREAKFAST

We have always had a love affair with breakfast, and it continues to intensify. When eating breakfast at a restaurant, we always find it thrilling to pick up a menu with a cheerful "good morning" printed on the front in letters large enough to accommodate our sleep-filled eyes. When we were younger, we were particularly vulnerable to the Yankee breakfasts we enjoyed at our favorite Boston cafeteria. Shrines to choices, these chains provided sticky buns, muffins, pancakes, or waffles; eggs any way we wanted them; and oatmeal with butter and salt or brown sugar. Later we would replicate these real American breakfasts at our own breakfast table, because it's the memory of eating at home that really appeals to us.

In this chapter, we salute the best of home breakfasts with the goal of reproducing everyone's family favorites. Looking through our collections of manuscript cookbooks, we find that the recipes for breakfast are predominantly sweet, and once again, it is the creators and the interpreters of these breakfast treats that continue to make them so interesting.

We found that a lady from New Hampshire faithfully listened to WJAR on her radio through the 1920s and 1930s. We learned that broadcasting from Providence, Rhode Island, Claire Wood dispensed her own brand of kitchen wisdom for 23 years, allowing housewives all over New England to jot down rules for cakes, cookies, and breakfast breads. Substituting ingredients, adjusting measurements, and catering to the idiosyncrasies of their own stoves, these listeners took Mrs. Wood's suggestions

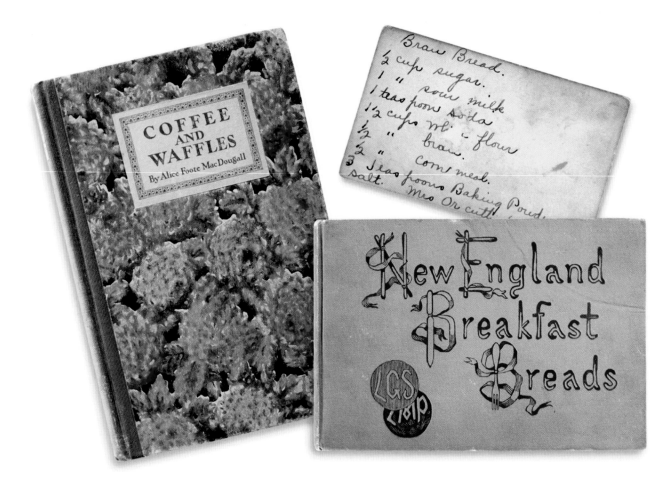

Coffee and Waffles, 1920s; *New England Breakfast Breads*, 1890; recipe for Bran Bread, 1918

and made them into their own personal recipes, such as a cake baked with homemade applesauce and plumped golden raisins.

Cranberry-Orange Cream Scones, delicious with either fresh blueberries or dried cranberries, come from the Carter family in Maine, whose collection spans almost 100 years and includes recipes for biscuits, steamed puddings, cakes, pies, and preserves. Elinor Jennings warns us not to serve bacon with her crisp, delicate Peanut Butter Waffles, while Melania Marasi, a great-grandmother from Cambridge, Massachusetts, who baked for more than 80 years, provides us with the recipe for her special biscotti, generous in size and flavor and amply suitable for dipping in a cup of breakfast coffee. We hope that you will enjoy baking the recipes in this chapter and continue to eat breakfast at home with the family.

Tin egg beater, early 1900s

Carrot Cream Cheese Muffins

MAKES 12 LARGE MUFFINS

FOR FILLING

8-ounce package cream cheese, softened in microwave on low for 40 seconds

¼ cup sugar

FOR MUFFINS

1¾ cups flour

½ teaspoon salt

1½ teaspoons baking powder

¾ teaspoon cinnamon

½ cup butter

¾ cup brown sugar

3 eggs, beaten

1 teaspoon orange extract

¼ cup orange juice

1 tablespoon grated orange zest

1¾ cups grated carrots

¾ cup raisins

¾ cup chopped walnuts

TIPS & TOUCHES

- Coat a melon baller with vegetable spray and use it to scoop the cream cheese.
- These muffins can be heated in a microwave before serving. They will not be as crisp, but they will be warm.

THIS RECIPE (PICTURED ON PAGE 23) CAME *from a modest collection spanning the 1960s through the 1980s. The woman who wrote these recipes entertained frequently, and her tersely written instructions illustrate the notes of an experienced home cook.*

1. Set oven rack in middle position. Preheat oven to 350°F. Coat cups and top surface of 12-cup muffin pan with vegetable spray.

2. To make filling: Place cream cheese in small bowl, add sugar, and mash with dinner fork until well blended. Cover with plastic wrap and place in freezer 10 minutes to chill.

3. To make muffins: Sift together flour, salt, baking powder, and cinnamon.

4. Cream butter and brown sugar in bowl of standing mixer fitted with paddle attachment. With mixer running, add eggs one at a time, beating after each addition. Add orange extract, orange juice, and orange zest. Add sifted dry ingredients and mix well. Fold in carrots, raisins, and walnuts.

5. Place 2 tablespoons batter in each muffin pan cup. Tap pan gently to distribute batter evenly in each cup. Add a generous tablespoon of filling to each cup. Add remaining batter until each cup is full. Spread and smooth batter with back of a spoon until filling is completely covered. Tap muffin pan again gently. Bake 20 to 22 minutes, or until tester inserted into muffins comes out clean. Cool on rack at least 20 minutes. Use tip of knife and your fingers to remove muffins from pan (don't tip pan and dump muffins out). Store cooled muffins loosely wrapped in wax paper in plastic container in refrigerator. Warm to room temperature before serving.

Penny's Cousin Pearl's Bran Muffins

{ *1930s* }

WE FOUND THIS RECIPE HANDWRITTEN IN A *copy of* Laboratory Recipes, *owned by Rachel W. Banks. We never learned very much about Penny or her cousin Pearl, but these bran muffins are as good as any we've ever tasted. They are generously portioned muffins, with the dark, sweet flavor of molasses and the signature candied cherry on top.*

1. Set oven rack in middle position. Preheat oven to 400°F. Coat cups and top surface of 12-cup muffin pan with vegetable spray.

2. Combine wheat bran, buttermilk, molasses, and egg in large bowl. Let stand 10 minutes. Add flour, sugar, salt, and baking soda and mix gently. Fold in raisins, being careful not to overstir. Fold in butter.

3. Fill each muffin cup with batter. Place candied cherry on top of each muffin. Bake 20 minutes, or until tester inserted in middle comes out clean. Store covered with paper towel and loosely wrapped in wax paper at room temperature.

$^3/_4$ cup wheat bran

1 cup buttermilk

1 tablespoon molasses

1 egg, beaten

1$^1/_4$ cups flour

$^1/_3$ cup sugar

$^1/_2$ teaspoon salt

1 teaspoon baking soda

$^1/_2$ cup raisins

$^1/_4$ cup butter, melted

12 candied cherries

TIPS & TOUCHES

- If you don't have candied cherries, you can use maraschino cherries. Dry them on a paper towel before placing them on top of muffins.

Pumpkin Walnut Muffins

MAKES 18 LARGE MUFFINS

{1940s}

ONE OF THOSE UNCLAIMED TREASURES WE FOUND *tucked between the pages of an old manuscript cookbook, this recipe, once again, demonstrates the choice of a baked sweet for breakfast. Although early baking was often limited by the selection and availability of ingredients, this muffin illustrates how something simple can still be wonderful.*

1. Set oven rack in middle position. Preheat oven to 400°F. Coat cups and top surface of 12-cup muffin pan and 6-cup muffin pan with vegetable spray.
2. Sift together flour, baking powder, salt, cinnamon, mace, and ginger in large bowl.
3. Place sugar in small bowl. Add egg, vanilla, milk, and heavy cream. Stir gently just until combined. Add egg mixture to sifted dry ingredients and stir. Fold in pumpkin and chopped walnuts. Fold in butter.
4. Fill each muffin cup with batter. Add 2 walnut halves to top of each cup and sprinkle with brown sugar. Bake 20 to 22 minutes, or until tester inserted into middle of muffins comes out clean. Cool in pan on rack 5 minutes before turning out. Serve muffins with butter and jam. Store loosely wrapped in wax paper at room temperature.

2 cups sifted flour

1 tablespoon plus 1 teaspoon baking powder

½ teaspoon salt

1 teaspoon cinnamon

1 teaspoon mace

1 teaspoon ginger

1 cup sugar

1 egg, beaten

2 teaspoons vanilla

½ cup milk

½ cup heavy cream

⅔ cup canned pumpkin

1 cup chopped walnuts

¼ cup butter, melted

36 walnut halves

½ cup dark brown sugar

Tips & Touches

- Use a wire whisk or wooden spoon to prepare the muffins, not an electric mixer. Do not overmix the batter.
- You can use either canned pumpkin or canned squash. The recipe originally called for squash, but it tastes just as good with pumpkin.
- We tried a variation of this recipe by folding a cup of dried cherries that we had heated in orange juice (and drained) into the muffin batter. We topped those muffins with brown sugar.

Pineapple Walnut Breakfast Bars

MAKES 24 2-INCH BARS

1½ cups flour, divided

1 teaspoon baking powder

½ teaspoon baking soda

¼ teaspoon salt

2 cups sugar

4 eggs

1 teaspoon vanilla

½ cup butter, melted

½ cup chopped dried pineapple

2 (8-ounce) cans pineapple chunks, well drained and chopped

1 cup finely chopped walnuts

THIS RECIPE WAS A TOUGH ONE TO UPDATE *because we couldn't taste the pineapple in it. We found that doubling the amount of canned pineapple as well as adding chopped dried pineapple made all the difference. Melted butter lightened the texture, while the added fruity crunch from the dried fruit did not coarsen the crumb. The pineapple flavor is rather subtle still, but it makes its presence known.*

1. Set oven rack in middle position. Preheat oven to 350°F. Line bottom and 4 sides of 9-inch by 13-inch pan with foil, shiny side up. Coat foil with vegetable spray.

2. Sift together 1¼ cups of the flour, baking powder, baking soda, and salt.

3. Beat sugar, eggs, and vanilla in bowl of standing mixer fitted with paddle attachment. With mixer running, add sifted dry ingredients. Add butter and mix thoroughly.

4. Combine remaining ¼ cup flour, dried pineapple, canned pineapple, and walnuts in medium bowl. Fold into batter. Pour batter into pan. Bake 35 minutes, or until tester inserted into cake comes out clean. Cool on rack and cut into 2-inch bars. Store loosely wrapped in wax paper at room temperature.

Mrs. Marasi's Biscotti

MAKES 25 BISCOTTI

{ 1950s }

Our friend Barbara told Marilynn about a *talented baker, Melania Marasi. The phone crackled as Barbara declared, "Mrs. Marasi always has a Scottie in a jar when her family visits." Marilynn found it hard to understand why Mrs. Marasi would keep a dog in a jar. Was she a taxidermist? Another call to Barbara cleared up the mystery. Mrs. Marasi always kept some biscotti in a jar for guests. Of course we asked for the recipe, which turned out to be a wonderful treat with the subtle flavor of anise.*

1. Set oven rack in middle position. Preheat oven to 350°F. Cover 14-inch by 16-inch baking sheet with foil, shiny side up. Coat foil with vegetable spray, or use silicone liner.

2. Sift together flour, sugar, baking powder, and salt.

3. Combine milk, oil, and anise extract. Add more anise extract if you like a strong anise flavor.

4. Lightly beat eggs in bowl of standing mixer fitted with paddle attachment. With mixer running, add milk mixture. Add sifted dry ingredients. Dough will be loose.

5. Divide dough in half using rubber spatula or oiled hands; shape into 2 flat loaves on baking sheet. Bake 20 to 25 minutes, or until edges are lightly brown and tester inserted in loaves comes out dry.

6. Cool 5 minutes. Transfer biscotti from baking sheet to cutting surface. Using serrated bread knife, cut diagonal slices $\frac{1}{2}$-inch to $\frac{3}{4}$-inch thick. Place slices, cut side up, on the same baking sheet and return to 350°F oven for 10 minutes. Remove baking sheet from oven, turn biscotti over, and return to oven to bake an additional 10 minutes. Transfer biscotti to rack to cool. Store between sheets of wax paper in covered tin.

2½ cups flour

1 cup sugar

3 teaspoons baking powder

⅛ teaspoon salt

¼ cup milk

½ cup vegetable or peanut oil

2 teaspoons anise extract

3 eggs

TIPS & TOUCHES

- Save broken or leftover biscotti to make into crumbs for cheesecake or crumb crusts.
- To make almond biscotti, substitute 1 teaspoon almond extract for anise and mix ½ cup chopped toasted almonds into dough.

Cranberry-Orange Cream Scones

{1920s}

MAKES 12 SCONES

2 cups flour (plus ¼ cup for kneading dough)

1 tablespoon baking powder

½ teaspoon salt

½ teaspoon cinnamon

¼ cup butter

½ cup sugar, divided

2 eggs

½ cup plus 2 tablespoons heavy cream

1 tablespoon grated orange zest

1 cup dried cranberries, plumped in 4 tablespoons orange juice (see "How to Plump Raisins" on page 33)

TIPS & TOUCHES

• We substituted a heaping cup of fresh blueberries for the cranberries, and the scones were equally wonderful. Sprinkle the blueberries on top of the dough after kneading it twice, and then continue with the instructions.

THIS OUTSTANDING RECIPE COMES FROM *a handwritten manuscript cookbook, from the collection of Marion A. Carter and M. E. Carter, that spanned the 1870s through the 1920s. A narrow notebook with a marbled maroon and grey cover, it was filled with tightly written segments on pages spattered with cooking stains. Since there is more than one handwriting in the book, we guess this was a collection compiled by two generations of the Carter family.*

1. Set oven rack in middle position. Preheat oven to 425°F. Cover 14-inch by 16-inch baking sheet with foil, shiny side up. Coat foil with vegetable spray, or use silicone liner.

2. Sift together flour, baking powder, salt, and cinnamon.

3. Cream butter and ¼ cup of the sugar in medium bowl. Combine eggs and ½ cup of the heavy cream and add to butter mixture. Add grated orange zest. Add sifted dry ingredients and stir until soft dough begins to form. Squeeze orange juice from cranberries and incorporate fruit into dough with your fingers.

4. Place dough on generously floured surface. Knead gently 5 times, turning corners of dough toward center. Pat dough into a ½-inch-thick circle. Using floured knife, cut dough into 12 equal wedges. Using floured wide spatula, transfer each wedge to baking sheet. Brush wedges with remaining 2 tablespoons heavy cream and sprinkle with remaining ¼ cup sugar. Bake 12 to 15 minutes, or until tops of scones are lightly brown and bottoms are golden brown. Place baking sheet on rack and cool about 10 minutes. Serve scones warm with butter and jam. They are best when eaten the day they are made.

Helen's Coffee Bans

{ 1930s }

FOR DOUGH

1 cup raisins

2 teaspoons instant coffee

²/₃ cup hot water

1½ cups sifted flour

½ teaspoon baking powder

½ teaspoon baking soda

¼ teaspoon salt

²/₃ cup butter

1 cup sugar

2 eggs

FOR TOPPING

½ cup sugar

½ teaspoon cinnamon

TIPS & TOUCHES

- These squares are very delicate. It's best to cut them on the day you bake them as soon as they have cooled. If you wait until the following day, you will find it hard to cut through the raisins.
- Helen recommended that her Coffee Bans be iced. We like them with the cinnamon and sugar on top, but a light glaze is also tasty.

THIS ORIGINAL RECIPE WAS HANDWRITTEN, SO WE'RE *not sure whether Helen meant to call them Coffee Bans or Coffee Buns. Because Helen's recipe doesn't call for yeast and these are bars rather than rolls, we've decided to stay with Bans. Whatever Helen meant to call them, they are light, delicious, and easy to make.*

1. Set oven rack in middle position. Preheat oven to 350°F. Line bottom and sides of 9-inch by 13-inch pan with foil, shiny side up. Coat foil with vegetable spray.

2. Place raisins and instant coffee in small bowl, add hot water, and stir. Allow raisins to plump at least 5 minutes.

3. Sift together flour, baking powder, baking soda, and salt.

4. Cream butter and sugar in bowl of standing mixer fitted with paddle attachment. With mixer running, add eggs one at a time. Add liquid coffee, straining out raisins. Add sifted dry ingredients. Fold in raisins by hand.

5. Pour batter into pan and smooth top with spatula. Combine sugar and cinnamon in small bowl and sprinkle over top of batter. Bake 20 minutes, or until tester inserted into cake comes out dry. Cool on rack. When cake is completely cool, cut into squares. Store loosely wrapped in wax paper at room temperature.

⇥ HOW TO PLUMP RAISINS ⇤

Raisins are like character actors in recipes. With the right plumping liquid, they can assume all kinds of roles in your baking. For a sophisticated taste, plump raisins in good brandy or port. For an old-world taste, plump raisins in tea. For a new-age organic taste, plump raisins in orange juice. For an uncomplicated taste but a velvety texture, plump raisins in hot water.

Brandy: Pour generous amount of brandy over raisins. Refrigerate overnight or for several days, shaking container at least once a day.

Tea, orange juice, or water: Bring liquid to a boil, immerse raisins, and remove from heat. Allow at least 30 minutes for raisins to absorb liquid. If you don't use raisins the same day you plump them, refrigerate and use within 1 week.

Depression glass juicer, 1930s

Dorothy Katziff Brass's Refrigerator Coffee Rolls

{ 1 9 3 0 s }

FOR DOUGH

1 package (2¼ teaspoons) active dry yeast

½ cup water, warmed to 115°F

1 tablespoon plus 1 cup sugar

4½ cups flour, divided

⅛ teaspoon salt

1 cup butter

3 eggs, beaten

1 cup sour cream

FOR COFFEE ROLL BASES

½ cup brown sugar

¾ cup walnuts, coarsely chopped

½ cup butter

FOR FILLING

½ cup butter, melted

1 cup brown sugar

1 teaspoon cinnamon

2 cups walnuts, coarsely chopped

1 cup raisins or dried cherries

1 egg, beaten

THESE COFFEE ROLLS WERE THE BREAKFAST PASTRY *of choice when we were growing up. Since the dough was made the night before, our mother always baked her coffee rolls the next morning in a flurry of rolling, sprinkling, and shaping. Marilynn remembers recuperating from a winter cold, wrapped in a down comforter, finally able to smell the melting butter and brown sugar of these rolls.*

1. To make dough: Dissolve yeast in warm water. Add 1 tablespoon of the sugar. Set in warm place to proof, about 10 minutes. Mixture will bubble when yeast is proofed.

2. Sift 4 cups of the flour, remaining 1 cup sugar, and salt into bowl of standing mixer fitted with paddle attachment. Add butter and mix to combine. Add proofed yeast, eggs, and sour cream and mix to combine.

3. Remove paddle attachment and attach dough hook. Knead dough about 5 minutes, adding up to ½ cup of remaining flour if needed to make a smooth, silky dough. Place dough in oiled bowl and turn so entire dough is coated with oil. Cover with towel and refrigerate overnight.

4. Remove dough from refrigerator. Dough should have risen to top of bowl. Punch down dough and allow to rise in warm place until doubled in bulk, about 1 hour. Punch down and divide in half.

5. Coat cups and top surface of two 12-cup muffin pans with vegetable spray.

6. To make coffee roll bases: Place 1 teaspoon brown sugar, 1 heaping teaspoon chopped walnuts, and 1 teaspoon butter in bottom of each cup of muffin pan.

7. To add filling: Roll out half of dough on floured wax paper or parchment paper. Brush surface with $\frac{1}{4}$ cup of the melted butter. Mix brown sugar and cinnamon in small bowl. Cover surface of dough with half of the sugar mixture, 1 cup of the walnuts, and $\frac{1}{2}$ cup of the dried fruit. Use paper to help lift and roll dough, jelly-roll style. Cut rolled dough into 12 equal pieces. Place each piece in muffin pan cup, cut side up. Repeat with remaining dough and filling ingredients.

8. Let rolled dough rise in warm place 30 minutes. Meanwhile, set oven rack in middle position. Preheat oven to 350°F. Brush tops of rolls with beaten egg. Bake 30 minutes, or until tops are golden brown. Cool in pan on rack 5 minutes and then invert pan over rack. If some of the base remains in bottom of muffin cups, scoop it out with spoon and place over inverted coffee rolls. Allow to cool completely. Store coffee rolls in plastic bag at room temperature.

Wire whisk, 1890; metal egg carrier, English, 1920s

Sugar Doughnuts

{1920s}

1 package (2¼ teaspoons) active dry yeast

½ cup water, warmed to 115°F

1 tablespoon plus ½ cup sugar

1 cup butter

2 eggs

3½ cups flour, divided

½ teaspoon nutmeg

½ teaspoon cinnamon

1 teaspoon salt

Vegetable or peanut oil, for frying

Sugar or confectioners' sugar

OUR LOVE AFFAIR WITH DOUGHNUTS STARTED EARLY *when we purchased them dredged in confectioners' sugar from Pearl's Bakery in Winthrop, Massachusetts. Later, we would venture into Boston with our parents to watch the doughnuts at Lord's coming off the line and dropping into their bath of hot fat. We'll never forget the smell of frying dough. We adapted this recipe for yeast dough to recapture the flavor of our youth.*

1. Dissolve yeast in warm water. Add 1 tablespoon of the sugar. Set in a warm place to proof, about 10 minutes. Mixture will bubble when yeast is proofed.
2. Cream butter, eggs, and remaining ½ cup sugar in bowl of standing mixer fitted with paddle attachment. Add proofed yeast and mix until combined.
3. Remove paddle attachment and attach dough hook. With mixer running, add 3 cups of the flour, 1 cup at a time, nutmeg, cinnamon, and salt and mix until dough holds together. Add remaining ½ cup flour if dough is too loose. Place dough in oiled bowl and turn so entire dough is coated with oil. Cover with towel and refrigerate 4 hours or overnight.
4. Remove dough from refrigerator. Allow dough to rest in warm place for 30 minutes. Divide dough in half. Place 1 half between 2 pieces of lightly floured wax paper or parchment paper. Roll out or pat dough into ½-inch-thick rectangle. Cut out doughnuts and holes using doughnut cutter dipped in flour. Transfer cut dough to parchment-covered baking sheet and allow to rest 15 minutes. Repeat with remaining dough.

5. Line a cooling rack with 3 layers of paper towels. Add 3 inches of oil to deep, flat-bottomed heavy pan or electric fryer. Heat oil to 375°F. Use greased spatula to carefully lower dough into hot fat. Fat may foam or bubble. Fry doughnuts in batches of 3 for approximately 1½ minutes on each side, or until golden brown. Fry doughnut holes in batches of 8 for 1 minute on each side or until golden brown. Place on lined rack to drain, and cover with additional paper towels. Roll doughnuts in granulated sugar while still warm, or dust with confectioners' sugar when slightly cool. Doughnuts are best eaten shortly after frying.

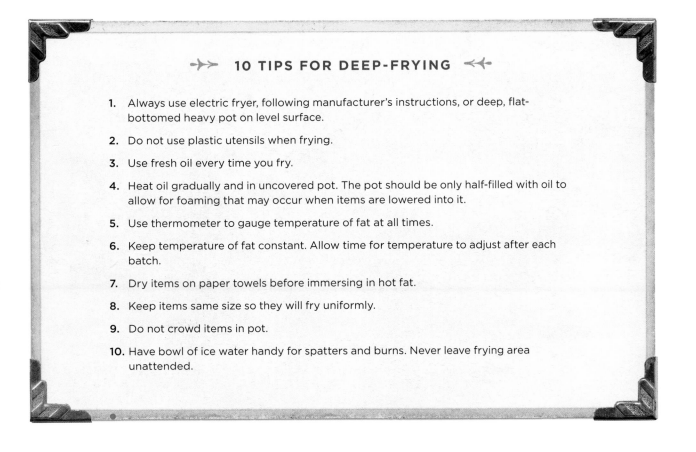

➤➤ 10 TIPS FOR DEEP-FRYING ◄◄

1. Always use electric fryer, following manufacturer's instructions, or deep, flat-bottomed heavy pot on level surface.

2. Do not use plastic utensils when frying.

3. Use fresh oil every time you fry.

4. Heat oil gradually and in uncovered pot. The pot should be only half-filled with oil to allow for foaming that may occur when items are lowered into it.

5. Use thermometer to gauge temperature of fat at all times.

6. Keep temperature of fat constant. Allow time for temperature to adjust after each batch.

7. Dry items on paper towels before immersing in hot fat.

8. Keep items same size so they will fry uniformly.

9. Do not crowd items in pot.

10. Have bowl of ice water handy for spatters and burns. Never leave frying area unattended.

Elinor's Peanut Butter Waffles

{ 1 9 4 0 s }

THIS RECIPE CAME FROM ELINOR JENNINGS, WHO *worked with Marilynn at MIT during the 1960s and 1970s. Elinor always said that she was not a cook but that she knew good food. She was particular about how these waffles were made and would lower her voice and gruffly proclaim them "luscious."*

1. Prepare and preheat waffle iron following manufacturer's instructions.
2. Sift together flour, baking powder, sugar, and salt.
3. Place butter in small glass bowl and microwave 10 seconds on low to soften. Transfer butter and peanut butter to medium bowl and cream with wooden spoon. Add eggs and stir to combine. Add sifted dry ingredients alternately with $1\frac{1}{2}$ cups of the milk, stirring just until mixed. If batter seems stiff, add 1 or 2 tablespoons milk.
4. When waffle iron reaches the ideal temperature, pour suggested amount of batter on each section of iron. Bake until waffles are soft and golden brown, not crisp. Serve immediately.

$1\frac{3}{4}$ cups flour

3 teaspoons baking powder

3 tablespoons sugar

$\frac{1}{4}$ teaspoon salt

$\frac{1}{4}$ cup plus 2 tablespoons butter, cut into 6 pieces

6 tablespoons crunchy peanut butter

2 eggs

$1\frac{1}{2}$ cups plus 1 or 2 tablespoons milk

 TIPS & TOUCHES

- Elinor advised against serving bacon with these waffles because she felt it interfered with their delicate flavor. We serve our waffles with fresh raspberries or stewed blueberries and yogurt.

Mrs. Orcott's Bran Bread

{ *1918* }

MAKES 14 SLICES

½ cup wheat bran

4 tablespoons honey, divided

½ cup buttermilk

½ cup butter, melted

2 eggs, beaten

1½ cups flour

½ cup cornmeal

3 teaspoons baking powder

1 teaspoon baking soda

1 teaspoon salt

½ cup sugar

¼ cup roasted, salted pepitas
(optional)

Tips & Touches

- Coat a tablespoon with vegetable spray before measuring the honey.

THIS RECIPE CAME FROM THE COLLECTION OF *Mrs. Orcott, an Ohio woman who was active in the Lakeside Women's Society during the 1950s. An avid home cook, she collected recipes wherever she went, often jotting them on the back of flyers. This recipe is an earlier one from her collection dating from 1918 and could possibly be a war bread. It has the texture of cornbread but the flavor of a good bran muffin. We think the pepitas bring it into the 21st century.*

1. Set oven rack in middle position. Preheat oven to 350°F. Line bottom and ends of 9-inch by 5-inch by 3-inch loaf pan with single strip of wax paper. Coat pan and wax paper liner with vegetable spray.

2. Place wheat bran, 3 tablespoons of the honey, buttermilk, butter, and eggs in large mixing bowl. Gently mix together. Let stand 10 minutes.

3. Place flour, cornmeal, baking powder, baking soda, salt, and sugar in small bowl. Whisk to combine.

4. Add dry ingredients to wheat bran mixture and stir just until combined. Using rubber spatula, give batter 2 quick turns.

5. Place batter in loaf pan. Tap pan twice on counter to level off batter and remove air bubbles. Drizzle remaining 1 tablespoon honey on top of batter and sprinkle with pepitas, if using. Press pepitas gently into batter with palm of your hand. Bake 45 to 50 minutes, or until tester inserted into center of loaf comes out clean. Set pan on rack until completely cool. Remove bread from pan and cut into slices. Store loosely wrapped in wax paper at room temperature.

Marion Freeman's Date and Nut Bread

MAKES 14 SLICES

{ 1 9 3 0 s }

THIS RECIPE CAME FROM THE COLLECTION OF *Mrs. George S. Sutton of Penny Farms, Florida. She requested it from Marion Freeman, who brought it to a "lunch" given by Mrs. Sutton on Christmas Day. We suggest spreading a warm slice with whipped cream cheese. The combination of dense, nut-studded sweet bread and tangy cream cheese is one that should not be overlooked.*

1. Set the oven rack in the middle position. Line the bottom and ends of a 9-inch by 5-inch by 3-inch loaf pan with a single strip of wax paper. Coat the pan and wax paper liner with vegetable spray.

2. Combine dates, butter, and boiling water in a small bowl. Let stand 25 minutes, or until at room temperature and most of the liquid is absorbed.

3. Sift together flour, baking powder, baking soda, and salt in a small bowl.

4. Mix sugar, egg, and vanilla in a large bowl. Add date mixture and combine. Add sifted dry ingredients and combine. Fold in pecans.

5. Pour batter into loaf pan. Bake 1 hour, or until top is browned and a tester inserted into bread comes out clean. Place pan on rack and cool at least 20 minutes. Turn out bread onto rack and allow to cool completely. Store covered with a paper towel and wrapped in wax paper at room temperature.

1 cup dates, chopped
1 tablespoon butter
1 cup boiling water
2 cups flour
1 teaspoon baking powder
1 teaspoon baking soda
½ teaspoon salt
1 cup sugar
1 egg, beaten
1 teaspoon vanilla
1½ cups chopped toasted pecans

➤➤ HOW TO TOAST NUTS ◄◄

Preheat the oven to 350°F. Spread nuts on foil-wrapped cookie sheet, shiny side up. Toast nuts for 5 minutes. Remove cookie sheet from oven, shake nuts to expose the other sides, and return pan to oven for another 5 minutes. Set baking sheet on rack to cool. We suggest you store any unused nuts in the refrigerator in sealed plastic bags labeled with the name of the nut, the quantity, and the date toasted.

Winchester Nut Bread

{1918}

FOR BREAD

½ cup brown sugar

¾ cup hot water

½ cup molasses

¾ cup milk

1 cup flour

2½ teaspoons baking powder

1¼ teaspoons salt

¾ teaspoon baking soda

1 teaspoon nutmeg

2 cups graham flour

¾ cup finely chopped walnuts

FOR NUT TOPPING

2 teaspoons butter, melted

⅓ cup finely chopped walnuts

TIPS & TOUCHES

- This bread should be handled as if it were a muffin batter, which means don't overmix it.
- Serve this bread with sweet butter and orange marmalade.

WE LOVE ANY RECIPE THAT HAS THE NAME *of a town or city in it, since we like knowing where our recipes come from. But there are a lot of Winchesters in the United States and Canada, so we can't be sure exactly where this nut bread originates. This is a very old recipe, and versions of it may have found their way into several community cookbooks. We found our handwritten version in an old manuscript cookbook, and we like to think of this wonderful coarse-grained bread as a personal adaptation by the woman who wrote it down.*

1. Set oven rack in middle position. Preheat oven to 350°F. Line bottom and ends of 9-inch by 5-inch by 3-inch loaf pan with single strip of wax paper. Coat pan and wax paper liner with vegetable spray.

2. Place brown sugar in medium bowl. Pour hot water over brown sugar. Add molasses and milk and stir.

3. Sift together flour, baking powder, salt, baking soda, and nutmeg into large mixing bowl. Whisk in graham flour. Add molasses mixture and mix gently with wooden spoon or wire whisk. Fold in walnuts.

4. Pour batter into loaf pan. Tap pan twice on counter to level off batter and remove air bubbles. Brush top of batter with melted butter. Sprinkle walnuts on top and press lightly into batter with palm of your hand. Bake 50 minutes, or until tester inserted into bread comes out clean. Cool completely in pan on rack before slicing. Store loosely covered with wax paper at room temperature.

Aunt Ida's Pecan Ring

MAKES 2 RINGS, 12 SLICES PER RING

{ *1930s* }

THESE WERE THE PECAN RINGS OUR AUNTIE IDA *made on her pink Formica table in Brookline, Massachusetts. Well into her nineties, Ida was still available for tea, sympathy, and some honest criticism—and she was never without a Pecan Ring in her postage stamp–sized freezer.*

1. Set oven rack in middle position. Preheat oven to 350°F. Cover 14-inch by 16-inch baking sheet with foil, shiny side up. Coat foil with vegetable spray, or use silicone liner.

2. To make dough: Dissolve yeast in warm water. Add 1 tablespoon of the sugar. Set in warm place to proof, about 10 minutes. Mixture will bubble when yeast is proofed.

3. Cream butter, eggs, remaining 3 tablespoons sugar, and salt in bowl of standing mixer fitted with paddle attachment. Add proofed yeast and combine. Remove paddle attachment and attach dough hook. Add 3 cups of the flour, 1 cup at a time, and knead about 5 minutes, or until dough holds together. Add remaining 1/2 cup of flour if necessary. Place dough in oiled bowl and turn so entire dough is coated with oil. Cover with towel and refrigerate 4 hours or overnight.

4. To add filling: Combine cinnamon, sugar, and brown sugar in bowl. Remove dough from refrigerator and allow it to sit in warm place for 30 minutes. Divide dough in half. Place half of dough between 2 pieces of wax paper or parchment paper sprinkled with flour and roll out into rectangle 1/4-inch thick. Brush surface of dough with some melted butter. Scatter half of pecans and half of sugar mixture over dough, allowing 1-inch margin on all sides. Roll up dough from top to bottom, jelly roll-style, using paper as aid. Place roll on baking sheet and join ends to form ring. Use scissors or knife to make 16 cuts in ring. Let rise for 20 minutes in warm place. Repeat with remaining dough.

5. Brush tops of rings with melted butter. Bake 30 to 33 minutes, or until golden brown. Remove from oven and cool on rack. Store loosely wrapped in wax paper at room temperature.

FOR DOUGH

1 package (2¼ teaspoons) active dry yeast

½ cup water, warmed to 115°F

¼ cup sugar, divided

1 cup butter

3 eggs

1 teaspoon salt

3½ cups flour, divided

FOR FILLING

1 teaspoon cinnamon

½ cup sugar

½ cup brown sugar

½ cup butter, melted

1 cup toasted pecans, coarsely chopped

Applesauce Cake

{ *1920s* }

MAKES 14 SLICES

1¾ cups flour

⅛ teaspoon salt

½ teaspoon cloves

1 teaspoon cinnamon

¼ teaspoon nutmeg

1 cup butter

½ cup sugar

½ cup brown sugar

2 teaspoons cold water

1 teaspoon baking soda

1 cup applesauce (use liquid
    measuring cup)

1 cup raisins plumped in orange
    juice (see "How to Plump
    Raisins" on page 33)

WE FOUND THIS RECIPE FOR APPLESAUCE CAKE *in a collection of handwritten recipes jotted down in a small notebook given out by the New Hampshire Fire Insurance Company. Because we're purists, we used our own homemade applesauce in this recipe (see "How to Make Applesauce") with grand success. However, we also baked the cake with commercial applesauce and found very little difference in texture or flavor.*

1. Set oven rack in middle position. Preheat oven to 350°F. Coat 9-inch by 5-inch by 3-inch metal loaf pan with vegetable spray. Line bottom and sides of pan with wax paper and spray again to coat liner.

2. Sift together flour, salt, cloves, cinnamon, and nutmeg.

3. Cream butter, sugar, and brown sugar in bowl of standing mixer fitted with paddle attachment.

Tin flour sifter, 1910; aluminum measuring cup, 1930s

4. Place cold water in small cup, add baking soda, and stir until dissolved. Pour mixture onto applesauce and stir briskly (mixture will foam up). Add applesauce to butter mixture and mix thoroughly. Add sifted dry ingredients and mix until well combined. Fold in raisins.

5. Pour batter into loaf pan. Bake 1 hour and 10 minutes, or until tester inserted into cake comes out dry. Cool on rack 15 minutes before turning out of pan. Serve warm or at room temperature. Store loosely covered with wax paper at room temperature.

TIPS & TOUCHES

- This cake is even better the next day. You can serve it with tea or coffee and a side of unsweetened whipped cream.
- We like to plump raisins by boiling them in orange juice, but you can skip this step and use raisins that have not been plumped. The orange juice does give an added nuance to the cake.

Lemon Poppy Seed Cake

MAKES 16 SLICES

{ 1 9 7 0 s }

THIS IS ONE OF THOSE UNASSUMING RECIPES *that often falls under the heading of "coffee cake," never mind that the batter is rich and looks like whipped cream. There are those who do not hesitate to point out its humble ingredients, but we love this cake and have been making variations on it for years. Chameleon-like, it's presented itself over the years as a Lemon Ginger Cake, Brown Sugar Pecan Cake, and Coconut Cake with Raspberry Butter Cream.*

1. Set oven rack in middle position. Preheat oven to 350°F. Coat 8-cup Bundt pan or 8-cup tube pan with vegetable spray or butter and dust with flour.

2. To make cake: Sift together flour, baking powder, and salt.

3. Cream butter and sugar in bowl of standing mixer fitted with paddle attachment. With mixer running, add eggs one at a time and sour cream. Add poppy seeds. Fold in sifted dry ingredients in thirds. Add lemon juice and lemon zest and mix well.

4. Pour batter into pan. Bake 50 to 60 minutes, or until cake pulls away from sides of pan and tester inserted into cake comes out clean. Cake may crack on top. Place pan on rack and cool about 20 minutes. Run butter knife around edges. Turn out cake onto rack and allow to cool completely.

5. To make lemon glaze: Mix together confectioners' sugar, lemon juice, and salt in small bowl. Slip sheet of wax paper under rack to catch drips. Use teaspoon or fork to drizzle glaze over top of cake. After glaze has set, store loosely covered with wax paper at room temperature. Cake can be frozen and reheated.

FOR CAKE

2 cups flour

1 teaspoon baking powder

¼ teaspoon salt

1 cup butter

2 cups sugar

2 eggs

1 cup sour cream

¼ cup poppy seeds

3 tablespoons lemon juice

2 teaspoons grated lemon zest

FOR LEMON GLAZE

1 cup confectioners' sugar

2 tablespoons lemon juice

Pinch of salt

TIPS & TOUCHES

* If you don't have time to make the lemon glaze, dust the top of the cake lightly with confectioners' sugar instead.

Brown Sugar Rhubarb Cake

{ 1 9 3 0 }

MAKES 12 SERVINGS

FOR CAKE

2 cups finely chopped rhubarb

2 cups sifted flour

$\frac{1}{4}$ teaspoon salt

3 teaspoons lemon zest

1$\frac{1}{2}$ cups brown sugar

$\frac{1}{2}$ cup vegetable oil

1 egg

1 teaspoon baking soda

1 cup buttermilk

1 teaspoon vanilla

3 tablespoons lemon juice

FOR TOPPING

1 cup brown sugar

1 teaspoon cinnamon

TIPS & TOUCHES

- This cake is best served the day it is baked. One day later, the rhubarb will turn into a layer of jam; the cake will still taste delicious, but the texture will change.
- To serve this cake as a dessert, add a scoop of rich vanilla ice cream.

FOUND WRITTEN ON A LINED INDEX CARD, *this little treasure has become part of our personal repertoire. When we first tried to make this recipe, the chopped rhubarb proved to be a challenge. We thought the cake would have a rather tangy taste, but the tart flavor of the rhubarb wasn't distinctive. Then we realized that the role of the rhubarb was to contribute moistness. We added lemon zest and lemon juice to the batter to bring out the true tartness of the rhubarb, and it worked!*

1. To make cake: Place chopped rhubarb in glass bowl, cover with plastic wrap, and refrigerate overnight. The next day, drain off and discard liquid. Squeeze rhubarb to extract remaining liquid. Mix together rhubarb, flour, salt, and lemon zest in bowl.

2. Set oven rack in middle position. Preheat oven to 350°F. Coat 9-inch by 13-inch glass baking dish with vegetable spray. Dust with flour and tap out excess.

3. Combine brown sugar, vegetable oil, and egg in bowl of standing mixer fitted with paddle attachment.

4. Dissolve baking soda in buttermilk. Add vanilla and stir. With mixer running, add buttermilk mixture to egg mixture. Add rhubarb mixture and beat in. Turn off mixer. Add lemon juice and stir twice with spatula. Pour batter, which will be very loose, into baking dish.

5. To make topping: Mix brown sugar and cinnamon in small bowl. Sprinkle topping on batter, avoiding edges to prevent sticking at sides of baking dish. Gently press topping into batter with palm of your hand. Bake 45 minutes, or until cake bubbles and topping has formed. Cool on rack. Serve slightly warm or at room temperature. Store loosely wrapped in wax paper in plastic container in refrigerator.

⇥ **ALL ABOUT RHUBARB** ⇤

Rhubarb is also called "pie plant" because it's used in so many pies. Select firm stalks that are no more than 1 inch in diameter. Cut the stalks into ½-inch pieces for ease in baking. Peel rhubarb stalks if they appear to be tough or stringy. Because it contains large amounts of fluid, chopped rhubarb should be allowed to drain for at least 30 minutes before using. Remember to use only the stalks of rhubarb—its leaves are toxic and should not be eaten.

Miniature canister set, 1920s

Mary Williams's Coffee Cake with Streusel

MAKES 16 SQUARES

FOR STREUSEL

½ cup brown sugar

2 tablespoons flour

½ teaspoon cinnamon

2 tablespoons cold butter

½ cup pecans, toasted and coarsely chopped

FOR CAKE

1½ cups flour

3 teaspoons baking powder

¼ teaspoon salt

¾ cup sugar

¼ cup butter

1 egg, beaten

½ cup milk

1 teaspoon vanilla

TIPS & TOUCHES

- Batter for coffee cake may be prepared up to 1 day ahead and refrigerated.

THIS RECIPE WAS GIVEN TO US BY *Elinor Jennings in the early 1970s. Several of the recipes she gave to us were from her mother, Daisy Inman, and reflect the cuisine of a Southern woman. Mary Williams was a friend of the Inman family. Her coffee cake is rich with butter and nuts.*

1. Set oven rack in middle position. Preheat oven to 350°F. Line bottom and sides of 8-inch by 8-inch metal pan with foil, shiny side up. Coat with butter or vegetable spray.

2. To make streusel: Place brown sugar, flour, and cinnamon in bowl. Work in butter with your fingers (wear disposable gloves if desired) until mixture resembles coarse sand. Add pecans and combine.

3. To make cake: Sift together flour, baking powder, and salt. Add sugar. Using pastry blender or 2 knives, cut butter into dry ingredients. Add egg, milk, and vanilla and combine. Place half of batter in pan. Sprinkle half of streusel on top of batter. Add rest of batter to pan and top with remaining streusel.

4. Bake 35 to 40 minutes, or until tester inserted into cake comes out clean. Cool on rack completely before cutting into squares. Serve plain or with butter. Store loosely wrapped with wax paper at room temperature.

CHAPTER 2

IN THE BEGINNING

Appetizers and first courses have always been an important part of every meal. They are the first act, the prelude to what is coming next. If the appetizer tastes good, then chances are the rest of the meal will be delicious. • Almost every language has a word for appetizers. In our family, we used the Yiddish word *farschpais* to refer to herring salad or chopped liver prepared to pique our appetites—we interpreted its meaning as something to spice up the meal. Italian families referred to their caponata (an eggplant-tomato spread) as the antipasto—something served before the rest of the meal. If we want to be fancy, we can call the recipe for savory Mystery Stuffed Mushrooms an hors d'oeuvre. These days, we often refer to these tempting first bites as something to whet or sharpen our appetites.

Reading through our growing collections of manuscript cookbooks filled with handwritten recipes, we've found a bounty of intriguing starters with interesting stories about the women who created them.

While not all starters are created equal, they should be simple and inexpensive to make and use easily obtainable ingredients. Some of the recipes in this chapter use similar ingredients such as cheese, eggs, or chicken livers, but they are used in very different ways. For example, the chopped liver of our childhood is very different from Ione Ulrich Sutton's sophisticated liver paté, with its buttery texture and hint of chopped sweet gherkins.

We found the recipe for Ione's paté as we leafed through a pile of faded handwritten recipes late at night in a New York bookstore. Ione Ulrich Sutton was a Renaissance woman. She was the financial officer of the Museum of Modern Art in the 1930s, and she worked on Wall Street in the 1940s and 1950s. Above all, she was a creative hostess who generously passed on her recipes for paté and zucchini pie to those who asked for them, often jotting them down on her own business stationery. We found that her recipes are as good today as they were when she served them at gatherings for her socially prominent friends.

Mrs. Yaffee's pierogi are meat-filled treasures in a crust rich with chicken fat. Baked, rather than boiled, these crusty starters came from the mother of our next-door neighbor, Thelma Hankin. Stopping by to visit on Sea Foam Avenue after a trip to Mexico, Mrs. Yaffee graciously shared her recipe with the women sitting on beach chairs in her daughter's driveway. We still have her recipe transcribed in our mother Dorothy's handwriting. Mama used to serve two or three pierogi with a bowl of home-made chicken soup, but we've made these smaller pierogi as appetizers.

A local yard sale provided Libby Corkery's Spicy Ribs with Barbecue Sauce. Our agent, Karen, gave us Libby's file of handwritten recipes. The telephone operator for the town of Groton, Massachusetts, for 35 years, Libby was a formidable home cook. These ribs are juicy, succulent finger food and a perfect start to a festive party.

Browsing in an antique store in Marblehead, Massachusetts, we found the recipe for Helen's Fried Cheese Balls, tasty little bites that are wonderful dipped in Chili Mayonnaise. As we handled the fragile pages of this manuscript cookbook, we found a precious love letter, written from Charles to Helen and dated June 27, 1897. In it, we read about the hopes the young couple had for a life together now that her father had given his blessing to the engagement. When Charles wrote his love letter, he had no idea that his "own darling little girl" would turn out to be such a gifted home cook and capable hostess.

Our friend Nick Malgieri provided us with the recipe for a savory cheese cracker that tasted very much like the ones Grandpa Katziff brought us from the family grocery store years ago. We adapted the recipe to include an extra level of flavor by substituting blue cheese for cheddar and adding the crunch of chopped walnuts. The taste of these crackers comes as close to the waffled cheese treats of our childhood as we can get.

We hope that you will enjoy reading the stories and preparing the recipes in this chapter, and that in making them your own, you will re-create the good times they represent.

Libby's Spicy Ribs with Barbecue Sauce

{ *1960s* }

4 pounds pork baby back ribs, separated

1¼ cups chopped onion

1 tablespoon salt

1 tablespoon pickling spice

1½ cups water

1 cup ketchup

¾ cup chili sauce

¼ cup firmly packed brown sugar

2 tablespoons Worcestershire sauce

1 tablespoon celery seed

¼ teaspoon garlic powder

⅛ teaspoon red pepper flakes

1 teaspoon ground mustard

Tabasco sauce (optional)

TIPS & TOUCHES

- For a spicier sauce, add more Tabasco sauce.
- Remove some of the cinnamon sticks from the pickling spice to reduce the cinnamon taste of the sauce.

SOME APPETIZERS JUST BRING A CROWD TOGETHER. *People don't stay strangers long when they're wiping barbecue sauce off their chins. Maybe that's what Libby Corkery, of Groton, Massachusetts, planned when she entertained—comfort food that was actually "finger-licking" good. This is a home cook's interpretation of barbecue. There are lots of pantry shelf ingredients in this recipe, so break out the ketchup, celery seed, and garlic powder.*

1. Place ribs in heavy 8-quart pot. Add onion, salt, and pickling spice. Add water to cover ribs. Cover pot and bring to a boil. Reduce heat and simmer 1 hour, occasionally stirring with wooden spoon and checking to make sure water doesn't evaporate. Replenish water if needed.

2. Set oven rack in middle position. Preheat oven to 325°F. Coat 9-inch by 13-inch ovenproof glass baking dish with vegetable spray.

3. In small saucepan, combine water, ketchup, chili sauce, brown sugar, Worcestershire sauce, celery seed, garlic powder, red pepper flakes, mustard, and Tabasco sauce, if using. Bring to a boil, reduce heat, and simmer 5 minutes. Place ribs in prepared dish, pour sauce over ribs, and turn ribs once in sauce to coat. Bake 1 hour, or until ribs are tender and falling off bone. Turn ribs at least twice during baking. To serve, spoon sauce on top and pass extra sauce on the side.

Mrs. Yaffee's Pierogi

MAKES 20 PIEROGI

FOR DOUGH

2 cups flour

2 teaspoons baking powder

½ teaspoon salt

½ cup chilled chicken fat or shortening

2 eggs, beaten

2 tablespoons ice water

1 egg, beaten, for glaze

FOR FILLING

¾ pound ground beef

2 tablespoons chicken fat or olive oil

1 cup finely chopped onion

1 cup finely chopped boiled potatoes

½ teaspoon salt

¼ teaspoon coarsely ground black pepper

THIS IS ONE OF THOSE GREAT RECIPES *that women exchange when visiting. We lived next door to Thelma Hankin, who held court with the ladies of Sea Foam Avenue during spring and summer afternoons in the 1940s. Her mother, Mrs. Yaffee, a talented home cook, could talk a good recipe. These meat- and potato-filled pastries (pictured on page 14) are like Jewish baked empanadas. The chicken fat in the dough gives these tender little savories a satisfying flavor. Originally made with shredded leftover pot roast or brisket, ours use ground beef.*

1. To make dough: Combine flour, baking powder, and salt in bowl of food processor fitted with metal blade. Add chicken fat or shortening and pulse until mixed. Add eggs and ice water. Process until dough pulls away from sides of bowl. Remove dough from bowl, divide in half, and shape each half into a disk. Place each disk in plastic bag. Chill until firm enough to roll, at least 2 hours.

2. To make filling: Sauté ground beef in large frying pan over medium heat until no trace of pink remains. Transfer cooked meat to large bowl. Do not drain fat from meat. Add chicken fat or olive oil to pan and return pan to medium heat. Add onion and sauté until translucent, 5 to 7 minutes. Add onion to bowl with meat. Add potatoes, salt, and pepper and stir to combine. Let cool.

➤➤ THE HISTORY OF PIEROGI ◄◄

Pierogi are small pastries filled with meat, onions, and potatoes. They are first cousins to *piroghi* (from Slovakia), *piroshki* (from Armenia), and *pelmeni* (from Russia). Mrs. Yaffee's Pierogi are baked, not boiled or fried. Not quite a dumpling, more of a small pie, the singular of *pierogi* is sometimes referred to as a *pierøg* or a *parog*. Pierogi have existed in some form since the 16th century and trace their origin to Russia and possibly to China. Pierogi can be filled with shredded cabbage, mushrooms, or farmer's cheese.

SOME THOUGHTS ON CHICKEN FAT

Chicken fat gives pierogi dough and chopped liver their distinctive flavor and texture. Traditionally, small amounts of chicken fat were collected from several kosher chickens. The raw fat was tightly wrapped and frozen. When enough fat was collected, it was defrosted and rendered with chopped onions on top of the stove.

Chicken fat is essential to many Jewish recipes. What lard is to Christian cooks, chicken fat is to Jewish cooks. Rendering chicken fat can be dangerous, but there is an alternative to simmering a large amount of fat on a hot stove. After roasting chickens, pour off the hot cooking liquid that collects in the pan and chill it in the refrigerator. Harvest the thick layer of golden fat that collects on the surface of this gravy, store it in an airtight container, and freeze it for future use. Small amounts of rendered chicken fat keep in the freezer for about 3 months and are available when needed. Rendered chicken fat can also be purchased at kosher markets.

3. Set oven rack in middle position. Preheat oven to 375°F. Line 14-inch by 16-inch baking sheet with foil, shiny side up, and coat with vegetable spray, or use silicone liner.

4. On lightly floured work surface, roll out 1 dough disk to $1/16$-inch thickness. Cut into circles using 4-inch round cookie cutter dipped in flour. Combine scraps and reroll to cut at least 10 circles total. Work remaining dough disk in the same way to cut 10 more circles.

5. Place heaping tablespoon of meat mixture in center of each dough circle. Using your finger, moisten edges of each circle with water and fold over dough to form half-moon. Use tines of salad fork to crimp folded edge. Place on prepared baking sheet and brush with beaten egg. Bake about 20 minutes, or until golden brown. Remove from oven, place baking sheet on rack, and cool 5 minutes. Serve immediately. Store leftover pierogi in covered container in refrigerator.

Tips & Touches

- Because pierogi are made with chicken fat, the dough is fragile. Handle it with care to prevent tears. Patch tears with thin pieces of extra dough.
- Baked pierogi can be frozen, defrosted, and reheated in a 375°F oven for 5 to 7 minutes.
- Pierogi can be served hot, warm, or at room temperature, as an appetizer or on the side with a bowl of chicken soup.

Mixed Olives with Lemon and Rosemary

MAKES 6 SERVINGS

Tᴴɪꜱ ɪꜱ ᴏɴᴇ ᴏꜰ ᴛʜᴏꜱᴇ ʀᴇᴄɪᴘᴇꜱ ᴡᴇ *made, when we were sweet young things, to take to parties in Cambridge, Massachusetts. It became Sheila's signature appetizer, and years later, there are those who still remember the mix of olives, the touch of citrus, and the use of the then exotic herb rosemary. The caper berries are an optional addition, enhancing the crunchy texture. This recipe uses olives very different from the canned black or bottled green ones we grew up with.*

1. Bruise rosemary sprigs with bottom of small metal saucepan and remove leaves.
2. Place rosemary, olives, olive oil, lemon juice, lemon zest, capers, red pepper flakes, caper berries (if using), and garlic in large nonreactive bowl. Mix thoroughly and cover with plastic wrap. Refrigerate for at least 2 days before serving.

2 sprigs fresh rosemary, each 5 inches long

1½ pounds assorted brined olives

¼ cup extra-virgin olive oil

1 tablespoon lemon juice

2 teaspoons grated lemon zest

1 tablespoon brined capers (not salt-cured)

¼ teaspoon red pepper flakes

½ pound caper berries (optional)

3 cloves garlic, smashed

Tɪᴘꜱ & Tᴏᴜᴄʜᴇꜱ

- We used a mix of Manzanilla, Kalamata, Sicilian, and Bella Cerignola Rosa olives for a good range of color and texture. Picholine and Calabrese olives can also be used for this recipe.
- We don't add salt because the olives are brined, but the seasoning can be adjusted.
- Olives can be garnished with thinly sliced rounds of lemon and sprigs of rosemary.

Auntie Dot's Chopped Liver

{ 1 9 3 0 s }

MAKES 2½ POUNDS CHICKEN LIVER

½ cup flour

2 pounds chicken livers, rinsed and patted dry

2 tablespoons chicken fat or olive oil, plus extra, if needed (see "Some Thoughts on Chicken Fat" on page 61)

2 cups chopped onion

4 eggs, hard-cooked, 1 yolk reserved for garnish, balance chopped

1 teaspoon salt

½ teaspoon coarsely ground black pepper

TIPS & TOUCHES

- Fry chicken livers in batches to avoid crowding the pan, which will result in uneven cooking.
- Use a metal egg slicer to save time chopping eggs.

THIS IS THE CHOPPED LIVER THAT OUR *mother, Dorothy, made when we were growing up. She always used a hand chopper and a wooden bowl and lots of homemade chicken fat. We use a food processor with excellent results, but don't expect a smooth, buttery paté. The variation in texture is what makes this appetizer so special. Chopped liver is delicious spread on a piece of rye bread, topped with a slice of raw onion. Marilynn was always responsible for the sieved egg yolk mimosa garnish.*

1. Place flour in plastic bag. Add chicken livers and shake until lightly coated. Shake floured livers in strainer over sink to remove excess flour. Set aside.

2. Heat chicken fat or olive oil in large heavy frying pan over medium heat. Add onion and cook until just translucent, 5 to 7 minutes. Remove to bowl and set aside. Working in batches, fry livers in chicken fat remaining in pan until bottoms are brown and crunchy, about 5 minutes. Turn and cook until second side is browned, another 5 minutes. Remove 1 liver from pan and cut into it. Livers are done when no pink remains in interior when you cut into liver. Add more fat during frying if pan gets dry.

3. Place onion and livers in bowl of food processor fitted with metal blade. Pulse until mixture is combined but still coarsely textured. Remove half of mixture and set aside. Pulse remaining mixture to a texture that is slightly coarser than paté. Combine liver mixtures and fold in chopped eggs. Add more chicken fat if texture is a little dry. Add salt and pepper; taste to adjust seasonings.

4. Refrigerate chopped liver in covered container until 15 minutes before serving. Serve in mound on platter surrounded by crackers and celery stalks. Press reserved yolk through fine sieve and scatter resulting mimosa on top of mounded liver. Do not leave out at room temperature for long periods of time.

New York Paté

{ *1930s* }

WE FOUND THIS LIVING RECIPE FOR *a sophisticated chicken liver paté on the personalized notepaper of Ione Ulrich Sutton, who was affiliated with the brokerage firm of Winslow, Cohu & Stetson, in New York. Further research told us that the personal papers of Ione, a career woman, writer, and active Republican, reside in the Eisenhower Library, in Abilene, Kansas. Just as important, Ione knew how to cook and entertain by preparing simple but memorable appetizers. Her guests often requested these recipes.*

8 tablespoons butter, softened to room temperature, divided, plus more if needed

2 pounds chicken livers, rinsed and patted dry

1 cup finely chopped onion

1 cup finely chopped sweet gherkins

1 tablespoon prepared yellow mustard

¾ teaspoon salt

½ teaspoon coarsely ground black pepper

1. Heat 2 tablespoons of the butter in large frying pan over medium heat. Working in batches, add as many chicken livers as will comfortably fit in pan and cook until well browned on 1 side, about 5 minutes. Turn with spatula and cook until the second side is browned, another 5 minutes. Add more butter if needed. Remove pan from heat and mash livers with fork in pan. Return pan to heat and continue cooking until livers are no longer pink, about 2 minutes more. Add onion and cook an additional 2 minutes.

2. Place liver mixture in bowl of food processor fitted with metal blade. Process until smooth. Add remaining 6 tablespoons butter, gherkins, mustard, salt, and pepper and pulse until blended. Line small molds or custard cups with plastic wrap with 1-inch overhang, spoon paté into molds, and chill until firm. Unmold 15 minutes before serving by lifting plastic wrap and placing paté on plates.

➤➤ HOW TO SELECT AND PREPARE CHICKEN LIVERS ◄◄

Buy chicken livers from a reputable butcher to ensure freshness. Always choose livers that are free of green spots or discolorations. To clean, remove membranes and any fat adhering to livers and separate the lobes. Chicken livers should be rinsed and patted dry with paper towels before frying.

Nick's Savory Blue Cheese and Walnut Crackers

{ 1 9 4 0 s — 1 9 9 0 s }   MAKES 40 CRACKERS

1 cup all-purpose flour

½ teaspoon salt

1 teaspoon coarsely ground
   black pepper

4 ounces blue cheese

½ cup cold butter, cut into 8 pieces

1 cup toasted walnuts,
   coarsely chopped

TIPS & TOUCHES

- This recipe is adapted from Nick Malgieri's Peppery Cheddar Coins from *Cookies Unlimited*.
- Blue cheese and walnuts give this cracker more of a bite, as well as a crunchy texture.

OUR GRANDPARENTS, CELIA AND JOSEPH KATZIFF, *ran a mom-and-pop grocery store on Shirley Street in Winthrop, Massachusetts, and when Grandpa Katziff wasn't taking Sheila to East Boston to buy hair ribbons or toys, he was bringing home special treats like waffled cheese crackers from their store. Our friend Nick Malgieri's recipe for Peppery Cheddar Coins comes the closest to replicating the taste of those treats from the 1940s. We substituted the blue cheese and walnuts, but you can make them with the original cheddar.*

1. Combine flour, salt, and pepper in bowl and set aside. Combine blue cheese and butter in bowl of food processor fitted with the metal blade. Pulse 5 or 6 times to combine. Add flour mixture and pulse until mixture forms ball.

2. Remove dough from bowl of food processor, form into log 1½ inches wide, and wrap in wax paper or plastic wrap. Refrigerate until firm, about 2 hours.

3. Set oven rack in middle position. Preheat oven to 350°F. Line three 14-inch by 16-inch baking sheets with foil, shiny side up, and coat with vegetable spray, or use silicone liners.

4. Cut dough into ¼-inch-thick slices. Place slices on baking sheets, no more than 16 crackers to a sheet. Sprinkle crackers with chopped walnuts. Cut 4-inch by 4-inch square of wax paper. Place wax paper on top of each cracker and press gently with bottom of glass to flatten. Bake 15 to 17 minutes, or until crackers are light golden color. Transfer to rack and let cool. Store between sheets of wax paper in covered tin.

Ione's Zucchini Pie

{1940s}

4 cups grated zucchini

1 cup coarsely chopped onion

½ cup chopped fresh parsley

1 teaspoon salt

½ teaspoon coarsely ground
  black pepper

¼ cup butter, softened to
  room temperature

2 eggs

9-inch pie shell, baked and cooled
  (see Sheila's Savory Pie Crust
  on page 306)

2 teaspoons mustard

WE DECIDED TO CALL THIS A ZUCCHINI PIE, *rather than a zucchini quiche, because there is no milk or cheese in the recipe. Painting the crust with mustard gives this simple but sophisticated pie a special zing. Easy to assemble, it's the type of elegant appetizer a New York career woman such as Ione Sutton would have prepared before leaving for work in the morning.*

1. Set oven rack in middle position. Preheat oven to 375°F.
2. Squeeze excess water out of zucchini and place in bowl. Add onion, parsley, salt, and pepper and stir to combine. Melt butter in large heavy skillet over medium heat. Add zucchini mixture and cook until vegetables no longer taste raw, 4 to 5 minutes.
3. Whisk eggs in bowl until yolks and whites are combined. Gradually pour into skillet with hot vegetables, stirring rapidly.
4. Paint bottom of pie shell with mustard. Spoon mixture into prepared pie shell and smooth top. Bake 25 to 30 minutes, or until tester inserted into middle comes out clean. Serve slices of zucchini pie on individual plates. Garnish with 1 tablespoon sour cream and sprig of fresh parsley.

TIPS & TOUCHES

- Be sure to stir eggs vigorously into hot vegetables so they don't pre-cook.

⤛ USING HERBS ⤜

Fresh herbs should be stored in a container with their stems in water in the refrigerator. Fresh parsley and other flat-leaved herbs can be chopped and frozen in a metal ice cube tray. Frozen cubes can be transferred to a plastic bag, dated, and stored in the freezer for up to 3 months. Add herb cubes to stews and soups during cooking, as needed.

Dried herbs have a more concentrated flavor than fresh herbs. Dried herbs should be kept in a cool, dark place, not near a source of heat such as a kitchen stove. Date the containers used for storing dried herbs and replace the herbs after 1 year.

Substitutions: 1 teaspoon of dried herbs = 2 tablespoons of fresh herbs

Mystery Stuffed Mushrooms

{ 1 9 6 0 s }

THERE IS A REAL HONEST-TO-GOODNESS MYSTERY HERE. *We found this recipe in our aunt Ida Katziff's recipe box, but we don't know where she found it. Ida once confessed to us that she was "an old-fashioned girl" and didn't use fancy seasonings like basil or oregano. So we can only guess that she tasted these mushrooms, thought very highly of them, and requested the recipe. Someday we hope to find who the originator of this recipe is.*

1. Set oven rack in middle position. Preheat oven to 375°F. Coat 9-inch by 13-inch ovenproof glass baking dish with vegetable spray.

2. Finely chop mushroom stems. Heat 5 tablespoons of the butter in skillet over medium heat. Add chopped stems and onion and cook until softened, about 4 minutes. Do not let vegetables burn. Add bread crumbs and continue to cook until bread crumbs are lightly browned, 2 to 3 minutes. Remove from heat. Add basil, salt, cayenne pepper, and walnuts and stir to combine.

3. Place mushroom caps in prepared dish. Use spoon to stuff with bread crumb mixture. Press down on stuffing gently to be sure caps are completely filled. Sprinkle filled caps with cheese and dot with remaining 1 tablespoon butter. Bake until filling bubbles, 20 to 30 minutes. Serve immediately. Store leftover mushrooms in a covered container in refrigerator.

1 pound large white mushrooms suitable for stuffing, caps and stems separated

6 tablespoons butter, softened to room temperature, divided

1 cup chopped onion

½ cup fine bread crumbs

½ teaspoon dried basil

½ teaspoon salt

¼ teaspoon cayenne pepper

¼ cup toasted walnuts, finely chopped

½ cup grated parmesan cheese

TIPS & TOUCHES

- If you want a slightly different flavor, oregano can be substituted for the basil.
- Mushrooms can be prepared ahead of time and refrigerated. Let them come to room temperature before baking. They may have to stay in the oven a little longer if refrigerated.
- Leftover mushrooms are also good eaten cold with a splash of red wine vinegar.

Stuffed Mushrooms

1 lb. large mushrooms
1 small onion, minced
5 tbsp butter
¼ tsp sweet basil

½ slice bread, crumbled
pinch cayenne
pinch salt
¼ cup chopped walnuts
grated fresh Parmesan cheese

Chop mushroom stems finely and sauté with the onion in the butter. Add the bread and toss until browned. Add spices and nuts. Stuff caps with mixture and top each with parmesan cheese. Dot with butter. Refrigerate until needed.

Salmon Mousse

MAKES 10 SERVINGS

{ 1 9 5 0 s }

We found this recipe for Salmon Mousse *on one of those cards that tell us "what's cookin'... from the kitchen of" but neglected to tell us whose kitchen. The underlining of the word* **blender** *seems to point to the 1950s, when using a blender was very innovative. Don't let the use of canned salmon deter you from trying this creamy appetizer. It's simple and delicious.*

1. Coat 9-inch by 5-inch by 3-inch loaf pan with vegetable spray or line bottom and sides of pan with plastic wrap; or lightly coat 4½-cup mold with vegetable spray.

2. Pick through salmon to remove skin and bones. Place salmon in bowl, flake with fork, and set aside.

3. In glass measuring cup, sprinkle gelatin on top of lemon juice. Whisk to combine. Let stand 5 minutes. Add boiling water, let stand 2 minutes, and whisk again.

4. Place salmon, onion or scallions, mayonnaise, dillweed or dill, paprika, salt, cayenne pepper, and gelatin mixture in bowl of food processor fitted with metal blade. Process on high until smooth. Add heavy cream and process to combine. Place mousse in prepared loaf pan or mold and chill for at least 2 hours, or until firm.

5. To unmold, dip bottom of pan or mold into bowl of warm water for a few seconds to loosen mousse. Invert serving plate over mousse. Quickly turn plate and mousse over. Mousse should slide out easily onto plate. Store covered with plastic wrap in refrigerator until ready to serve.

1 (12¾-ounce) can pink salmon

1 (¼-ounce) envelope unflavored gelatin

3 tablespoons lemon juice

½ cup boiling water

¼ cup finely chopped onion or scallions

½ cup mayonnaise

1 teaspoon dried dillweed, or 1 teaspoon chopped fresh dill

1 teaspoon paprika

Salt to taste

⅛ to ¼ teaspoon cayenne pepper

1 cup heavy cream

 Tips & Touches

- Draining salmon and removing the skin reduces the strong flavor.
- Sprinkle mousse with paprika, garnish with fresh dill, and serve with crackers or toast fingers.

Helen's Fried Cheese Balls with Chili Mayonnaise

{ *1900* }

FOR CHEESE BALLS

1 cup grated sharp cheddar cheese

½ cup fine bread crumbs

5 drops Worcestershire sauce

1 egg, beaten

Vegetable oil, for frying

FOR CHILI MAYONNAISE

1 cup mayonnaise

6 tablespoons chili sauce

1 teaspoon lemon juice

½ teaspoon salt

½ teaspoon cayenne pepper or
   chopped, brined hot peppers

TIPS & TOUCHES

- We often use commercially brined chopped hot peppers because they can be kept refrigerated and ready to use.
- Crowding cheese balls during frying will result in lowered oil temperature (see "10 Tips for Deep-Frying" on page 37).

THESE LITTLE CHEESE BALLS REMIND US OF *crunchy little crab balls but without the crab. We found this recipe in a manuscript cookbook whose pages crumbled as we touched them. We added the perky Chili Mayonnaise dipping sauce. The cookbook contained a love letter from Worcester, Massachusetts, written from Charles to Helen on June 27, 1897. Conservative by today's standards, the letter reflected the joy of a young couple looking forward to their marriage.*

1. To make cheese balls: Cover cooling rack with 3 layers of paper towels. In bowl, combine cheese, bread crumbs, Worcestershire sauce, and beaten egg. Roll dough into balls about 1 inch in diameter. Set aside.

2. To make chili mayonnaise: Combine mayonnaise, chili sauce, lemon juice, salt, and cayenne pepper or chopped peppers in bowl and mix well. Cover and chill until ready to use.

3. Heat 1½ inches of oil to 375°F in heavy, deep, flat-bottomed pan or electric fryer. Use slotted spoon to transfer balls, one at a time, into hot oil. Fry balls in batches of 4 (to keep oil temperature from dropping), turning once, until both sides are golden brown, about 2 minutes on each side. Remove with slotted spoon to prepared rack. Cover with additional paper towels and allow to drain. Serve immediately or keep warm in 200°F oven until ready to eat. Serve with Chili Mayonnaise.

Corn Pancakes with Sour Cream and Chives

MAKES 16 MINI PANCAKES

{ 1 9 1 0 }

WE FOUND THIS HANDWRITTEN RECIPE ON *a faded index card in the file of The Church Lady of Mansfield, Ohio. These savory corn pancakes are meant to be served with chicken or pork, but we decided to make them silver dollar–size and garnish them with sour cream and snipped chives. This is one of the earliest recipes from The Church Lady's collection, which spanned the early 1900s through the 1950s.*

1. Place flour, baking powder, salt, and pepper in mixing bowl and set aside. Beat egg yolks in another bowl. Beat in milk and melted butter. Add dry ingredients and stir gently to combine. Fold in corn.
2. Beat egg whites until stiff in bowl of standing mixer fitted with whisk attachment. Fold egg whites into batter.
3. Melt 2 tablespoons butter in large frying pan over medium heat. Spoon 1 tablespoon batter into pan for each pancake, pressing down gently on pancakes once they are formed to make them thinner. Cook pancakes until tops begin to bubble around edges, about 2 minutes. Turn and cook until undersides are golden brown, about 2 minutes more. Serve immediately, topped with sour cream and chives, or keep warm on tray in 200°F oven for not more than 15 minutes. Store leftover pancakes in covered container in refrigerator. Reheat in frying pan with melted butter over low heat.

1 cup flour

2 teaspoons baking powder

¾ teaspoon salt

¼ teaspoon coarsely ground black pepper

2 eggs, separated

½ cup milk

1 tablespoon butter, melted

1 cup canned or cooked corn

2 tablespoons butter, softened to room temperature

1 cup sour cream

¼ cup snipped chives

TIPS & TOUCHES

- Corn pancakes are best on the day they are made.
- These pancakes are also good served with fresh snipped dill on top instead of chives.
- Serve pancakes on a warmed platter.

Chickpea and Potato Cholay

{ 1 9 7 0 s }

1 (19-ounce) can chickpeas

1 (28-ounce) can whole tomatoes

2 medium potatoes, boiled

1 tablespoon butter, softened to room temperature

2 tablespoons vegetable oil

1 teaspoon cumin seeds

1 teaspoon garam masala

1 teaspoon curry powder

¼ teaspoon red chili powder

1 cup chopped onion

1 large clove garlic, minced

½ teaspoon salt

2 tablespoons lemon or lime juice

THIS IS THE CHICKPEA AND POTATO CHOLAY *that our friend Katy first tasted as a young girl in England, where she was raised. Katy learned how to cook from her mother, Viru, who is an expert in Indian cuisine. Although sometimes thought of as a vegetable stew, cholay is very adaptable and is a good appetizer when served with untoasted wedges of pita bread.*

1. Drain chickpeas in colander and rinse with cold water. Transfer to bowl and set aside.
2. Drain tomatoes in colander, cut into ½-inch dice, and set aside in another bowl.
3. Peel and cut potatoes into 1-inch pieces and place in third bowl.
4. Melt butter with oil in saucepan over low heat. Add cumin seeds. Turn heat up slightly and stir with wooden spoon until cumin seeds sizzle. Add garam masala, curry powder, and chili powder and stir to mix. Add onion and garlic and continue cooking until softened, 2 to 3 minutes. Stir in diced tomatoes. Add chickpeas, potatoes, and salt and cook, stirring, until chickpeas and potatoes are heated through, 4 to 5 minutes. Remove cholay to serving dish and let cool to room temperature. Pour lemon or lime juice on top before serving.

→→ GARAM MASALA ←←

Garam masala originated in the kitchens of India, where it varies by region. It has a sweeter, hotter, more assertive taste than curry powder. Although Indian cooks prepare their own blends of garam masala, a good commercial blend can be found in the spice sections of grocery stores or food markets carrying international foods. Garam masala is a strong spice mix, and a little goes a long way. One of the advantages of cooking with garam masala is the wonderful aroma that scents the kitchen. Although curry powder may contain some of the same spices as those found in garam masala, substituting curry powder will not give the same depth of flavor as using garam masala. Reddish brown in color, garam masala is best added toward the end of cooking.

Rose and Natalie's Caponata

MAKES 6 CUPS

WE FIRST TASTED THIS RECIPE AT A GATHERING *20 years ago. We loved the sour-sweet eggplant spread and discovered that it had been passed down through the D'Ambosio–Peluso family from Ozone Park, Queens. Rose Peluso Slobodzinski recalls that when she was a child, her aunts competed for the best caponata recipe at family gatherings, but she always voted for the version made by her mother, Natalie D'Ambosio. Rose taught her youngest child, Natalie Pangaro, how to make her caponata, and thus this recipe continues through three generations of a Neapolitan–American family.*

1. Wash eggplant and pat dry with paper towel. Cut into $\frac{1}{2}$-inch cubes (you should have about 6 cups).
2. Heat $\frac{1}{2}$ cup of the olive oil in large frying pan over medium heat. Add eggplant and sauté until tender and golden brown, 5 to 7 minutes. Remove eggplant and set aside. Add remaining 2 tablespoons oil to pan. Add onion and celery and sauté until tender, about 5 minutes.
3. Return eggplant to pan. Stir in tomato sauce, tomato paste, and raisins. Bring mixture to a boil. Lower heat, cover, and simmer for 15 minutes. Add vinegar, salt, pepper, brown sugar, capers, and olives. Simmer, covered, stirring occasionally, for 20 minutes more. Cool to room temperature. Refrigerate overnight in covered container to allow flavors to marry.

1 large eggplant, unpeeled

$\frac{1}{2}$ cup plus 2 tablespoons olive oil, divided

$1\frac{1}{4}$ cups diced onion

1 cup diced celery

1 (15-ounce) can tomato sauce

1 tablespoon tomato paste

$\frac{1}{2}$ cup golden raisins

$\frac{1}{4}$ cup red wine vinegar

$\frac{1}{2}$ teaspoon salt

$\frac{1}{2}$ teaspoon coarsely ground black pepper

1 to 2 tablespoons firmly packed brown sugar

2 tablespoons capers, drained

20 pitted, brined black olives, cut in slivers or quartered

TIPS & TOUCHES

- Be sure to use red wine vinegar, not balsamic vinegar.
- The addition of brown sugar balances the flavor.
- Caponata can be served on top of pasta but should be thinned with a little tomato sauce before being heated.

Toy enamelware colander, early 1900s

SALADS and SANDWICHES

Being a collection of
150 tested recipes
for home cookery.
arranged by months

ORIGINATED AND PUBLISHED BY
WOMAN'S WORLD MAGAZINE CO.
CHICAGO, U.S.A.

Wesson
Oil
ONE QUART NET
For Making
Good Things to Eat

Saladtime

with 615 Recipes
By Marion Harris Neil

32ND Ann
Cook
Book

BROADCASTING STATION WNAX
—302.8 Meters—990 Kilocycles

Recipes

Fleis
Re

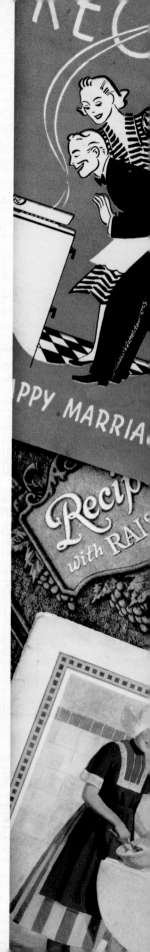

CHAPTER 3

SALAD DAYS

There's something bright and breezy about the title "Salad Days." It reminds us of spring lunches on front porches with the scent of lilacs in the air or backyard Victory Gardens with their bounty of homegrown greens. We grew up in a community where the best vegetables were hand selected for us at the local market or presented to us by local gardeners. As budding home cooks, we learned early that salads should be crisp and colorful, pleasing to both the eye and the palette. When we browsed through our collection of manuscript cookbooks, we found that home cooks treated their salad plates as if they were canvases, creating a picture of what was seasonally appealing as well as what tasted good. We learned that with a few deft passes of a knife, these women could make carrots into pennies and radishes into roses. Tomatoes picked off the vine, while still warm from the sun, could be cut into wedges or generous slices.

We found that salads could be light or substantial—a jellied tease full of fruit and marshmallows could serve as a first course for a bridge party or a hearty bowl with an abundance of chopped bacon, eggs, and vegetables could be put before the men in the family. Some of these home cooks practiced the tradition of their Mediterranean heritage and served a few greens dressed with oil and vinegar as palette cleansers after the main course and just before dessert.

When these women created their salads, they honored the changing seasons by selecting the best ingredients available. The lettuces and berries of summer gave way to the robust cranberries and yams of autumn, while winter salads using rice and nuts promised contentment, as did coleslaws of shredded cabbage, peppers, and onions. Spring brought its plates of Sunshine Potato Salad, golden with egg yolks, welcome after the dark days of winter, as well as offerings of early greens touched with fruited mayonnaise.

When making salads, home cooks had to be creative in the kitchen because they had to use what they had in their pantries or root cellars. What might be leftovers to some became a delicious, perhaps daring, salad plate to others. The boiled dressing,

Salad dressing pamphlet, American

forgotten for so many years, can become an easy ally of today's home salad maker, just as it added a touch of richness to Mrs. Julian's Shrimp Salad, a handwritten recipe from the 1920s. It seems that no one could forget the darling candle salads of the 1950s, which are just as fascinating to today's children as they were two generations ago.

Most of the salads we selected are memorable not just for their ingredients and creativity but because they have become the legacy of the women who served them. A colorful and significant chopped salad, prepared every October by a friend who held her annual Finally Fall Brunch to celebrate the cooler weather of the changing seasons, is as good today as when she first started making it 25 years ago. Although she has left us, we will always remember her when serving her signature salad.

A recipe called Mock Chicken Salad has become a tradition in the Paxton-Grigor-Hails Family, from Pennsylvania. Originally made from veal and pork because chicken was more expensive, this thrifty substitute became a family favorite for the picnics that accompanied swimming parties.

The secret of Mrs. Fredman's Coleslaw has finally been revealed, and her achievement can now be shared with all of the customers who ate at her Shirley Street delicatessen, in Winthrop, Massachusetts, more than 55 years ago. Her friendly culinary rivalry with Mrs. Nat of Nat's Delicatessen is still remembered fondly, with a nod of respect to both ladies, as is the memory of Mr. Fredman, in his slippers and cap, smoking a cigar and reading a Yiddish newspaper while his wife dished out coleslaw and corned beef sandwiches to generations of young Winthropites.

We hope you'll try Dot Luke's Hawaiian Jellied Salad with its pineapple and mandarin oranges. Now hostesses can serve this creamy pale green salad at their own family picnics, even if they don't eat it with chopsticks the way everyone did on the Island of Oahu in the 1950s.

And finally, we praise a winter salad made with rice, honey, and walnuts, which is still remembered 40 years after a young resident brought it to a Sunday potluck supper at the Cambridge, Massachusetts, YWCA.

Mayonnaise maker, mixer, American, 1920s–1930s

Sunshine Potato Salad

MAKES 6 TO 8 SERVINGS

6 waxy potatoes (about 3 pounds)

½ cup extra-virgin olive oil

¼ cup apple cider vinegar

1 tablespoon water

2 teaspoons salt

½ teaspoon coarsely ground
black pepper

⅓ cup diced red bell pepper

⅓ cup diced green bell pepper

1 cup finely chopped celery

1½ cups finely chopped onion

3 eggs, hard-cooked and
coarsely chopped

⅓ cup coarsely chopped
dill pickles

½ cup mayonnaise

1 tablespoon prepared
yellow mustard

Red and green bell pepper rounds,
for garnish

TIPS & TOUCHES

* Cook potatoes only until tender.
* Toss ingredients gently to prevent
potatoes from falling apart.

WE HAVE TO GIVE TWO HOME COOKS *credit for this recipe because their versions of it were so similar. Constance Etz Ferdon, from our collection of Martha's Vineyard living recipes, and Elizabeth Corkery, from Groton, Massachusetts, came up with virtually the same recipe for a marinated potato salad, made golden with mustard and egg yolks. This is the first potato salad we've ever made that uses both an oil-and-vinegar marinade and mayonnaise. Diced red and green peppers make the potato salad crunchy.*

1. Place potatoes in steamer basket over simmering water, cover, and steam just until tender when pierced with small knife, 15 to 20 minutes. Do not overcook. Remove to large bowl. Peel when cool enough to handle. Cut into 1-inch cubes.

2. In another bowl, whisk together olive oil, vinegar, water, salt, and black pepper. Pour dressing over warm potatoes and stir gently to coat. Cover and place in refrigerator to marinate at least 6 hours, or overnight. Stir and shake occasionally for even marinating.

3. Pour off any excess marinade. Add red and green peppers, celery, onion, eggs, and dill pickles and toss gently to combine. In small bowl, stir together mayonnaise and mustard. Add to salad and toss to coat vegetables. Cover and refrigerate until ready to serve. Serve garnished with rounds of red and green pepper. Store leftover potato salad in covered container in refrigerator.

Mrs. Fredman's Coleslaw

{ *1930s* }

MAKES 8 CUPS

8 cups shredded cabbage (about 2 pounds)

2 cups shredded carrots (about 3 large carrots)

1½ teaspoons kosher salt

3 tablespoons apple cider vinegar

¾ cup Miracle Whip salad dressing

¼ cup sugar, or as needed

Salt and coarsely ground black pepper

TIPS & TOUCHES

- The original recipe made a large amount of coleslaw.
- We added more carrots in proportion to cabbage because we like a colorful coleslaw.

MRS. FREDMAN WAS KNOWN FAR AND WIDE *for the coleslaw she served at Fredman's Delicatessen on Shirley Street, in Winthrop, Massachusetts. She and Mrs. Nat, of Nat's Delicatessen, a few doors down, had a friendly competition over who made the best coleslaw and potato salad. Both coleslaws were superior, but customers were fiercely loyal to one or the other. Larraine Byne Yaffee was able to provide this recipe because her aunt, Alice Ceder, worked for Mrs. Fredman during the 1950s.*

1. Combine cabbage, carrots, and salt in large nonreactive glass or stainless steel bowl and mix thoroughly. Add vinegar, salad dressing, and sugar and mix to combine. Cover bowl with plastic wrap and refrigerate overnight.
2. Drain off any liquid collected in bottom of bowl. Season to taste with salt and pepper. Store leftover coleslaw in covered glass container in refrigerator.

Food chopper, American, early 1900s

Sweet Potato Salad

MAKES 8 SERVINGS

THIS COLORFUL, TASTY SALAD IS PERFECT FOR *autumn gatherings. We suggest that you start this salad early in the day so that the flavors will come together. Steam the sweet potatoes the night before. The sweet potatoes should still be a bit firm when you make the salad.*

1. To make salad: Place sweet potatoes in steamer basket set over simmering water. Cover and steam about 20 minutes (see Tips & Touches). Remove to large bowl and allow to cool.

2. When cool enough to handle, cut potatoes into ³/₄-inch dice and return to bowl. Add orange marmalade, apricot jam, and red pepper and toss to coat.

3. To make vinaigrette: Place olive oil, vinegar, orange juice, and mustard into container with cover. Cover and shake to combine. Remove cover; add salt, black pepper, garlic or garlic powder, hot pepper flakes, and orange zest. Replace cover and shake to combine.

4. Pour vinaigrette over salad and stir gently with wooden spoon. Mound salad on platter or place in large bowl, cover with plastic wrap, and refrigerate for at least 4 hours to allow flavors to marry.

5. Remove salad from refrigerator 15 minutes before serving. Serve sprinkled with pecans. Store leftover salad in covered container in refrigerator.

FOR SALAD

3 pounds sweet potatoes, peeled and cut into 2-inch chunks

¼ cup orange marmalade

¼ cup apricot jam

1 cup diced red bell pepper

1 cup toasted pecans, coarsely chopped

FOR VINAIGRETTE

¼ cup extra-virgin olive oil

1 tablespoon apple cider vinegar

⅓ cup orange juice

1 tablespoon prepared mustard

½ teaspoon kosher salt

¼ teaspoon coarsely ground black pepper

2 cloves garlic, minced, or ³/₄ teaspoon garlic powder

⅛ teaspoon hot pepper flakes

Grated zest of 1 orange

TIPS & TOUCHES

- Steaming sweet potatoes for 20 minutes is an arbitrary amount of time. The best way to know when they're cooked is to test them: They should still be a bit firm. If you overcook them, they will fall apart.

- Do not use baked sweet potatoes for this salad.

- Do not mix pecans into salad or they will become soggy.

Food chopper, American, 1890s

Barbara Carey's Chopped Salad

{ *1970s* }

THIS IS THE CHOPPED SALAD RECIPE OUR *friend Barbara Carey used when she held her annual Finally Fall Brunch. Barbara loved the colder weather, and after a hot New England summer, she gathered family and friends to celebrate the coming of autumn. This is a great salad because the ingredients and their amounts can be adjusted for the number of people you will be serving. Barbara always finely chopped or shredded the ingredients.*

1. Place romaine and iceberg lettuce in bottom of 10- to 12-cup clear glass bowl with generous diameter (ours is 8 inches in diameter and 4 inches high) and set aside.
2. Finely chop bacon and eggs. Layer bacon, eggs, and onion separately over shredded greens. Add layer of peas and layer of carrots. Mix mayonnaise and sour cream together and spread on top of salad. Top with cheese and serve. Store leftover salad covered with plastic wrap in refrigerator.

2 cups shredded romaine

2 cups shredded iceberg lettuce

4 ounces cooked bacon

4 eggs, hard-cooked

1 cup chopped red onion

1 cup fresh or frozen peas, boiled until tender

1 cup grated carrots

1 cup mayonnaise

1 cup sour cream

½ pound shredded Swiss cheese

↠ PUTTING TOGETHER A CHOPPED SALAD ↞

Chopped salad is a wonderful choice for a gathering because you can tailor it to the season or to the tastes of your guests. You can omit the bacon, cheese, and eggs and go for a lighter dish, or you can leave them in for a more substantial one. Always choose a large-diameter bowl to accommodate the layers of chopped ingredients and show them off nicely. The bowl should be shallow enough to allow guests to scoop through the layers of cheese and dressing on top to sample all the layers. You can also serve the salad layered in individual clear glass bowls or martini glasses.

Candle Salad

MAKES 4 SERVINGS

8 leaves Boston lettuce

4 canned pineapple slices

4 bananas

4 strips green bell pepper

4 maraschino cherries, or 4 strips
  (½-inch long) pimento

¼ cup sour cream, or ¼ cup
  mayonnaise

TIPS & TOUCHES

• It can be a bit tricky to get
  a banana "candle" to stand up
  in the middle of a pineapple
  ring. Try a dab of cream cheese
  "glue" or fill part of the hole with
  torn lettuce.

THIS IS ONE OF THOSE 1950s FANTASY *salads that appeal to children of all ages. Growing up in a Jewish household, we were treated to the Jewish version of candle salad, made with sour cream and a maraschino cherry, for Sunday night supper. Our Christian friends enjoyed a similar salad made with mayonnaise and a piece of pimento for the flame. This was a pretty sophisticated salad for a 7-year-old.*

1. Arrange 2 leaves of lettuce on each of 4 plates. Place 1 pineapple ring on each plate. Peel bananas, cut off ends, and stand upright in center of pineapple rings to make "candles." Tuck strips of pepper into pineapple at base of candles to look like candle-holders. Split cherries and place split side down on top of bananas to simulate flame (or use pimento strips).

2. Drizzle sour cream or mayonnaise down sides of bananas to represent melted candle wax.

Blue milk glass salt; glass Liberty Bell cherry jar, American, 20th century

Mock Chicken Salad

MAKES 4 SERVINGS

MOCK CHICKEN SALAD DOES NOT CONTAIN ANY *chicken. This rec-ipe, found in a tattered manuscript cookbook, calls for chopped roast pork. Laced with some good-quality mayonnaise or boiled dressing, this salad filled the need for a quick, tasty yet inexpensive meal.*

Combine roast pork, celery, bell pepper, olives, mayonnaise or boiled dressing, salt, and black pepper in large bowl. Cover and refrigerate for at least 2 hours before serving. Store leftover salad in covered container in refrigerator.

4 cups coarsely chopped roast pork

1 cup chopped celery

$^3/_4$ cup chopped red bell pepper

$^1/_2$ cup chopped pimento-stuffed green olives (about 6 olives)

$^1/_2$ cup mayonnaise or Boiled Salad Dressing (page 94)

$^1/_2$ teaspoon salt

$^1/_2$ teaspoon coarsely ground black pepper

➤➤ HOW MOCK CHICKEN SALAD WAS INVENTED ◄◄

It's always a challenge to make "mock" anything because you have to have a reliable substitute in your home kitchen. Mock chicken salads were made from cubes of roast pork or roast veal, both of which were less expensive than chicken, which was a source of eggs for the farm family. Some heirloom cooks ground their roast pork or veal and bound it with mayonnaise to make their mock chicken salad sand-wiches. Preparing mock chicken salad allowed inventive homemakers to conserve the hens that lay the eggs, which they often sold to supplement their income.

Barbara's Rice Salad with Cumin and Walnuts

{ 1 9 7 0 s }

FOR SALAD

2 ½ cups cooked wild rice, cooled (cook according to package directions)

3 cups cooked long grain white rice, cooled (cook according to package directions)

1 cup toasted walnuts, coarsely chopped

FOR VINAIGRETTE

¼ cup extra-virgin olive oil

¼ cup vegetable oil

1 teaspoon salt (omit if rice is salty)

¼ teaspoon coarsely ground black pepper

¼ cup plus 1 tablespoon honey

¼ cup plus 2 tablespoons lemon juice

2 teaspoons ground cumin

¼ teaspoon cinnamon

WE FIRST TASTED THIS SALAD WHEN MARILYNN *was living at the YWCA in Cambridge. The Y did not serve a supper on Sunday nights, so the girls would get together and do a communal meal. Marilynn's friend Barbara had lived on a kibbutz in Israel, and she put this salad together using a hot plate in the resident kitchen to make the rice. We added the wild rice, and this salad is as good today as it was when we first tasted it.*

1. To make salad: Combine wild rice, white rice, and walnuts in large bowl. Stir together with wooden spoon.

2. To make vinaigrette: Whisk together olive oil, vegetable oil, salt (if using), pepper, honey, lemon juice, cumin, and cinnamon in small bowl. Pour vinaigrette over salad and toss with 2 serving spoons. Cover bowl with plastic wrap and refrigerate for at least 2 hours to mellow flavors. Serve at room temperature. Store leftover salad in covered container in refrigerator.

Silver nut cups, American, 20th century

TIPS & TOUCHES

*   To cook wild or white rice, use water or low-sodium chicken stock and follow the cooking instructions on the rice package.
*   Coat measuring cups and measuring spoons with vegetable spray before measuring honey. It will be easier to add to a recipe.

Mrs. Julian's Shrimp Salad

MAKES 8 SERVINGS {1920s}

HERE'S ANOTHER RECIPE FROM THE MANUSCRIPT COOKBOOK *of the lady who brought us* Mock Chicken Salad *(page 89) and* Crispy Norwegian Potatoes *(page 121). A grand home cook, this lady handwrote her recipes in an unassuming little composition book with tattered pages that have inspired us in so many ways.*

1. In large bowl, combine macaroni, shrimp, onion, celery, pimento, parsley, salt, pepper, and eggs.
2. Add mayonnaise or boiled dressing and toss until all ingredients are well coated. Chill before serving. Store leftovers in covered container in refrigerator.

3 cups cooked macaroni, cooled

3 cups cooked shrimp, cut into ½-inch dice

½ cup finely chopped onion

1 cup chopped celery

1 cup chopped pimento

3 tablespoons chopped fresh parsley

1 teaspoon salt

½ teaspoon coarsely ground black pepper

3 eggs, hard-cooked and coarsely chopped

¾ cup mayonnaise or Boiled Salad Dressing (page 94)

✈ QUICK SALAD DRESSINGS ✦

Almost all manuscript cookbooks have recipes for boiled dressing, mayonnaise, and French dressing. Several of these dressings take extra time to prepare and call for the use of a double boiler and eggs. Others suggest that you add whipped cream just before serving. For generations, home cooks have taken the easy way out by working with their favorite commercial brand of mayonnaise, enhancing its taste and texture with pureed fruit, ketchup, mustard, jam, capers, chopped pickles, or relishes. A dash of lemon juice or a bit of orange zest is often helpful, combined with a touch of sugar, to balance the flavor of these inventive dressings.

TIPS & TOUCHES

- The ingredient amounts can be adjusted to make the salad your own.
- Any salad containing eggs and mayonnaise should not remain unrefrigerated for long periods of time.

Boiled Salad Dressing

{ *1920s* }

MAKES 2 CUPS

¼ cup sugar

2 teaspoons salt

¼ cup sifted flour

1 tablespoon dry mustard

⅛ teaspoon cayenne pepper

3 tablespoons white vinegar

1½ cups hot water

2 eggs or 4 yolks

2 tablespoons vegetable oil or
heavy cream

THIS IS THE SALAD DRESSING RECIPE WE *found with the Mock Chicken Salad. This is very much like a homemade cooked mayonnaise. It's worth the effort to make and serve this creamy salad dressing. The manuscript cookbook also had the recipe for Crispy Norwegian Potatoes (page 121).*

1. Combine sugar, salt, flour, mustard, and cayenne pepper in top of double boiler. Add vinegar and whisk. Gradually whisk in hot water.

2. Bring about 1 inch of water to a simmer in bottom of double boiler. Set top of double boiler over bottom and cook, stirring constantly with wooden spoon, until mixture is thick and smooth, about 3 minutes.

3. Remove top of double boiler from heat. Whisk eggs or yolks lightly in another bowl. Add a little of the hot mixture to the eggs, whisking briskly to temper. Then whisk eggs back into top of double boiler with hot mixture. Place top of double boiler on bottom and cook 1 minute, stirring with wooden spoon. Transfer dressing to clean bowl. When cool, thin with oil or cream.

➤➤ HOW TO USE PREPARED AND DRY MUSTARD ◄◄

When we refer to "prepared mustard," we are talking about a condiment made from ground mustard seeds, salt, and vinegar. Dry mustard is a powdered spice made from pulverized mustard seeds. Heirloom cooks often added prepared mustard to their dishes to enhance the flavor because it was an inexpensive, readily available ingredient. However, certain heirloom recipes call for dry mustard, which has been milled from mustard seeds and sold commercially for almost 200 years.

SUBSTITUTION: 1 tablespoon prepared mustard = 1 teaspoon dry mustard

Fruit "Mayonnaise"

MAKES APPROXIMATELY 2 CUPS

WE FOUND THAT THIS HEIRLOOM RECIPE FOR *a fruit mayonnaise based on pineapple and orange juice was wonderful with Dot Luke's Hawaiian Jellied Salad (page 96). It's light and fruity, and the addition of whipped cream at the end makes it soft and cloudlike.*

2 eggs

¼ cup sugar

¼ cup pineapple juice

¼ cup orange juice

1 teaspoon orange zest

2 tablespoons white vinegar

3 tablespoons water

½ cup heavy cream, whipped

1. Whisk eggs in bowl until lightened. Gradually whisk in sugar and set aside.

2. Combine pineapple juice, orange juice, orange zest, vinegar, and water in top of double boiler. Bring about 1 inch of water to a simmer in bottom of double boiler. Set top of double boiler on bottom and cook, stirring with wooden spoon until heated through. Add small amount of hot liquid to eggs and whisk briskly to temper. Return egg mixture to hot juice and continue to cook, stirring until mixture thickens and coats back of spoon, about 2 minutes more.

3. Remove mayonnaise to another nonreactive container and allow to cool for 5 minutes. Place plastic wrap on surface of mayonnaise and refrigerate. Fold in whipped cream just before serving. Store mayonnaise in covered container in refrigerator. Leftover mayonnaise may deflate slightly.

Dorchester Pottery mixing bowl, American, early 20th century

Dot Luke's Hawaiian Jellied Salad

{ *1 9 5 0 s* }

2 (3-ounce) packages lime gelatin

1 cup pineapple juice, heated

Juice of 2 limes

Juice of 1 orange

1 cup canned pineapple chunks, drained and diced

1 (11-ounce) can mandarin orange segments, drained

6 ounces cream cheese, softened

1 cup heavy cream, whipped

½ cup mayonnaise

1 cup mini marshmallows

½ cup toasted pecans, chopped

Iceberg lettuce, shredded, for serving

TIPS & TOUCHES

* This salad is very good with Fruit "Mayonnaise" (page 95).

THIS RECIPE CAME FROM DOT LUKE, THE *mother of our friend Liane Welch. Liane grew up in Honolulu, on the Island of Oahu. Dot passed away in 2006 at the age of 84. When Liane went through her mother's papers, she found her recipe for a jellied lime salad, which brought back fond memories of a refreshing treat on hot afternoons. Dot often made it for potluck picnics and large family gatherings. Her family and friends always ate this salad with chopsticks.*

1. Coat 10-cup mold with vegetable spray.
2. Dissolve gelatin in hot pineapple juice in 2-cup measure. Add lime juice, orange juice, and enough water to equal 2 cups of liquid. Pour gelatin into bowl, stir well, cover, and chill until nearly firm.
3. Lightly whisk chilled gelatin mixture. Fold in diced pineapple, orange segments, cream cheese, whipped cream, mayonnaise, mini marshmallows, and pecans. Pour into prepared mold and chill 3 to 4 hours, or until firm.
4. To release, dip bottom of mold in bowl of hot water for a few seconds. Invert plate on top of mold, then turn plate and mold over. Salad should unmold easily. Arrange lettuce on individual salad plates and place slice of jellied salad on top.

Mary Bradshaw's Egg and Gherkin Salad

{ *1 8 8 0 s* }

1 cup gherkins

6 eggs, hard-cooked

1 teaspoon salt

¼ teaspoon cayenne pepper

2 teaspoons lemon juice

¼ cup butter, softened

Shredded iceberg lettuce, for garnish

Sliced radishes, for garnish

4 pieces toasted white bread, cut into fingers and generously buttered

Tips & Touches

* This salad has the consistency of an egg paste and is very delicate.

THIS SALAD IS FROM THE MANUSCRIPT COOKBOOK *of Mary Bradshaw, an English woman who recorded her personal recipes from the 1880s to the 1920s. Mary provides us with recipes for tea sandwiches, meat pies, comforting servings of milk toast, and dainty salads, as well as menus for Bible study groups and World War I knitting instructions. This is a very ladylike salad. We suggest that you double the recipe if you are expecting some gentleman guests.*

1. Line four ½-cup ramekins with plastic wrap and set aside.
2. Place gherkins in bowl of food processor fitted with metal blade. Pulse until finely chopped. Remove gherkins to large bowl. Place eggs in food processor and pulse until finely chopped. Add eggs to bowl with gherkins. Add salt, cayenne pepper, and lemon juice and stir to combine. Add butter and mash to soft paste. Divide mixture among prepared ramekins, smooth tops, cover with plastic wrap, and chill at least 2 hours.
3. Run knife around inside of ramekins to loosen salad. Unmold salad from each ramekin onto bed of shredded iceberg lettuce. Serve with thinly sliced radishes and buttered toast fingers.

Mrs. O'Brien's Cranberry Delight Salad

MAKES 10 SERVINGS

{ 1 9 5 0 s }

THIS IS A RECIPE FROM THE MANUSCRIPT *cookbook of Geneva Bellevue O'Brien, of Belmont, Massachusetts. A lively woman of French-Canadian heritage, she and her mother held "baking days" twice a week, during which they produced enough bread to feed Geneva's husband, Eugene, and their 4 children. Mrs. O'Brien always kept 2 tins decorated with circus carousels filled with cookies and cake on her kitchen counter. Cranberry Delight Salad was featured at Thanksgiving and Christmas.*

1. Pour orange juice into measuring cup and add enough cold water to equal 1 cup. Pour into heavy-bottomed saucepan. Add cranberries, raisins, and orange zest and mix with wooden spoon to combine. Add sugar and stir.
2. Place pan over medium heat, bring to a boil, and cook, stirring constantly, until mixture begins to thicken, about 13 minutes. Cool completely. Stir in walnuts. Spoon onto plates lined with Boston lettuce leaves and garnish with mandarin orange segments.

Juice and grated zest of 2 oranges

4 cups cranberries

1 cup raisins

2 cups sugar

½ cup toasted walnuts, coarsely chopped

10 Boston lettuce leaves, for garnish

Mandarin orange segments, for garnish

TIPS & TOUCHES

- Add a little more cold water to the cranberry mixture if needed.
- For a fancy presentation, hollow out half of an orange rind, fill with Cranberry Delight Salad, and serve on a bed of lettuce.

Green Depression glass measuring cup, 1930s; tin advertising bank, 1920s

Banana Nut Salad

{ 1 9 2 0 s }

MAKES 4 SERVINGS

6 cups chopped or torn lettuce

4 firm bananas

1 cup sugar

1 cup hot water

Juice of 1 lemon

¼ teaspoon salt

½ cup mayonnaise

1 cup toasted walnuts,
   coarsely chopped

TIPS & TOUCHES

- Either iceberg or Boston lettuce can be used for this salad. Iceberg lettuce should be shredded, and Boston lettuce should be torn.
- Sprinkle salads with maraschino cherries or dried cherries for additional color.

THIS RECIPE CAME FROM THE MANUSCRIPT COOKBOOK *of the lady who provided us with the recipes for Mock Chicken Salad (page 89), Mrs. Julian's Shrimp Salad (page 93), and Boiled Salad Dressing (page 94). This lady loved her salads. This is a very simple dish to put together, great for those days when you have all that ironing to do.*

1. Divide lettuce among 4 salad plates. Peel bananas and cut into 1-inch-thick rounds. Cover with wax paper and set aside.

2. Place sugar and hot water in heavy-bottomed saucepan. Bring to a boil over medium heat, stirring with wooden spoon. Boil 5 to 6 minutes, stirring constantly, until mixture thickens and becomes syrupy. Add lemon juice and boil 2 to 3 minutes more, still stirring constantly.

3. Remove pan from heat. Add bananas to pan, turning with slotted spoon until bananas are evenly coated with syrup. Divide banana slices among prepared plates, setting slices on top of lettuce. Sprinkle bananas with salt and drizzle with remaining syrup. Add dollop of mayonnaise to each and sprinkle with walnuts.

Majolica lemon reamer, Japanese, 1920s-1930s

Herring Salad

{ *1930s* }

CHOPPED HERRING IS THE TRADITIONAL *appetizer eaten during the Jewish holidays. Although other herring salads sometimes include chopped beets and sour cream, this simple savory salad uses only herring, onions, and apples. We've substituted diminutive pieces of herring in wine sauce for the large, salty slices of herring that our mother had to repeatedly soak, skin, and bone. A touch of cinnamon enhances the slightly sweet flavor of the wine sauce. This salad is very nice served on a bed of Boston lettuce, garnished with slices of hard-cooked egg and dill pickles or sliced Granny Smith apples.*

1. Drain herring and onions in colander, rinse under cold water, and place in large bowl. Cover with cold water and soak for at least 3 hours, changing water at least once. Rinse in cold water and gently squeeze to remove excess liquid.

2. Place soda crackers in bowl of food processor fitted with metal blade. Pulse until finely crumbed. Remove to small bowl.

3. Place herring and onions in bowl of food processor fitted with metal blade. Process until well ground but not to a paste. Remove to large bowl. Add cracker crumbs and grated apple and mix well. Chop hard-cooked eggs, reserving 1 yolk for garnish (refrigerate until ready to use). Add chopped eggs, sugar, and cinnamon and mix to combine. Refrigerate salad at least 2 hours or overnight in covered nonreactive container to allow flavors to blend.

4. Form salad into mound on serving plate. Press reserved yolk through fine sieve and sprinkle over herring.

1 (32-ounce) jar herring tidbits and onions in wine sauce

8 soda crackers

1 large apple, peeled, cored, and grated

4 eggs, hard-cooked

1 tablespoon sugar

1/8 to 1/4 teaspoon cinnamon

TIPS & TOUCHES

- Cover bowl containing grated apple with plastic wrap to prevent discoloration.
- Chopped herring was originally made using a metal handheld chopper. To replicate the texture of the original recipe, save 5 pieces of herring, chop by hand, and add to processed herring salad.

for
... ES
... TOES

...king methods,
...est a full quota
... values — with
... Home Canning.

"HOOK-UP"
COOK BOOK   No 7

The
VEGETABLE
Being a collection of tes...
...ipes of fresh and canned...
...les—showing their dieteti...
...d giving sensible methods...
...y and service

AND PUBLISHED BY
... MAGAZINE CO. INC.
..., U.S.A.

...CH
BOOK

275 Recipes for
MEALS
WITHOUT MEAT

Now is the time — and here are
countless ways—to prepare substantial Meatless Main Dishes.

A "HOOK-UP"
COOK BOOK

No 6

DELL

...r of Dinners"
...5 Recipes
...y Marion Harris Neil
...cluding Crisco

CHAPTER 4

SIDE DISHES

Just because side dishes, such as vegetables, are good for you, this doesn't mean they shouldn't taste good. There are even people like us who eat our vegetables before the main dish. Whether they're raw, chunky, pureed, or fried, we love them. The good news is that it's easier to learn to love vegetables when someone puts a little extra effort into bringing out their natural goodness. We know that there are some of you who shun the thought of using canned vegetables, so we've tried to substitute fresh and frozen ones. However, canning is an accepted method of preserving food and was once a part of every home cook's repertoire. There are still some hearty, well-organized souls who have the time and patience to home-can the bounty of their gardens or the seasonal surplus of their local markets. For some, canning is still the middle step between growing and serving what one eats.

As the methods of commercial canning and freezing of vegetables became more advanced, and as we went from being members of farming communities to urban dwellers with larger freezers, the type of vegetables we served changed. Although there's a special joy in eating a firm, flavorful tomato just off the vine, canned plum tomatoes can be the next best thing for some recipes when tomatoes are not in season. It's not always what one serves but how one serves it. Frozen corn and lima beans, briefly steamed and seasoned with a squeeze of lemon juice and a touch of butter, taste almost as good as fresh. To be more specific, the home cooks whose recipes we feature here knew that when vegetables are dressed up a bit—whether by sauce or marinade, baking au gratin, or frying—they are more appealing and memorable than those that are merely boiled until they become a pale, sodden mass.

Children's dishes, English, early 20th century

PACKING SUPPLY SHORTAGE

Ice Box Pickle

14 Cups Slice Cucumbers
2 c Slice Onions
2 Green Peppers Sliced
4 tsp salt
4 Cup Sugar
2 Cup vinegar White
2 tsp Celery seed
Mix good and let stand 30 min
dont eat before 4 day —
Keep in Ice box

Corn Souffle
1 T. butter
2 T. Flour
1 cup milk
1 can corn
1¼ t Salt pepper
2 Eggs Separated.

Melt butter add
flour gradually
the milk bring
to boil add corn
Seasonings & beaten
yolks last beaten
Whites — (beat until
dry.) Turn in
to buttered dish bake moderate
oven 25 to 40 min 350°

Exploring the vegetable recipes of home cooks has shown us the almost miraculous feats women could perform by presenting humble beans and squash with their own fanciful touches. A gratin of yellow summer squash turns into an almost ethereal dish with the addition of a rosy paprika sour cream sauce. A recipe for Baked Butternut Squash from Michigan, with its buttery brown sugar glaze, satisfies the traditionalist in us all.

We salute two Church Ladies—Jean Downey, the minister's wife, who achieved wonders with her Marinated Vegetables, and Louella MacPherson, for her Church Cauliflower, with its blanket of buttery bread crumbs and cheese.

We also acknowledge those who believe that a pickled cucumber is a green vegetable by sharing a recipe for crisp Icebox Pickles from North Carolina, an easy road to travel for almost instant pickle gratification. We can't say enough good things about the rosy goodness of Elizabeth Corkery's Stovetop Pickled Beets, with a color and taste that brighten up any meal.

We invite you to think of the following recipes as a movable feast as you travel from Massachusetts to New York to Michigan to North Carolina, sampling the best of the harvest.

Jane Bullard's Yellow Squash Casserole

{ *1930s* }

FOR CASSEROLE

3 cups cut-up (¼-inch pieces) yellow squash

1 tablespoon extra-virgin olive oil

¾ cup chopped shallots

½ cup sour cream

4 tablespoons butter, softened to room temperature

1 teaspoon salt

½ teaspoon coarsely ground black pepper

1 tablespoon fresh thyme leaves

½ teaspoon paprika

¼ cup grated parmesan cheese

¼ cup grated Romano cheese

1 egg, beaten

FOR TOPPING

1 cup soft bread crumbs (see "How to Make Soft Bread Crumbs" on page 241)

2 tablespoons butter, melted

1¼ cups grated parmesan cheese

THIS DISH IS ACTUALLY CALLED *Summer Squash Au Gratin, which means that it is a casserole with a top layer of buttered bread crumbs and cheese, browned in the oven. Whatever name it goes by, plain or fancy, it's delicious. The paprika-flavored sour cream sauce is outstanding. We found this recipe in a gift bundle of living recipes from our friend Bonnie Slotnick, who runs a cookbook shop in New York.*

1. Set oven rack in middle position. Preheat oven to 350°F. Coat 9-inch by 13-inch ovenproof glass baking dish with vegetable spray.

2. To make casserole: Place squash in steamer basket, set over simmering water, and cover. Steam just until tender, 10 to 12 minutes. Do not overcook. Cool and pat dry with paper towels. Set aside.

3. Heat olive oil in small frying pan over medium heat. Add shallots and cook, stirring with wooden spoon, until translucent, about 5 minutes. Set aside.

4. Combine sour cream, butter, salt, pepper, thyme leaves, and paprika in large saucepan over medium heat. Cook, stirring, until butter melts and mixture is smooth, 3 to 4 minutes. Add parmesan cheese and Romano cheese and stir until smooth. Remove from heat and whisk in egg. Fold in sautéed shallots. Add squash and gently stir to combine. Place in prepared dish and level top.

5. To make topping: Mix bread crumbs with melted butter and parmesan cheese in small bowl and sprinkle over squash. Bake about 30 minutes, or until bread crumbs are golden brown and cheese is bubbling. Serve hot. Store leftovers covered with wax paper in refrigerator.

Caramelized Potatoes
(Brunede Kartofler)

{ 1 9 5 0 s }

THIS IS A TRADITIONAL DANISH RECIPE FOR *preparing potatoes, which we received from Edward Steenberg. Ed prepares his specialty—Danish Roast Goose Stuffed with Apples and Prunes (page 236)—for family and friends at Thanksgiving and Christmas. He always serves these potatoes and Red Cabbage (Rødkål) (page 122) as accompaniments. Ed learned to cook when he was just 15 years old, following the death of his mother, Erma Horn Steenberg.*

2 pounds small new potatoes (about 12)

2½ teaspoons salt, or to taste, divided

¼ cup sugar

¼ cup butter, softened to room temperature

¼ teaspoon coarsely ground black pepper

1. Place potatoes in saucepan with 2 teaspoons of the salt. Add water to cover potatoes by about 1 inch. Bring water to a boil, reduce heat, and simmer 15 to 20 minutes, or until tip of knife can be inserted into potatoes easily. Do not overcook.

2. Drain potatoes in colander, rinse under cold water, and peel. Cut potatoes into quarters, or wedges, if potatoes are large.

3. Place sugar in heavy frying pan over low heat and cook, stirring constantly with wooden spoon, for about 3 minutes, or until sugar turns golden brown (not black). Add butter and stir until smooth. Add as many potatoes as will fit easily in 1 layer. Using spoon, roll potatoes in sugar and butter mixture until coated and golden. Cook about 6 minutes, or until small particles of brown caramel adhere to potatoes.

4. Remove potatoes to heatproof bowl. Repeat to caramelize remaining potatoes. Sprinkle potatoes with remaining ½ teaspoon salt (or to taste) and pepper and serve.

TIPS & TOUCHES

- You can use larger waxy potatoes, quartered.
- This is a very rich dish, and it is a traditional complement to Danish Roast Goose Stuffed with Apples and Prunes.

Libby's Stovetop Pickled Beets

MAKES 4 CUPS

{ 1950s }

THIS VERY SIMPLE RECIPE FOR PICKLED BEETS *from Elizabeth Corkery, of Groton, Massachusetts, helped us overcome our fear of beets. The cooking process prevents the bleeding usually associated with working with beets and is much easier than roasting beets in the oven and peeling them afterwards. These beets get better as they sit in the refrigerator. They look very pretty in a pressed-glass dish.*

1. Wash beets. Trim any long stems, leaving about 1 inch of stem. Do not trim tails. Bring pot of water to a boil over medium heat, add beets, and return to a boil. Cook about 35 minutes, or until blade of small knife can be inserted into beets easily. Remove beets from pot and let cool. Peel and cut into $1/4$-inch-thick rounds.

2. Combine vinegar, water, sugar, salt, and cloves in nonreactive heavy-bottomed saucepan. Bring to a boil, reduce heat, and simmer 5 minutes, stirring with wooden spoon. Add beets and onion and simmer another 5 minutes. Remove from heat and place in glass container. Cool completely, cover, and refrigerate overnight. Pickled beets are best served the next day. Store leftover beets in refrigerator.

6 medium beets

1 cup white vinegar

$2/3$ cup water

$1/2$ cup sugar

$1/4$ teaspoon salt

$1/4$ teaspoon whole cloves

1 cup sliced onion

TIPS & TOUCHES

- Leaving part of the top stem and tail on beets prevents them from bleeding during cooking.
- Golden beets or candy cane beets make a nice presentation with less bleeding.

➤➤ PICKLING SPICE ◂◂

Pickling spice is a mix of spices used to preserve vegetables such as cucumbers, tomatoes, and cauliflower or to flavor condiments such as chutneys. The main ingredients in pickling spice are bay leaves, peppercorns, cinnamon sticks, mustard seeds, and whole cloves. Pickling spice can vary as to composition and quantities of ingredients. It is also used for curing meats and cooking corned beef or pot roasts.

Icebox Pickles

14 cups pickling cucumbers,
unpeeled and sliced
¼-inch thick

2 cups sliced onions

2 green bell peppers, sliced

2 cups white vinegar

3½ cups sugar

4 teaspoons salt

2 teaspoons celery seed

⅛ teaspoon cayenne pepper

⅛ teaspoon ground cloves

2 bay leaves (fresh if possible)

WE FOUND THIS RECIPE IN A MANUSCRIPT *cookbook from North Carolina. It's simple and quick and produces a crisp pickle. Don't hesitate to make half the recipe. These pickles keep for several weeks in the refrigerator. The lady who created this recipe may actually have used an icebox. Be sure to use glass or stainless steel containers that will not react with the vinegar.*

1. Layer cucumbers, onions, and green peppers in medium nonreactive glass bowl and set aside.
2. Combine vinegar, sugar, salt, celery seed, cayenne pepper, cloves, and bay leaves in nonreactive stainless steel saucepan. Bring to a boil, pour over cucumbers, and let stand 30 minutes. Pack into 1-gallon glass jar. When completely cool, place in refrigerator. Pickles will keep about 4 weeks stored in glass jar in refrigerator.

TIPS & TOUCHES

- Icebox Pickles are ready to eat within 4 hours, but for improved flavor, the original recipe suggests waiting 4 days.

➤➤ SUGGESTIONS FOR ◄◄ PICKLING CUCUMBERS

- It's better to use small pickling cucumbers.

- If you use large cucumbers, peel them first. They won't be as crisp as pickling cucumbers, but they will taste good.

- Do not eat bay leaves.

- Pickled cucumbers can be transferred to smaller clean glass jars and refrigerated.

- A special pickling salt prevents pickles from turning dark and the pickling liquid from turning cloudy. This recipe uses table salt.

Baked Butternut Squash

{ 1 9 5 0 s }

MAKES 6 SERVINGS

2 pounds butternut squash, peeled and cut into 1-inch cubes

4 tablespoons butter, softened to room temperature

²/₃ cup firmly packed brown sugar

1 (20-ounce) can pineapple chunks (about 2 cups), drained

¾ teaspoon salt

½ teaspoon coarsely ground black pepper

1 teaspoon dried ginger

½ cup toasted walnuts, coarsely chopped

TIPS & TOUCHES

- Shake nuts in a strainer to remove nut dust.

THIS RECIPE WAS WRITTEN ON AN INDEX *card from the Midwest. We love the sauce made with butter and brown sugar, with its touch of ginger. Butternut squash is a favorite autumnal dish, especially in New England, but it's perfect for Thanksgiving dinner all over the country. The crunchy walnuts add balance to the tender squash.*

1. Set oven rack in middle position. Preheat oven to 425°F. Line 17-inch by 11-inch jelly roll pan with foil, shiny side up, and coat with vegetable spray. Place squash in large bowl.

2. Melt butter in saucepan over medium heat. Add brown sugar and stir with wooden spoon until combined. Add pineapple, salt, pepper, and ginger. Bring to a boil, reduce heat to medium, and cook until mixture is syrupy, about 15 minutes.

3. Pour pineapple mixture over squash and toss to coat. Spread squash on prepared pan. Bake 20 minutes, shaking pan after 10 minutes for even cooking, or until squash is soft when pierced with small knife. Sprinkle with walnuts and serve immediately. Store leftover squash in covered container in refrigerator.

Toy tin saucepan, German, 1890s

Louella's Church Cauliflower

MAKES 6 SERVINGS

LOUELLA MACPHERSON WAS A FRIEND OF *Mary Johnson, our agent Karen's mother. Mary and Louella attended The First Congregational Church in Kenosha, Wisconsin. Louella's recipe for cauliflower in a cheese sauce was a much-loved regular at the annual Harvest Home Dinner and became a staple in the Johnson home. Mary added the butter to the bread crumb topping.*

1. Place cauliflower florets and 1 teaspoon of the salt in heavy saucepan. Add water to cover. Bring to a boil, reduce heat, cover, and cook until cauliflower is tender when pierced with small knife, 10 to 12 minutes. Drain and set aside.

2. Melt 1 tablespoon of the butter in saucepan over low heat. Add bread crumbs and mix to combine. Set aside.

3. Melt remaining ¹/₃ cup butter in large frying pan over low heat. Add mushrooms, green pepper, remaining 1 teaspoon salt, and black pepper. Cook 5 minutes, stirring constantly with wooden spoon. Remove from heat, add flour, and mix thoroughly. Return pan to heat, increase to medium heat, add milk, and cook, stirring, until mixture begins to thicken. Remove from heat.

4. Set oven rack in middle position. Preheat oven to 350°F. Coat 1¹/₂-quart round ovenproof casserole with vegetable spray.

5. Place half of cooked cauliflower in prepared dish. Pour half of mushroom-pepper sauce over cauliflower and sprinkle with half of cheese. Repeat to layer remaining cauliflower, sauce, and cheese. Sprinkle with bread crumb mixture.

6. Place baking dish on cookie sheet and bake 25 to 30 minutes, or until casserole is golden brown and bubbling. Serve hot. Cool any leftover cauliflower in baking dish, cover with paper towel and plastic wrap, and refrigerate. To reheat, remove paper towel and plastic wrap and place in 300°F oven until warmed through, 10 to 15 minutes.

1 head cauliflower (1½ pounds), cut into small florets

2 teaspoons salt, divided

1 tablespoon plus ¹/₃ cup butter

½ cup fine bread crumbs (see "How to Make Fine Bread Crumbs" on page 204)

½ pound sliced white mushrooms

¼ cup chopped green bell pepper

1 teaspoon coarsely ground black pepper

¼ cup flour

2 cups scalded milk

1¹/₃ cups medium-sharp cheddar cheese, grated

TIPS & TOUCHES

- Milk is scalded when small bubbles form around edges.

Zucchini Cheese Bake

{ 1 9 4 0 s }

MAKES 8 SERVINGS

2 pounds zucchini

1 cup finely chopped onion

8 tablespoons butter, melted

1¼ cups fine bread crumbs (see "How to Make Fine Bread Crumbs" on page 204)

⅓ cup heavy cream

4 eggs, beaten

1¼ cups grated American cheese

1 teaspoon salt

½ teaspoon coarsely ground black pepper

½ teaspoon chopped fresh dill

Tips & Touches

* Squeeze as much liquid as possible from the zucchini and onion before assembling the casserole. The dish will be watery if you don't.

THIS WAS ONE OF THOSE LITTLE HEIRLOOM *gems we found while browsing through some scraps of paper late at night at our friend Bonnie Slotnick's cookbook shop in New York. This handwritten recipe made imaginative use of 2 popular inexpensive ingredients, zucchini from the garden and American cheese. We brought this recipe into the 21st century by using a food processor to grate the zucchini, but a handheld grater will do the job.*

1. Set oven rack in middle position. Preheat oven to 350°F. Coat 1½-quart ovenproof soufflé dish with vegetable spray or butter.

2. Wash and peel zucchini. Trim both ends. Grate with metal grating blade of food processor. Wring out grated zucchini in dish towel over sink to remove as much liquid as possible. Squeeze zucchini again by hand to remove any remaining liquid. Set zucchini aside in large bowl.

3. Squeeze chopped onion by hand to remove as much liquid as possible. Add to bowl with zucchini. Add melted butter, bread crumbs, and cream. Add eggs and mix thoroughly. Fold in cheese, salt, pepper, and dill until completely combined.

4. Spoon mixture into prepared dish and bake about 1 hour and 15 minutes, or until golden brown on top and bubbling around edges. If zucchini seems to be browning too quickly, cover with foil. Serve hot. Cover leftovers with layer of paper towels and then wax paper and store in refrigerator. Pour off any liquid that collects before reheating.

Jean Downey's Marinated Vegetables

{ *1940s* }

MAKES 6 CUPS

1 (15½-ounce) can cut green beans, liquid reserved (see step 1)

1 (15½-ounce) can cut wax beans, liquid reserved (see step 1)

1 (17-ounce) can lima beans, liquid reserved (see step 1)

1 cup finely chopped red onion

½ teaspoon coarsely ground black pepper

Pinch of salt

¼ teaspoon chopped, brined hot chilies

¼ cup extra-virgin olive oil

¾ cup sugar

¾ cup white vinegar

1 large clove garlic, finely chopped

¼ cup chopped fresh parsley

THE RECIPE FOR THIS MARINATED VEGETABLE SALAD *comes from Jean Downey, who served with her minister husband at churches in Indiana, Kentucky, and Massachusetts. An unflappable cook, Jean, along with her husband, ran a summer church camp when they were newly married, and she made all of the meals for summer church youth groups. She also cooked for countless Unitarian Universalist teas, lunches, and suppers in Westford and Groton, Massachusetts.*

1. Set strainer over bowl and drain green beans, wax beans, and lima beans. Reserve ½ cup bean liquid; discard remainder. Combine drained beans, onion, pepper, salt, chilies, and olive oil in large bowl and set aside.

2. Combine sugar, vinegar, reserved bean liquid, and garlic in saucepan over medium heat and stir with wooden spoon until mixture starts to boil. Remove from heat and pour over bean mixture. Stir thoroughly. Add parsley and toss. Place in nonreactive container and let cool. Cover and refrigerate overnight. Drain before serving.

TIPS & TOUCHES

- We use chopped chilies in brine to add a bit of bite to the salad.
- Be sure to drain salad before serving. Reserve liquid to store leftover salad.

Toy colander, American, 1920s

Marinated Fresh Bean Salad

MAKES APPROXIMATELY 6 CUPS

THIS VERSION OF THE MARINATED VEGETABLE SALAD *uses fresh and frozen vegetables.*

1. Cook lima beans according to package directions and place in large bowl.
2. Place green beans, wax beans, and salt in saucepan. Add cold water to cover. Bring to a boil and boil 6 minutes, add mini corn, and boil 1 additional minute. Drain vegetables in colander. Immerse in bowl of cold water to stop cooking. Let stand 5 minutes. Drain well. Add to bowl with lima beans. Add onion, black pepper, chili peppers, and olive oil.
3. Combine sugar, vinegar, water, and garlic in saucepan over high heat and stir with wooden spoon until mixture starts to boil. Remove from heat and pour over bean mixture. Stir thoroughly. Add parsley and toss. Place in nonreactive container and let cool. Cover and refrigerate overnight. Drain before serving.

1 (12-ounce) package frozen lima beans

9 ounces fresh green beans

9 ounces fresh wax beans

1 teaspoon salt

1 cup fresh mini corn, cut in rings

1 cup chopped red onion

1/2 teaspoon coarsely ground black pepper

1/2 teaspoon chopped chili peppers in brine

1/4 cup extra-virgin olive oil

3/4 cup sugar

3/4 cup white vinegar

3/4 cup cold water

1 large clove garlic, finely chopped

1/4 cup finely chopped fresh parsley

Miniature baskets, American, 1920s–1930s

Mrs. Carter's Baked Stuffed Onions

MAKES 6 SERVINGS

{ 1 9 0 5 }

THIS RECIPE COMES FROM THE MANUSCRIPT COOKBOOK *of the Carter family, from Portland, Maine. Marion A. Carter was the originator of the manuscript cookbook, filled with heirloom recipes covering three generations.*

1. Coat 9-inch by 13-inch ovenproof glass baking dish with vegetable spray.

2. To prepare onions: Peel and trim onions but do not cut off root ends. Slice off ½ inch from stem ends and set aside for stuffing. Bring large saucepan of water to a boil. Add whole onions, cover, and return water to a boil. Reduce heat and simmer about 15 minutes, or until tester inserted into onions penetrates easily.

3. Drain onions and allow to cool. Hollow out onions by first cutting around interiors with small knife, leaving wall about ¼-inch thick (at least 3 layers of onion). Then scoop out insides with spoon or melon baller. If an onion falls apart, reinforce with layer of onion scooped from another onion. Chop scooped-out insides and reserved slices from tops and set aside for stuffing. Place onions, root ends down, in prepared pan.

4. To make stuffing: Heat olive oil in large frying pan over medium heat. Add ground beef and cook until no longer pink. Drain and remove to bowl. Add salt, pepper, parsley, thyme, reserved chopped onion, bread crumbs, and 3 tablespoons of the chicken stock and mix to combine.

5. Set oven rack in middle position. Preheat oven to 375°F.

6. Spoon stuffing into hollowed-out interiors of onions, pressing down gently to pack well and mounding stuffing over tops. Add any leftover stuffing to bottom of pan. Add remaining ½ cup chicken stock to bottom of pan.

7. To make topping: Mix bread crumbs and olive oil in small bowl. Sprinkle over onions. Cover with foil and bake 25 minutes. Uncover and bake 15 minutes more, or until onions are nicely browned on top. (Larger onions may need to bake a little longer.) Serve onions hot along with any extra stuffing from bottom of baking dish. Store leftover baked onions in covered container in refrigerator. Reheat in low oven or microwave until hot.

FOR ONIONS

6 large sweet onions

FOR STUFFING

2½ tablespoons extra-virgin olive oil

¾ pound ground beef

¼ teaspoon salt

½ teaspoon coarsely ground black pepper

1½ tablespoons chopped fresh parsley

1 teaspoon dried thyme

¼ cup fine bread crumbs (see "How to Make Fine Bread Crumbs" on page 204)

3 tablespoons plus ½ cup low-sodium chicken stock

FOR TOPPING

⅓ cup fine bread crumbs (see "How to Make Fine Bread Crumbs" on page 204)

¼ cup extra-virgin olive oil

Mrs. E. R. Brown's Corn Soufflé

{ 1 9 2 0 s }

½ teaspoon salt

¼ teaspoon coarsely ground black pepper

¼ teaspoon dry mustard

4 eggs, separated

4 tablespoons butter, softened to room temperature

¼ cup flour

1 cup milk

¼ cup half-and-half

1 cup fresh, frozen and thawed, or canned corn, drained

TIPS & TOUCHES

- Using white pepper means no black flecks in your soufflé.
- Run your finger around the rim of a soufflé before placing it in the oven to form a "high hat" when baked.

FOUND ON A 2-CENT POSTCARD SENT TO *Susan Adams, Grand Central, New York, this fluffy but substantial corn soufflé is equally acceptable as a savory luncheon dish or as an accompaniment to a stew or braise. It really stars when paired with gravy. Another recipe from the file of The Church Lady of Mansfield, Ohio.*

1. Set oven rack in middle position. Preheat oven to 400°F. Butter 1½-quart glass or ovenproof baking dish or coat with vegetable spray.

2. Combine salt, pepper, and mustard in small bowl and set aside. Place egg yolks in medium bowl. Place egg whites in bowl of standing mixer fitted with whisk attachment.

3. Melt butter in heavy-bottomed saucepan over low heat. Remove from heat, add flour, and stir with wooden spoon until combined. Return pan to heat, increase heat to medium, and add milk and half-and-half, stirring, until sauce has thickened. Add salt mixture and stir to combine. Remove sauce from heat and spoon into large bowl. Beat yolks with fork to combine. Pour small amount of sauce into yolks, whisking to temper yolks, then return yolk mixture to bowl with sauce, whisking to combine quickly. Fold corn into sauce mixture.

4. Beat egg whites until stiff peaks form. Fold egg whites into sauce mixture until completely combined.

5. Turn down oven to 350°F. Pour soufflé mixture into prepared dish. Bake 1 hour, or until soufflé rises, turns golden brown on top, and pulls away from sides of baking dish. A tester inserted into center should come out clean. Soufflé will deflate within a few minutes, so serve immediately. Soufflé is best served the same day. Place any leftovers in container, cover with plastic wrap, refrigerate, and eat as a personal snack.

Crispy Norwegian Potatoes

MAKES 8 SERVINGS { 1920s—1930s }

THIS RECIPE SHOULD PROBABLY BE CALLED *Norwegian Potatoes and Carrots* because both vegetables have leading roles in this dish. The potatoes and carrots, flavored with nutmeg and onions, are actually twice baked, once in liquid and once on a jelly roll pan, to produce crunchy, buttery nuggets. We found this handwritten recipe tucked in among dessert recipes from the early part of the 20th century.

1 cup butter, divided

2 cups coarsely chopped onion

3 pounds potatoes, peeled and cut into ½-inch chunks (8 cups)

4 cups sliced (¼-inch rounds) carrots

2 teaspoons salt

1½ teaspoons coarsely ground black pepper

1 teaspoon nutmeg

1. Set oven rack in middle position. Preheat oven to 350°F. Coat 9-inch by 13-inch ovenproof glass baking dish with vegetable spray. Set aside.

2. Bring 4 cups of water to a boil.

3. Melt ½ cup of the butter in Dutch oven or heavy-bottomed casserole over medium heat. Add onion and cook until translucent, 5 to 7 minutes. Add potatoes, carrots, salt, pepper, and nutmeg. Cook 1 minute, stirring with wooden spoon. Remove to prepared baking dish. Add enough boiling water to cover vegetables. Cover with foil and place in oven. Bake about 40 minutes, or until vegetables are tender when pierced with tip of knife. Remove from oven.

4. Drain vegetables in colander.

5. Line 17-inch by 11-inch jelly roll pan with foil, shiny side up, and coat with vegetable spray. Arrange vegetables in even layer in prepared pan. Melt remaining ½ cup butter and pour over vegetables. Return to oven and bake for 55 minutes, shaking pan every 15 minutes, or until brown and crispy. Serve immediately. Store leftover vegetables in covered container in refrigerator.

Silver nutmeg grater, English, early 1800s

Red Cabbage *(RødKål)*

MAKES 6 TO 8 SERVINGS

¼ cup butter, softened to room temperature

½ cup diced (½-inch) red onion

20 ounces shredded red cabbage (about a 1½-pound cabbage)

½ cup white vinegar

½ cup sugar

2 teaspoons salt

¼ cup currant jelly

THIS HEIRLOOM RECIPE FOR DANISH RED CABBAGE *is an accompaniment to Ed Steenberg's roast goose recipe (page 236). It is easy to make, and the red cabbage, red onions, and currant jelly turn the vegetables a glistening garnet color. The slight acidity of the red cabbage nicely balances the richness of the goose. Red cabbage should be made the day before because the flavor is even better when it is reheated.*

1. Brown butter lightly in Dutch oven or heavy pot over low heat, stirring with wooden spoon. Add onion and cabbage. Stir well. Add vinegar, sugar, and salt. Cover and simmer 1 hour and 20 minutes, or until cabbage is soft, stirring occasionally. Add currant jelly in last 10 minutes of cooking and stir to combine.

2. Cool cabbage to room temperature and refrigerate in covered container overnight before serving. Rewarm over medium heat.

✈ SOME SUGGESTIONS ✦
FOR COOKING RED CABBAGE

Red cabbage can be shredded with a food processor or by hand. You can also use two 10-ounce packages of shredded cabbage. To reduce cabbage odor, bring mixture to a boil, then place in 325°F oven in covered pot. Cook, stirring with wooden spoon every 15 minutes, until cabbage is soft, from 1½ to 2 hours.

Mrs. Hodges's Savory Sweet Potato Puff

{ 1 8 9 4 }

3 eggs, separated

8 tablespoons butter, softened to room temperature

½ cup firmly packed brown sugar

½ cup heavy cream

2 tablespoons sherry

½ teaspoon salt

½ teaspoon coarsely ground black pepper

½ teaspoon dried ginger

1 teaspoon grated lemon zest

2 tablespoons ginger jam

1 tablespoon grated fresh ginger

⅓ cup ricotta

1 cup cooked riced sweet potatoes (from about 3 medium sweet potatoes)

We found this handwritten recipe for a *sweet potato puff* in a copy of Mrs. John G. Carlisle's Kentucky Cook Book, *owned by Mrs. Harriette G. Hodges. It was originally referred to as a sweet potato pudding, but we renamed it. This puff is both sweet and savory, with 3 kinds of ginger. If you omit the pepper, it can serve as a dessert with whipped cream or vanilla ice cream. Both Mrs. Hodges and Mrs. Carlisle were true Southern cooks, and they both knew their stuff.*

1. Set oven rack in middle position. Preheat oven to 350°F. Coat 1½-quart ovenproof glass or china baking dish with vegetable spray or butter.
2. Place egg whites in bowl of standing mixer fitted with whisk attachment. Beat until soft peaks form. Set aside.
3. Cream butter and brown sugar in bowl of standing mixer fitted with paddle attachment. Add egg yolks and mix thoroughly. Add cream, sherry, salt, pepper, ginger, lemon zest, ginger jam, and grated ginger. Mix until well combined. Add ricotta and sweet potatoes. Fold in reserved egg whites.
4. Pour into prepared pan and bake 45 minutes, or until tester inserted into puff comes out clean. Serve immediately. Puff will deflate a little on standing. Cover any leftovers with plastic wrap and store in refrigerator. Warm in low oven before serving.

Tips & Touches

• To steam sweet potatoes: Peel 3 sweet potatoes, cut into 1-inch chunks, and place in steamer basket over simmering water. Cover pot and steam for about 20 minutes, or until tip of knife can penetrate easily. Put sweet potatoes through ricer and measure 1 cup.

French Risotto
(White Rice)

MAKES 6 SERVINGS

THIS DISH IS NOT A TRUE RISOTTO. *It's just the way we make the white rice that accompanies many of the home plates in* Heirloom Cooking. *Years ago, we discovered that Julia Child made her rice the same way, by coating the grains with oil. Since she called it "French Risotto," we did, too. This is one of the few recipes that we make with dried onion flakes, which absorb any extra moisture left after the rice has finished cooking. Although onion flakes are optional, they give the rice a bit of crunch.*

1. Heat olive oil in saucepan over medium heat. Add rice and stir with wooden spoon until all of the grains are coated with oil, about 1 minute.

2. Add stock or water, salt, pepper, and parsley. Stir once or twice and bring to a boil. Cover, reduce heat to very low, and cook 18 minutes, or until rice is tender. Remove pan from heat, uncover, and stir in dried onion flakes. Cover rice and cool for 2 minutes. Remove cover, stir, and serve.

1 tablespoon extra-virgin olive oil

1 cup long grain white rice

2 cups low-sodium chicken stock or water

½ teaspoon salt

½ teaspoon coarsely ground black pepper

1 tablespoon dried parsley

2 tablespoons dried onion flakes (optional)

TIPS & TOUCHES

- You can use chopped fresh parsley instead of dried parsley.

Food chopper, American, 1890s–1920s

CHAPTER 5

SOUP OF THE DAY

We've always had an intimate relationship with soup. It warms us when we're cold, cools us when we're hot. It feeds us when we're hungry, and, most important, soup comforts us when the going is rough. There is something very appealing and universal about that round, steaming bowl placed before us. When we were growing up, it seemed that everyone's mother knew how to make soup, some better than others. Some home cooks had more ingredients to work with, including meat, fish, or chicken. For those who couldn't afford meat, there were always free soup bones from a generous butcher. Chicken feet and chicken backs were indispensable ingredients of choice by the thrifty, but they also made a darn good soup. Liquid masterpieces were also created from beans, corn, and root vegetables.

As we read through the handwritten recipes that we had gathered, we realized that every bowl of soup represents someone's story, whether it is the story of the person who made the soup or the person who ate it. It seems that everyone loves soup, even a person as awe-inspiring as the principal of our grammar school, Preston L. Chase, who made a cup of soup mixed with crumbled soda crackers his permanent choice for lunch at the local spa.

For us, there were the Friday morning aromas of our mother's chicken soup, with its abundance of celery, carrots, onion, and parsnips, which she made for the Sabbath. Our honorary aunt, Rose Levy, produced an admirable vegetable soup, made with dried split peas, barley, noodles, and big chunks of soup meat, while sharing her kitchen with an elderly white cat named Lucky.

On hot summer nights on Sea Foam Avenue, our mother used to make quick versions of cold soup for our father using canned tomato soup or glass jars of beets for her cream of tomato soup and her borscht. She mixed these handy ingredients with generous portions of old-fashioned sour cream and garnished them with a sprinkling of chopped green onions.

And so we became acquainted with all manners of soup, both hot and cold. In time, we began to understand that soup was more than just a hearty main dish served in a thick crockery bowl. We learned that some soups were better served in delicate double-handled bowls on damask tablecloths laid with silver spoons. Soup could be a starter or even a dessert. The late Gloria Schleiger Story, a 91-year-old home cook from Nebraska, provided us with a recipe for *Schnit Suppe*, a soup from her German-Russian heritage, made from dried prunes and apricots. This hearty sweet soup is served for dessert during the cold Nebraska winters.

Advertising bean crock, Durgin-Park Restaurant, American, 1950s

Although we traditionally relate the stories of inspired home cooks, in this chapter we also celebrate the story of our friend Arthur, who as a young Swedish-American teenager had to leave school in the middle of the Depression to help support his family. His culinary journey started as he waited in line outside the kitchen of the stylish Statler Hotel in Boston. Selected to work with the hotel chefs, Arthur started out by washing pots and pans and later was allowed to wash vegetables. Clever and industrious, he acquired kitchen wisdom and eventually became a chef at the hotel. Upon retirement, he brought his culinary talents to the kitchen of a prestigious women's college. We recently found, tucked away, a copy of his recipe for clam chowder made with minced salt pork and heavy cream, an example of the best of New England chowders.

Margaret Yarranton, transplanted from the Isle of Wight, brought her home cooking skills to Belmont, Massachusetts, where she replicated a very traditional English cream of parsnip soup for her young family. Although more modest than Arthur's Clam Chowder, Margaret's soup makes a memorable meal when accompanied by a green salad and homemade bread and butter.

We revisit the home kitchen of Virginia P. Lima, of Providence, Rhode Island. In this working-class Portuguese household, Mrs. Lima produced her long-simmering red bean and chorizo soup. A flavorful meal in a bowl, it is still remembered today by her children. Mrs. Lima sometimes simmered the chorizo in her soup and sometimes served it on the side.

And finally we pay tribute to some classic heirloom soups: Scotch Broth, Split Pea Soup, and Baked Bean Soup. We encourage you to make your bowl of soup even better by presenting some recipes for crisp White Hall Crackers (see page 173) and buttery Homemade Croutons (see page 172).

Scotch Broth

{ *1 8 8 0 s* }

MAKES 8 SERVINGS

4 tablespoons extra-virgin olive oil, divided

1 to 1½ pounds lamb shanks

2 cups chopped onion

2 cups chopped celery

1½ cups chopped carrot

1 teaspoon kosher salt

½ teaspoon coarsely ground black pepper

9 cups low-sodium beef broth

2 bay leaves

2 teaspoons dried parsley

⅓ cup barley

1½ pounds waxy potatoes, cut in quarters

2½ cups chopped frozen turnips

TIPS & TOUCHES

* The potatoes and the turnips may fall apart and thicken the soup.
* Fresh turnips can be substituted for frozen, but they may take a little longer to cook.

WE FOUND SEVERAL RECIPES FOR SCOTCH BROTH. *Simple, easy, and inexpensive, this is a lovely warm soup perfect for cold winter days and nights. Just a touch of lamb, a good helping of barley, and some aromatics make this comforting soup appealing.*

1. Heat 2 tablespoons of the oil in large heavy frying pan over medium-high heat. Add lamb shanks and cook until well browned on all sides. Remove to large Dutch oven or heavy-bottomed pot.

2. Add remaining 2 tablespoons oil to frying pan and reduce heat to medium. Add onion, celery, and carrot and cook until onion is translucent, about 7 minutes. Scrape into pot with lamb. Add salt, pepper, beef broth, bay leaves, parsley, and barley. Cover and bring to a boil. Reduce heat and simmer 1 hour.

3. Add potatoes and turnips and cook until soft, another 30 minutes. Allow soup to cool. Remove and discard bay leaves. Remove meat from pot. Pull meat from bones and discard bones. Shred or chop meat and return to pot. To serve, bring soup to a simmer and ladle into warmed soup bowls. Store leftover soup in covered container in refrigerator.

Spongeware mixing bowl, American, early 20th century

Arthur's Clam Chowder

MAKES 12 CUPS

WE FIRST TASTED THIS CLAM CHOWDER MORE *than 25 years ago. A rich, milky chowder, loaded with clams and potatoes, it is simple to make and easy to serve. Arthur worked in the kitchens of the Statler Hotel, in Boston, as a teenager during the Depression. He became a seasoned chef who graciously shared his recipes. Arthur's recipe called for salt pork, but we suggest using bacon or pancetta. The butter–and–flour mixture is called a roux.*

1. Melt 2 tablespoons of the butter in Dutch oven or heavy-bottomed 5-quart pot over medium heat. Add onion and cook, stirring with wooden spoon, until translucent, 5 to 7 minutes. Stir in bacon or pancetta and cook until fat begins to melt into onion, about 5 minutes. Turn down heat if bacon or pancetta begins to burn.

2. Add flour, reduce heat to low, and stir briskly to make roux. Cook roux 1 minute. Add pepper. Add broth and reserved clam liquid to roux, continuing to stir until chowder begins to thicken. Add clams. Remove chowder from heat.

3. Heat milk and cream in separate 1½-quart pot over medium heat until small bubbles form around edges. Add to chowder, set chowder pot over medium heat, and bring to a simmer, stirring briskly. Stir in potatoes. Add remaining 2 tablespoons butter and cook, stirring gently, until melted. Do not allow chowder to boil. Serve in heated soup bowls, garnished with fresh parsley, crumbled common crackers, or Pilot crackers. Store leftover chowder in covered containers in refrigerator. Reheat gently. Do not boil or cream will curdle.

4 tablespoons butter, divided

2 cups coarsely chopped onion

4 slices bacon or 3 ounces pancetta, diced

½ cup flour

¼ teaspoon coarsely ground black pepper

2 (8-ounce) bottles clam broth

3 (10½-ounce) cans chopped clams, drained and liquid reserved

2 cups milk

2 cups cream

1½ pounds potatoes, peeled, cooked, and diced (about 4 cups)

¼ cup chopped fresh parsley (optional)

TIPS & TOUCHES

- Serve with Souffléed Common Crackers (page 187).
- If you use salt pork, it is important to remove the tough layer of skin before dicing.
- Each can of clams will yield a little over 5 ounces of clam liquid, which should be added to the bottled clam broth.
- If you like a thicker chowder, mix 2 tablespoons of flour with softened butter and whisk into chowder.

Katherine's Savory Tomato Peanut Butter Soup

{ 1 9 2 0 s }

1 (28-ounces) can tomato puree

¾ cup creamy peanut butter

1 teaspoon salt

½ teaspoon coarsely ground
  black pepper

½ teaspoon paprika

1 cup low-sodium beef stock

2 tablespoons butter, softened to
  room temperature

Pinch of red pepper flakes

Tips & Touches

* Serve hot with buttered
  Homemade Croutons (page 172).
* Serve cold with a touch of sour
  cream and a sprinkling of red
  pepper flakes or paprika.

We found this recipe in a cunningly *illustrated recipe journal from the 1920s. This soup is good served either hot or cold. The peanut butter adds richness to the soup, yet it is not readily identifiable upon tasting. This soup takes on a whole new personality when served cold.*

1. Combine tomato puree and peanut butter in large heavy-bottomed pot and blend with wooden spoon or whisk until smooth. Add salt, black pepper, and paprika.

2. Add stock and bring to a boil. Reduce heat and simmer 10 minutes. Add butter. Add red pepper flakes and stir to blend. Allow to sit 5 minutes to marry flavors. Serve hot or cold. Store leftover soup in covered container in refrigerator.

Folding wire basket, American, early 20th century

Fred's Creamy Potato Soup with Thyme

MAKES 6 CUPS

4 medium boiling potatoes
   (2 pounds), peeled and
   quartered

2 teaspoons salt, divided

½ cup chopped celery leaves

1 cup sliced onion

1 bay leaf

½ cup heavy cream

2 tablespoons butter, cut into dice

½ teaspoon coarsely ground
   black pepper

½ teaspoon dried thyme

½ teaspoon chopped chilies
   in brine

1 cup milk

Homemade Croutons, for garnish
   (page 172)

TIPS & TOUCHES

• Save the leftover potato stock
  for gravies or soups.

THIS RECIPE CAME FROM A MANUSCRIPT COOKBOOK *given to Katherine and Fred by Ceil and Betty. This little treasure was loaded with recipes, including Tomato Peanut Butter Soup, Corned Beef Hash, and Shepherd's Pie— all hearty heirloom recipes designed to please a husband. This soup is thick and satisfying and can be enjoyed either hot or cold. It's great hot with buttery Home- made Croutons (page 172) or with finely chopped chives or some fresh thyme leaves if served cold. We suggest using fresh thyme, if you have some, for the potato soup.*

1. Place potatoes in large pot and add water to cover (about 6 cups). Add 1 teaspoon of the salt, celery leaves, onion, and bay leaf. Cover and bring to a boil. Reduce heat to medium and simmer until potatoes are fork tender, about 15 minutes.

2. Drain potato mixture in colander, reserving cooking liquid. Dis- card bay leaf. Place potato mixture, heavy cream, and butter in bowl of food processor fitted with metal blade. Pulse until pota- toes are smooth and creamy. (Or puree soup in blender.) Add remaining 1 teaspoon salt, black pepper, thyme, chili peppers, and milk and pulse to blend. Add some of the reserved potato stock or additional milk to thin soup to the desired consistency.

3. To serve, ladle soup into warmed soup bowls and garnish with croutons. Store in covered container in refrigerator. Reheat soup on low, adding more milk or potato stock to thin, as needed. Serve hot or cold.

German Dessert Fruit Soup
(*Schnit Suppe*)

MAKES 6 CUPS

{ *1900s* }

THIS IS AN AMERICANIZED VERSION OF THE *hearty German dessert soup that a community of Germans living in Russia brought with them to Nebraska. Schnit Suppe is delicious hot or cold. It's sweet and spicy and similar to the Jewish dessert compote. Serve it hot in the cold winter months with a bit of whipped cream and sliced toasted almonds on top. Our thanks to Sue Truax and her mother, Gloria Schleiger Story, who gave us the recipe for this soup.*

1½ cups dried apricots

1½ cups dried pitted prunes

½ cup raisins, tightly packed

1 quart cold water

1 tablespoon flour

½ cup dark corn syrup

²/₃ cup heavy cream

⅛ teaspoon salt

¼ teaspoon ground cloves

1. Combine apricots, prunes, and raisins in large saucepan. Add water to cover. Cover with lid and bring to a boil. Reduce heat and simmer, stirring occasionally with wooden spoon, until fruit is tender, 10 to 12 minutes. Combine flour and corn syrup, add to soup, and stir until soup thickens. Remove soup from heat and allow to cool 20 minutes.
2. Stir ½ cup of the soup liquid into heavy cream. Return cream mixture to soup. Add salt and cloves and stir well. Let stand for 5 minutes to let flavors marry.
3. To serve, warm soup over medium heat (do not boil) and ladle into warmed soup bowls. Store leftover soup in covered container in refrigerator.

TIPS & TOUCHES

- Fruit soup can be made with different combinations of mixed dried fruit. You can also add canned sweet cherries to the soup.

Pink Depression glass serving pieces, 1930s

Garden Salad Soup

{ *Early 1900s* }

SUE TRUAX, FROM OMAHA, NEBRASKA, TOLD US *about this simple soup prepared with ingredients picked from the family garden. Sue stayed with her Uncle Rheinhold and Aunt Grace when her husband, Glenn, did his National Guard duty. Uncle Riney and Aunt Grace were 1st-generation descendants of the Czar's Germans, from Odessa, Russia. Sue remembers building her own bowl of fresh greens, warm potatoes, and cold buttermilk, garnished with sweet spring onions. We made this soup with sour cream, and it was outstanding. This was a spring luncheon dish when the new potatoes were ready for digging.*

1¼ pounds new potatoes, unpeeled

1 head fresh Boston lettuce, romaine, or oak leaf lettuce

2 cups buttermilk, or 1 cup sour cream

3 green onions or scallions, sliced into ¼-inch rounds

⅛ teaspoon kosher salt

⅛ teaspoon coarsely ground black pepper

1. Place potatoes in 4-quart pot, add salted water to cover, and bring to a boil over medium heat. Boil 15 to 20 minutes, or until potatoes are soft and tip of knife penetrates easily. Drain and slice ¼-inch thick.

2. Rinse and spin-dry lettuce. Tear into small pieces and divide among soup bowls. Mound ¾ cup warm potatoes in each bowl. Pour ½ cup buttermilk or spoon ¼ cup sour cream into each bowl. Sprinkle with green onions or scallions, salt, and pepper.

Bok Choy and Corn Soup

MAKES 12 CUPS

2 ounces pancetta, diced

5 tablespoons extra-virgin olive oil, divided

2 cups chopped onion

2 cups chopped leeks

½ cup chopped shallots

4 cups chopped bok choy

4 cups corn kernels
(3 to 4 ears fresh corn), or
4 cups frozen corn

½ teaspoon salt

½ teaspoon coarsely ground black pepper

¼ cup butter, softened to room temperature

¼ cup flour

2 cups low-sodium chicken stock

¼ cup chili sauce

2 tablespoons chopped fresh parsley

1 cup milk

TIPS & TOUCHES

- Pancetta is optional, but it gives a nice salty balance to the soup. If you leave out the pancetta, increase salt to ¾ teaspoon.
- Reheat soup slowly on low heat so that milk will not curdle.
- Recipe can be halved.

THIS RECIPE GREW OUT OF OUR INTEREST *in the availability of fresh vegetables and ethnic ingredients such as pancetta and bok choy. The search for healthy food fueled our use of naturally sweet vegetables such as onions, bok choy, and corn when we cooked for family and friends. The crispy pancetta contrasts nicely with the mild flavor of the onions, leeks, and shallots. We suggest that you make this soup when corn is in season.*

1. Sauté pancetta in large heavy saucepan over medium heat until crisp, about 5 minutes. Remove to large bowl and set aside. Add 1 tablespoon of the olive oil to pan. Add onion, leeks, and shallots and cook until translucent, 5 to 7 minutes. Remove to bowl with pancetta. Wipe pan with paper towel.

2. Return pan to heat and add 2 tablespoons of the olive oil. Add bok choy and cook until leaves are wilted and stems are soft, about 4 minutes. Remove to bowl with pancetta and onion. Add remaining 2 tablespoons oil to pan, add corn, and cook until softened, about 4 minutes. Remove to bowl. Sprinkle vegetables with salt and pepper and stir.

3. Melt butter in 4-quart saucepan over low heat. Remove pan from heat. Add flour and stir with wooden spoon to form roux. Return pan to low heat and cook, stirring, for 1 minute. Remove pan from heat. Add stock. Return to heat, increase heat to medium, and cook, stirring until mixture thickens and small bubbles form around edges, 3 to 5 minutes.

4. Fold in pancetta and vegetables. Add chili sauce and parsley. Add milk. Pour in batches into bowl of food processor fitted with metal blade. Pulse until soup is almost smooth but still has some texture. (Or puree soup in blender.) Serve hot in warmed soup bowls. Store leftover soup in covered container in refrigerator. Thin with a little milk when reheating.

BaKed Bean Soup

MAKES 10 CUPS

WE FOUND THIS RECIPE IN A DARLING *little book, designed and illustrated by Louise Perrett, called* Recipes, My Friends' and My Own. *It was created to record handwritten recipes. This soup is very satisfying on a cold winter day. It's also simple to prepare and makes a speedy, comforting bowl. Garnish with crumbled bacon and sour cream if desired.*

1. Combine 4 cups of the baked beans and onions, celery, and beef stock in heavy-bottomed pot. Bring to a boil, reduce heat, and simmer 30 minutes.

2. Add tomato puree and stir to combine. Pour in batches into bowl of food processor fitted with metal blade. Pulse until completely blended. (Or puree soup in blender.) Return soup to pot. Add remaining 1 cup beans and cook over low heat, stirring, until warmed through. Serve in warmed soup bowls. Store leftover soup in covered container in refrigerator.

5 cups canned baked beans, drained, divided

2 medium onions, sliced (2 cups)

2 stalks celery, sliced (1 cup)

6 cups low-sodium beef stock

1½ cups canned tomato puree

TIPS & TOUCHES

- We used pork and beans in tomato sauce for our soup.

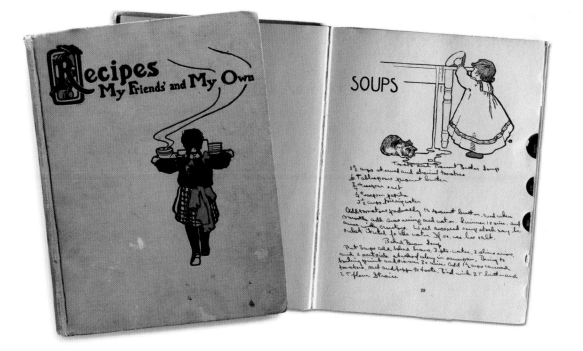

Portuguese Red Kidney Bean Soup

{ 1 9 2 0 s }

MAKES 14 CUPS

1 pound dried kidney beans, rinsed

4 tablespoons extra-virgin olive oil, divided

2 cups coarsely chopped onion

1 cup coarsely chopped celery

2 tablespoons tomato paste

7 cups low-sodium chicken stock

1 teaspoon salt

1/2 teaspoon coarsely ground black pepper

1/2 teaspoon paprika

1/2 cup loosely packed chopped fresh parsley

1 1/2 cups canned tomato puree

8 ounces (1 link) chorizo sausage, peeled and coarsely chopped

1 1/2 cups elbow macaroni

1 tablespoon red wine vinegar

TIPS & TOUCHES

- If you want a stronger sausage flavor, add 2 links of chorizo.

THIS THICK, CHUNKY SOUP IS BASED ON *the Portuguese red kidney bean soup that David Lima's mother prepared in the kitchen of their home in Providence, Rhode Island. Virginia P. Lima was famous for her Portuguese sweet bread and her wonderful soups and stews. We added the chorizo as seasoning. This is comfort food at its best.*

1. Place beans in bowl, add cold water to cover, and let soak overnight. The next day, drain beans and rinse under cold running water. Set aside.

2. Heat 3 tablespoons of the olive oil in Dutch oven or heavy-bottomed pot over medium heat. Add onion and celery and sauté until translucent, 5 to 7 minutes. Whisk tomato paste with chicken stock and add to pot. Add salt, pepper, paprika, parsley, tomato puree, and drained beans and stir with wooden spoon to mix. Cover and bring to a boil over medium heat, stirring occasionally. Reduce heat to low and simmer, covered, for 1 hour.

3. Heat remaining 1 tablespoon oil in frying pan over high heat. Add chopped chorizo and cook about 15 minutes, or until slightly crispy.

4. Add cooked chorizo and browned bits from bottom of pan to soup pot. Cover and continue cooking another 30 minutes. Add macaroni and vinegar. Simmer, covered, another 30 minutes, stirring occasionally, until beans are tender. If beans are still a little firm, continue cooking 15 minutes more. Store leftover soup in covered container in refrigerator.

Mama's Chicken Soup

{1930s}

4 whole cloves, or pinch of ground cloves

1 large onion, peeled, cut into quarters

4½- to 5-pound chicken, cut in pieces with the skin on

5 stalks celery with leaves, coarsely chopped

4 carrots, cut into 1-inch pieces

2 parsnips, cut into 1-inch pieces

2 cloves garlic, peeled, cut into small pieces

3 bay leaves

2 teaspoons kosher salt

½ teaspoon coarsely ground black pepper

16 cups water

Tips & Touches

- Chicken fat is wonderful for making savory pastry, such as Mrs. Yaffee's Pierogi (page 60); store rendered chicken fat in a covered container in the freezer up to 3 months.
- Heat a bit of chicken fat with the soup for a richer taste and higher cholesterol.

THIS IS THE CHICKEN SOUP OUR MOTHER, *Dorothy, made for us when we were growing up. If it was Friday, it was chicken soup. Mama made great pots of it and served some of the chicken in the soup. The remaining chicken she dusted with flour, paprika, and pepper and fried in vegetable oil along with a cut-up onion. We didn't know fried chicken had skin until we were adults. We remember fondly Mama's chicken soup. We make it just the way she did, but we add 4 whole cloves to the onion. The recipe makes a lot of chicken soup, but it's wonderful to have the extra chicken stock on hand. Cubed or shredded cooked chicken makes a nice salad or stir-fry.*

1. Stick clove, if using, in each onion quarter and place in large soup pot (or place ground cloves and onion quarters in pot). Add chicken, celery, carrots, parsnips, garlic, bay leaves, salt, pepper, and water to pot. Cover and bring to a boil. Use ladle to skim white solids that float to surface of soup. Reduce heat, leave cover ajar, and simmer, skimming periodically as more solids rise to surface, until chicken is thoroughly cooked, 2 to 2½ hours.

2. Remove from heat. Uncover, and cool 15 minutes. Remove chicken from soup with slotted spoon; set aside. Strain soup into large, clean pot. Remove and reserve carrots and parsnips; discard all other solids. Pour soup carefully into containers and let stand until cool. Cover and refrigerate.

3. Remove and discard skin and bones from chicken. Place chicken and reserved carrots and parsnips in 2 separate covered containers and refrigerate.

4. When soup has chilled, scrape fat from surface with spoon and reserve in covered container.

5. To serve, bring soup to a simmer in saucepan. Add some of the reserved chicken and vegetables and a bit of the reserved chicken fat, if desired. Taste and adjust seasonings. Serve in warmed soup bowls.

Margaret's Cream of Parsnip Soup

MAKES 10 CUPS

{1970s}

MARGARET YARRANTON WROTE THIS RECIPE FOR HER *English cream of parsnip soup on the back of a discount ticket to an antique show and sale. A good friend and an antique dealer, she often invited us for Thanksgiving dinner at her home in Belmont, Massachusetts. One Thanksgiving, she served this velvety parsnip soup. Margaret came from the Isle of Wight and lived through the rationing of World War II. She has been known to churn her own butter and bake her own Scottish Baps (page 177) for Thanksgiving dinner.*

1. Melt butter in Dutch oven or heavy-bottomed pot over medium heat. Add parsnips, onion, and celery and cook, stirring with wooden spoon, until softened, 5 to 10 minutes. Add chicken stock, bay leaf, and nutmeg and simmer 30 minutes.

2. Add lemon juice and stir. Pour soup into large bowl. Remove and discard bay leaf. Pour 2 cups of soup mixture in bowl of food processor fitted with metal blade. Pulse until smooth. (Or puree soup in blender.) Return soup to clean pot. Continue working in batches to puree all of the soup.

3. Add half-and-half, salt, and pepper. Cook over low heat, stirring with wooden spoon, until warmed through. Do not boil. Taste soup and adjust seasonings. Serve in warmed soup bowls. Store in covered container in refrigerator.

2 tablespoons butter, softened to room temperature

4 cups chopped parsnips

1 cup chopped onion

1 cup chopped celery

6 cups low-sodium chicken stock

1 bay leaf

1/4 teaspoon nutmeg

1 tablespoon lemon juice

1 cup half-and-half

1 1/2 teaspoons salt

1/2 teaspoon coarsely ground black pepper

TIPS & TOUCHES

- Boiling the soup after adding the half-and-half can cause the soup to curdle.
- This soup is wonderful served with a plate of sliced turkey and a green salad the day after Thanksgiving.

Toy enamelware ladle, early 1900s

Auntie Rose's Vegetable Beef Soup

MAKES 14 CUPS   {1930s}

ROSE LEVY WAS OUR MOTHER DOROTHY'S BEST *friend and honorary sister. Auntie Rose's vegetable soup was outstanding, and when our mother made it, the kitchen on Sea Foam Avenue was perfumed with the aroma of simmering legumes and root vegetables. Fishel Zwieg, one of the many kosher butchers on Shirley Street in Winthrop, was known for his generosity in giving loyal customers free soup bones. Our version uses chunks of chuck, or as we liked to call it, "soup meat."*

1. Place green and yellow split peas in strainer and pick over for gravel or husks. Rinse under cold water. Drain and set aside in bowl. Do the same for barley and set aside in separate bowl.

2. Heat olive oil in large Dutch oven or heavy-bottomed pot over medium-high heat. Add beef chuck, working in batches so as not to crowd pan, and cook until well browned on all sides. Remove meat to bowl and set aside.

3. Add onion to pot and cook until translucent, about 5 minutes. Return beef to pot. Add green and yellow split peas, carrots, celery, garlic, salt, pepper, bay leaves, and 8 cups of the stock. Stir, cover, and bring to a boil. Reduce heat and simmer 1 hour, stirring occasionally.

4. Add barley and 1 more cup of the stock. Return soup to a boil, reduce heat, and simmer, covered, for 15 minutes. Add frozen lima beans and simmer another 15 minutes. Remove beef from soup with slotted spoon, shred, and return to pot.

5. Add remaining 2 cups stock and noodles and cook another 15 minutes, or until dried peas dissolve and barley is soft. Remove from heat and let stand 15 minutes. Soup will thicken on standing. Remove and discard bay leaves. To serve, ladle into warm soup bowls. Store leftover soup in covered container in refrigerator.

1 cup green split peas

1 cup yellow split peas

½ cup barley

2 to 3 tablespoons extra-virgin olive oil

1 to 1¼ pounds beef chuck, cut into 2-inch pieces

1½ cups coarsely chopped onion

4 carrots, cut into 1-inch pieces

3 stalks celery, chopped

2 large cloves garlic, minced

1 teaspoon salt

½ teaspoon coarsely ground black pepper

3 large bay leaves

11 cups low-sodium beef stock, divided

1 cup frozen lima beans

6 ounces dried egg noodles

TIPS & TOUCHES

- If the peas and barley are not completely cooked after 1 hour and 45 minutes, soup can be simmered another 15 minutes.

Split Pea Soup

{1890s}

1 pound split green peas

1 quart water

1 quart low-sodium chicken stock

1 cup coarsely chopped celery
    with leaves

3 bay leaves

1 tablespoon dried parsley

½ teaspoon coarsely ground
    black pepper

6 ounces pancetta

1 tablespoon extra-virgin olive oil

2 cups coarsely chopped onion

1 cup coarsely chopped carrot

1 clove garlic, peeled and chopped

TIPS & TOUCHES

* Do not fry pancetta until crispy.
  It should retain enough of its
  shape to melt into the soup.
* You can use a blender instead
  of a food processor.

THIS IS A VERY OLD RECIPE, WHICH *originally called for a ham bone. Since not everyone has a ham bone in the freezer, we tried it with pancetta, that salty Italian rolled bacon. We found that the nuggets of pancetta lend a rich, velvety feel to the soup (pictured on page ii) and provide a sweeter taste than the ham bone. One of our favorite trendy crepe restaurants used to serve a similar soup, Potage St. Germaine, with a small container of cream or sherry. We like this soup just the way it is.*

1. Place split peas in strainer and pick over for gravel or husks. Rinse under cold water. Place in Dutch oven or large heavy-bottomed pot. Add water and chicken stock and stir. Add celery and leaves, bay leaves, parsley, and black pepper and set aside.

2. Cut pancetta into ½-inch cubes. Place in frying pan over medium heat and cook 5 to 7 minutes, or until pancetta is just beginning to release fat but before it begins to brown. Scrape into pot with peas. Add olive oil to frying pan and return to medium heat. Add onion, carrot, and garlic and cook 5 to 8 minutes, stirring with wooden spoon, until onion is just translucent. Scrape into soup pot.

3. Cover soup, place over medium heat, and bring to a boil. Reduce heat and simmer 1 hour and 15 minutes to 1 hour and 30 minutes, or until peas dissolve and vegetables are tender. Stir every 10 minutes to prevent peas from sticking to bottom of pot.

4. Remove pot from heat and allow soup to cool slightly. Remove bay leaves and discard. Soup will thicken as it stands. Pour 2 cups into bowl of food processor fitted with metal blade. Pulse until blended. (Or puree soup in blender.) If there are still some pieces of pancetta in soup, leave them. Return soup to clean pot. Continue working in batches to puree all of the soup.

5. To serve, rewarm soup gently over low heat and serve in warmed soup bowls. Store leftover soup in covered container in refrigerator.

Vermont Corn Chowder

MAKES 8 CUPS

{ *1 9 3 0 s* }

We found this recipe in a modest *box of handwritten recipes in Concord, Massachusetts. The origin of the recipes was Martha's Vineyard, a small island off the coast of Cape Cod. Mixed in with the recipes for Almond Granola and Cranberry Pudding was this "Vermont" Corn Chowder. This collection of living recipes also contained a genealogy chart for the family of the Vineyard cook. This simple chowder uses one of the staples of the pantry shelf, canned creamed corn.*

1. Melt butter in Dutch oven over low heat. Increase heat to medium, add onion and celery, and cook until tender, 5 to 7 minutes. Add salt, pepper, and paprika and stir with wooden spoon. Add potatoes, milk, and corn and stir until soup is heated through.

2. Remove Dutch oven from heat and stir in cheese until melted. If necessary, place soup over low heat and cook, stirring, until all of the cheese is melted. Do not boil.

3. Ladle soup into bowls and sprinkle with chopped parsley. Store leftover soup in covered container in refrigerator.

2 tablespoons butter, softened to room temperature

1 cup chopped onion

½ cup chopped celery

½ teaspoon salt

½ teaspoon coarsely ground black pepper

¼ teaspoon paprika

1¼ pounds potatoes, cooked, peeled, and diced

2 cups milk

2 (14¾-ounce) cans cream-style corn

8 ounces cheddar cheese, shredded (about 3 cups)

2 tablespoons chopped fresh parsley

Toy enamelware cooking pot, American, 1920s

CHAPTER 6

STAFF
OF LIFE

This chapter is very close to our hearts because bread baking so completely defines the home kitchen. We've always thought of the women whose manuscript cookbooks we've discovered and treasured as the bakers of the bread and the keepers of the hearth because bread, more than any other food, is what nourishes us both as individuals and as families. Bread is sacred. We talk of a companion as someone with whom we share our bread; we break bread together. We refer to bread as the staff of life—the food that supports and sustains us. • Bread is included in many religious rituals. In Judaism, a blessing is said over the Sabbath challah. Christians receive Communion wafers or Communion bread. In the Greek Orthodox tradition, the Easter bread,

Lambropsomo, cushions eggs dyed a deep red, symbolizing resurrection and rebirth. These are just a few of the examples of how bread feeds us both spiritually and physically.

During periods of natural disaster or war, the lack of bread can mean the loss of life. When a man supports his family, he is said to put bread on the table. He is referred to as a good provider or a breadwinner. When there was no man in the house, the woman in charge of the family had to find a way to provide bread. She had to secure shelter so she could have a place to bake the bread, and she needed to earn the money to purchase ingredients and fuel. Often women became breadwinners as well as bread bakers. Although many of them brought work home or eventually went out to work, their kitchens were still the center of family life. Nothing changed. The smell of baking bread still means home to most people.

In our search for traditional bread recipes, we found that women and men brought their bread-baking skills and their recipes with them when they immigrated to America. When Margaret Yarranton and her family came to the United States from England more than 50 years ago, she started the tradition of baking and serving her Scottish Baps at Thanksgiving. Simple raised yeast rolls, they are wonderful with butter and jam or as a sandwich roll.

Erika Geywitz brought her mother Emma's recipe for Christmas stollen with her when she came to this country from Germany in the 1960s. A casual conversation with her son, Michael, on a train from Boston to New York, provided us with the recipe for this satisfying yeast bread with its candied fruit and almonds. The recipe for Oma Emma's Stollen can be made any time of the year, but it brings a special cheer to

Tin baking pan, American, early 20th century

winter holidays. So dedicated is her grandson, Michael, that he even makes his own candied lemon and orange peel for his version of her stollen.

Although Grandma Gaydos's Gum Boots may not be thought of as bread, they are definitely staff of life material. The story of a 14-year-old girl named Helen Sochko, from Vlahovo, Austria-Hungary, who married John Gaydos, a Greek Orthodox priest, and raised five children in the mining communities of West Virginia, Ohio, and Pennsylvania, is one of courage and faith. With a limited food budget, Helen found ways to feed her children simple, delicious food. They called this dish of farmer's cheese and farina dumplings rolled in buttered bread crumbs Gum Boots because they couldn't pronounce its Czechoslovakian name. Three generations later, the Gaydos family still marvels at the feats of a young girl who washed and pressed the church linen, had the bishop to dinner, and tended to the needs of a large congregation.

One of the most moving stories about bread comes from the Arfa family, whose patriarch left Poland in 1938 as a young baker. He immigrated to America, served in World War II, and started a bakery in Chicago in 1947. For years, the bakery produced outstanding bagels, cakes, and rugelach. The tradition continues because we have adapted the recipe for the Arfa Family's Bagels for your home kitchen. Every time someone takes a pan of these golden bagels from a kitchen stove, the story of a family's search for a new homeland and a better life lives on.

Sally Lunn

1 (¼-ounce) package dry yeast

1 teaspoon plus ½ cup sugar

¼ cup water, warmed to 115°F

1¼ cups milk

½ cup butter, cut into 8 pieces

1½ teaspoons salt

3 eggs

3½ cups flour

TIPS & TOUCHES

- Sally Lunn can be served toasted with butter and jam or made into French toast or bread pudding.

MAKES 16 SLICES

SALLY LUNN ACTUALLY ORIGINATED IN THE 18TH *century, in England, and was brought to America by the colonists. Over the next 3 centuries, this sweet, buttery bread evolved into a quick bread made without yeast. We like the yeast version better because it reminds us of French brioche. There is still some confusion about the origin of the name Sally Lunn. Some sources say it was the name of the young girl who sold the bread on the streets of Bath. Others say it found its name from the French* sol et lune, *sun and moon, because it was baked in a round pan.*

1. Dissolve yeast and 1 teaspoon of the sugar in warm water. Set in warm place for about 10 minutes to proof.

2. Place milk in saucepan and warm over medium heat until bubbles form around edges. Remove from heat, add butter, and stir with wooden spoon until melted. Add remaining ½ cup sugar and the salt and stir until sugar has dissolved. Remove from heat and allow to cool slightly.

3. Beat eggs in bowl of standing mixer fitted with paddle attachment. Add milk mixture and proofed yeast mixture and beat until combined. Add flour, approximately 1 cup at a time, beating well after each addition. Mix until there are no lumps and dough is smooth, about 2 minutes. Cover bowl with clean dish towel and put in warm place to rise for about 1 hour, or until double in size.

4. Coat 10-inch by 4¼-inch tube pan with vegetable spray or butter. Lightly dust with flour and tap to remove excess. Stir dough with wooden spoon to deflate. Place dough in prepared pan. Cover with clean dish towel and allow to rise for another hour until double in size.

5. Set oven rack in middle position. Preheat oven to 350°F. Bake Sally Lunn 35 to 40 minutes, or until golden brown. Let cool in pan on rack for at least 30 minutes. Turn out onto rack and cut into slices. Store wrapped in wax paper at room temperature.

Ila's Canadian Banana Bread

MAKES 14 SLICES   { 1 9 2 0 s }

WE FOUND THIS HANDWRITTEN RECIPE ON A *yellowed piece of paper with "From the desk of ILA D. BERRY" printed in red ink on the upper left corner. There was a notation that said "a Canadian receipt." What makes this living recipe remarkable is that the writer was a workingwoman early in the 20th century who still had time to exchange recipes with coworkers. This banana bread is moist and delicious and perfect with the Banana Nut Salad (page 100).*

1. Set oven rack in middle position. Preheat oven to 350°F. Line bottom and narrow ends of 9-inch by 5-inch by 3-inch loaf pan with single strip of wax paper or parchment paper. Coat pan and paper liner with vegetable spray.

2. Cut bananas and pear into 1-inch slices, place in bowl, and mash until blended. Set aside. (There should be about 1½ cups mashed fruit.)

3. Sift flour, salt, baking soda, and pumpkin pie spice into another bowl and set aside.

4. Cream butter, sugar, and honey in bowl of standing mixer fitted with paddle attachment until fluffy. Add mashed fruit mixture and beat to combine. Add dry ingredients in thirds, beating after each addition. Fold in walnuts with a spatula. Pour batter into prepared pan.

5. Bake 50 to 55 minutes, or until tester inserted into middle of bread comes out clean. Remove from oven and place on cooling rack. Let stand 15 minutes and then turn out onto rack to cool. Store covered with paper towels and wax paper at room temperature. This bread is even better the next day.

2 large ripe bananas

4 ounces peeled, cored pear (about ½ large pear)

1½ cups flour

½ teaspoon salt

1 teaspoon baking soda

½ teaspoon pumpkin pie spice

¼ cup butter, softened to room temperature

1 cup sugar

2 tablespoons honey

1 cup toasted walnuts, coarsely chopped

TIPS & TOUCHES

* Ila's Canadian Banana Bread is good sliced, buttered, and cut into quarters and served with salads.

Aunt Ruth's Dilly Casserole Bread

{ 1 9 5 0 s }

MAKES 1 ROUND LOAF

1 (¼-ounce) packet dry yeast

¼ cup water, warmed to 115°F

1 cup large curd cottage cheese, heated to lukewarm

2 tablespoons sugar

1 tablespoon onion flakes

1 tablespoon butter, softened to room temperature

2 teaspoons dill seed

½ teaspoon salt

¼ teaspoon baking soda

1 large egg

2 to 2½ cups flour

Softened butter, for brushing

Coarse sea salt, for sprinkling

THIS RECIPE CAME FROM OUR AGENT *Karen Johnson's aunt Ruth, a wonderful Midwestern cook and baker. Ruth has been making her Dilly Casserole Bread for many years. This handwritten recipe was part of Karen's kitchen inheritance from her mother, Mary. Recently, at a flea market, Karen happily found a bowl to replace the one she broke that she had been using for baking her Dilly Bread.*

1. Dissolve yeast in water and set aside in warm place to proof for about 10 minutes. Mixture will bubble when yeast is proofed.

2. Mix cottage cheese, sugar, onion flakes, butter, dill seed, salt, baking soda, egg, and proofed yeast in bowl of standing mixer fitted with paddle attachment. Add flour gradually, beating well after each addition, to make stiff dough. Cover with clean dish towel and allow to rise in warm place until double in size, about 1 hour.

3. Punch down dough and turn into well-buttered 8-inch round ovenproof casserole. Cover and let rise in warm place for 1 hour.

4. Set oven rack in middle position. Preheat oven to 350°F.

5. Bake 40 to 50 minutes, or until golden brown. Turn bread out of dish, brush top with soft butter, and sprinkle with salt. Cool bread on rack for at least 10 minutes before serving. Store leftover bread wrapped in wax paper at room temperature.

TIPS & TOUCHES

- Use large curd creamed cottage cheese if you can find it because it has more moisture and gives the bread a richer flavor.

Clara J. Warren's Refrigerator Rolls

{ 1 9 3 0 s }

FOR YEAST SPONGE

1 (¼-ounce) package dry yeast

¼ cup water, warmed to 115°F

1 teaspoon sugar

FOR DOUGH

½ cup butter, cut into 8 pieces

1 cup boiling water

1½ teaspoons salt

¼ cup sugar

2 eggs, beaten

4 cups flour

Melted butter, for brushing

TIPS & TOUCHES

- After brushing the tops with butter, sprinkle kosher salt or poppy seeds on the rolls, if desired.

THIS RECIPE WAS TYPED ON A MANUAL *typewriter. We found it among some recipes from the Midwest, and we are glad that we have the name of the originator. There is even a typed line for Clara's name. We wonder if she typed this herself and signed the recipe. Clara knew how to bake with yeast, and these rolls are wonderful with butter or jam.*

1. For yeast sponge: Dissolve yeast in warm water. Add sugar. Set in warm place for 10 minutes to proof.
2. For dough: Whisk butter into boiling water to melt. Add salt and sugar and mix well. Let cool.
3. Mix cooled butter mixture, eggs, and proofed yeast sponge in bowl of standing mixer fitted with paddle attachment. Add 2 cups of the flour and mix well. Add remaining 2 cups flour and mix to form soft dough.
4. Coat medium bowl with butter or vegetable spray. Place dough in greased bowl. Coat piece of plastic wrap with vegetable spray (to prevent sticking) and place it loosely over dough. Place in refrigerator and let rise for at least 2 hours or overnight.
5. Coat cups and top surface of 12-cup muffin pan with butter or vegetable spray. Turn dough out onto floured work surface. Pat or gently roll to 10-inch by 10-inch square. Cut into 12 equal pieces with floured knife. Roll dough pieces into balls, place in prepared muffin pan, and let rise in warm place for 30 to 60 minutes, or until double in size.
6. Set oven rack in middle position. Preheat oven to 400°F.
7. Brush rolls with melted butter and bake 20 to 25 minutes, or until golden brown. Turn rolls out onto metal rack to cool. Store rolls wrapped in wax paper at room temperature.

Arline's Farm House Rye Bread

MAKES 2 LOAVES

{ 1 9 4 0 s }

WE FOUND THIS MIDWESTERN RECIPE ENTITLED *Farm House Bread* on a handwritten index card. It is not a dark pumpernickel bread, nor is it a Jewish light rye; it is simply an honest loaf, dense and cocoa-colored. It is good spread with butter or jam, and it satisfies when one wants a slice of bread that is both homey and filling. Arline also provided us with the recipe for Swedish meatballs (page 219).

1. To make dough: In medium heavy-bottomed pan, heat milk, sugar, and salt over medium heat until small bubbles form around edges. Remove from heat, add butter, stir until melted, and add 1/2 cup warm water. Let cool to room temperature.

2. To make sponge: Dissolve yeast in warm water. Add sugar. Let stand, uncovered, in warm place for about 10 minutes to proof.

3. Sift all-purpose flour, rye flour, and cocoa into medium bowl.

4. Mix proofed yeast and cooled milk mixture in bowl of standing mixer fitted with paddle attachment. Beat in dry ingredients, 1 cup at a time, until well mixed. Change to dough hook and knead for 3 to 4 minutes, or until dough comes together and is smooth and shiny.

5. Coat medium bowl with vegetable spray or butter. Place dough in greased bowl. Coat piece of plastic wrap with vegetable spray (to prevent sticking) and place it loosely over dough. Allow dough to rise until double in size, about 1 hour. Punch down dough and divide in half.

6. Coat two 9-inch by 5-inch by 3-inch loaf pans with vegetable spray. Shape dough into 2 loaves on lightly floured work surface. Place loaves in prepared pans and let rise until double in size, about 1 hour.

7. Set oven rack in middle position. Preheat oven to 375°F.

8. Bake breads until crusty, about 40 minutes. Turn bread out of pans onto rack and cool to room temperature. Store loosely wrapped in wax paper at room temperature.

FOR DOUGH

1 cup scalded milk

2 tablespoons sugar

1 1/4 teaspoons salt

2 tablespoons butter, softened to room temperature

1/2 cup water, warmed to 115°F

3 3/4 cups all-purpose flour

1 3/4 cups rye flour

1/4 cup cocoa

FOR YEAST SPONGE

2 (1/4-ounce) packages dry yeast

1/2 cup water, warmed to 115°F

1 teaspoon sugar

Virginia P. Lima's Portuguese Sweet Bread

MAKES 2 LOAVES

THIS LIVING RECIPE IS FROM DAVID LIMA, *who often assisted his mother when she made her signature Portuguese Sweet Bread for Christmas, for Easter, and as holiday gifts for family and friends. David recalls his mother tying a large washbasin to a stool so that she could mix the dough. It was a tradition to put 2 shots of whiskey in the dough, pour a shot of whiskey for the baker, and make the sign of the cross over the bread.*

1. Set oven rack in middle position. Preheat oven to 350°F. Coat two 9-inch cake pans with vegetable spray or butter.

2. Warm milk in microwave for 40 seconds at low. Set aside.

3. Dissolve yeast in warm water. Add 1 tablespoon of the sugar. Set in warm place to proof, about 10 minutes. Mixture will bubble when yeast is proofed.

4. Mix 5½ cups of the flour, butter, salt, and remaining 1 cup sugar in bowl of standing mixer fitted with paddle attachment. Add eggs. Add yeast mixture and whiskey or lemon extract. Add up to ¾ cup milk gradually, continuing to work dough. If dough continues to be sticky, add remaining ½ cup flour until dough firms up. Change to dough hook and continue to knead for 5 minutes at medium speed.

5. Butter large bowl. Place dough in bowl and turn dough so that all surfaces have film of butter. Put in warm place and allow to rise until double in size, about 1 hour. Punch down dough and divide in half. Shape into 2 rounds, using a little flour if necessary. Place in cake pans and let rise for 30 minutes. Make slit on top. Brush with beaten egg. Bake 40 to 45 minutes, or until crust is golden brown. Cool on rack. Slice bread with serrated knife. Store in plastic bag when completely cool.

¾ cup milk

2 packages (4½ teaspoons) quick-rising yeast

½ cup water, warmed to 115°F

1 tablespoon plus 1 cup sugar

5½ to 6 cups flour

½ cup butter

2 teaspoons salt

3 eggs, beaten

2 tablespoons whiskey or 1 teaspoon lemon extract

1 egg, beaten, for glaze

TIPS & TOUCHES

- To make mini-loaves (as pictured), divide dough in half and then form into 6 round portions each. Fit 6 rounds into each of two 9-inch prepared cake pans and bake as for loaves.

Cheddar Cheese and Dill Biscuits

MAKES 10 LARGE OR 15 SMALL BISCUITS

1 cup flour

2 teaspoons baking powder

¼ teaspoon salt

1 teaspoon fresh dill

2 tablespoons cold butter, cut into
½-inch cubes

2 tablespoons cold lard, cut into
½-inch cubes

¾ cup freshly grated cheddar
cheese (can grate in food
processor)

⅓ cup milk

1 egg, beaten

Tips & Touches

- Do not handle dough
  too much or biscuits will
  be tough.
- Brushing unbaked biscuits
  with beaten egg gives them
  a brown color.

THE RECIPE FOR THESE BISCUITS WAS TUCKED *into a manuscript cookbook from the 1930s and 1940s. Since rationing was going on in the 1940s, this home cook might have used more lard than butter in the recipe. We like using a combination of both because it lends a rich texture to the biscuits. These are both sophisticated and elegant. Serve them with lots of butter.*

1. Set oven rack in middle position. Preheat oven to 450°F. Cover 14-inch by 16-inch baking pan with foil, shiny side up. Coat foil with vegetable spray or use silicone liner.

2. Place flour, baking powder, salt, and dill in bowl of food processor fitted with metal blade. Pulse three times to mix. Add butter, lard, and cheese and pulse 3 times. Add milk and pulse until dough comes together.

3. Place dough on lightly floured wax paper or parchment paper. Roll out to ½-inch thickness. Dip round 2-inch or 3-inch biscuit cutter in flour and cut circles of dough. Press cutter straight down and lift up; do not twist cutter in dough or biscuits will not rise. Use spatula to lift and transfer dough to baking sheet. Gather up scraps and reroll to cut more biscuits. Biscuits made from rerolled scraps may not be as tender, but they will still be good.

4. Brush biscuits with beaten egg. Bake 12 minutes for large biscuits, 10 minutes for small biscuits. Place on rack to cool. Serve while still warm. Store leftover biscuits loosely covered with wax paper in container in refrigerator. Reheat before serving.

Buttermilk Biscuits

{ *1900s* }

MAKES 9 BISCUITS, 2½ INCHES IN DIAMETER

2 cups flour

½ teaspoon baking soda

2 teaspoons baking powder

½ teaspoon salt

6 tablespoons cold butter,
cut into dice

¾ cup buttermilk

MARILYNN MADE BISCUITS FOR WHAT SHE THOUGHT *was the first and last time when she was 12. Although her age may have been tender, her biscuits weren't. Faced with the challenge of writing this book, Marilynn decided it was time to make biscuits again. After consulting several of our collections of living recipes, we found this simple no-nonsense recipe that yielded stellar results. Marilynn has now conquered her fear of biscuits!*

1. Set oven rack in middle position. Preheat oven to 450°F. Prepare 14-inch by 16-inch baking sheet by greasing it or using silicone liner.
2. Combine flour, baking soda, baking powder, and salt in large bowl. Work in butter with your fingers (wear disposable gloves, if desired) until butter pieces are size of small peas. Add buttermilk and work in gently. Knead twice in bowl.
3. Place dough on floured surface. Knead gently 2 times. Sprinkle lightly with flour and pat into circle ½-inch thick. Cut out 2½-nch biscuits using biscuit cutter dipped in flour. Press cutter straight down and lift up; do not twist cutter in dough or biscuits will not rise. Transfer biscuits to baking sheet using wide floured spatula. Gather up scraps, reshape dough, and cut out more biscuits. Biscuits made from scraps may not be as tender, but they will still be good.
4. Bake 12 to 13 minutes, or until lightly browned. Biscuits are best eaten within an hour of baking. Serve with butter and jam.

Dixie Dinner Rolls

MAKES 12 ROLLS

THIS RECIPE WAS A PLEASANT SURPRISE. We *had never baked with self-rising flour before and always envisioned Southern farmhouse kitchens when we found recipes that called for this type of flour. Less than 5 minutes to "throw together" and only 12 minutes to bake, these biscuitlike dinner rolls are a great success. Your home will smell like an old-fashioned farmhouse kitchen while these are baking in the oven!*

2 cups self-rising flour

½ teaspoon sugar

1 cup milk

¼ cup mayonnaise

1. Set oven rack in middle position. Preheat oven to 450°F. Coat cups and top surface of 12-cup muffin pan with vegetable spray.
2. Mix flour, sugar, and milk in medium bowl. Add mayonnaise and mix until just combined. Fill muffin sections two-thirds full. Bake 12 minutes, or until lightly browned. Remove from oven and cool on rack 10 minutes. Serve while still a little warm with butter or jam.

Grandma Hails's Buns

{ 1 8 8 0 s }

FOR YEAST SPONGE

2 (¼-ounce) packages quick-rising yeast

1½ cups water, warmed to 115°F

1 tablespoon sugar

FOR DOUGH

5 cups flour

3 tablespoons sugar

1½ teaspoons salt

2 teaspoons finely chopped fresh rosemary leaves (optional)

½ cup solid shortening

Milk, for brushing

TIPS & TOUCHES

- You can split the dough and make a dozen rolls and 1 loaf of bread. Bake loaf at 425°F in 9-inch by 5-inch by 3-inch loaf pan, coated with vegetable spray, for 30 minutes.

MAKES 2 DOZEN ROLLS, OR 1 DOZEN ROLLS AND 1 LOAF OF BREAD

THIS RECIPE COMES FROM DONNA HENSIL TAUB, *who is the fifth generation of her family to bake these rolls. Donna learned how to make them from her mother, Cheryl, and her grandmother, Lorraine Paxton. The recipe originated with Donna's great-great grandmother, Sarah Toal Hails, who came to the United States from England. These were the rolls the Paxton–Grigor–Hails Family took on Fourth of July picnics at Ten Mile Creek in Washington County, Pennsylvania. These buns are wonderful for hamburgers, and the dough will also yield a tender loaf.*

1. To make sponge: Dissolve yeast in warm water. Add sugar and set in warm place for 10 minutes to proof.

2. To make dough: Mix flour, sugar, salt, rosemary (if using), and shortening in bowl of standing mixer fitted with paddle attachment. Add proofed yeast sponge and beat to combine. Change to dough hook and knead for 3 to 4 minutes, or until dough comes together and is smooth.

3. Coat medium bowl with vegetable spray or butter. Place dough in greased bowl. Coat piece of plastic wrap with vegetable spray (to prevent sticking) and place it loosely over dough. Put dough in warm place to rise until double in size, 30 minutes to 1 hour.

4. Line two 14-inch by 16-inch baking sheets with foil, shiny side up, and coat with vegetable spray, or use silicone liners. Punch down dough and divide into 2 dozen equal pieces. Roll each piece into a ball on lightly floured surface and place balls on prepared baking pans. Let rolls rise until double in size.

5. Set oven rack in middle position. Preheat oven to 425°F.

6. Brush tops of rolls with milk. Bake 15 to 20 minutes, or until rolls are golden brown. Let cool on metal racks. Store wrapped in wax paper at room temperature.

Chili Cheese Cornbread

MAKES NINE 3-INCH SQUARES

{ 1950s }

Eating this chili cornbread is like walking *through the door of a ranch house, sitting down at a Formica-topped table in the rumpus room, kicking off our loafers, and hitching up our poodle skirts. This is as good as it gets from the 1950s. This is from the manuscript cookbook of the lady from North Carolina.*

1. Set oven rack in middle position. Preheat oven to 375°F. Line bottom and sides of 9-inch by 9-inch pan with foil, shiny side up. Coat foil with butter or vegetable spray.

2. Remove casing from chorizo and coarsely chop. Add chorizo to frying pan, set over medium to high heat, and sauté until lightly browned, 5 to 7 minutes. Remove chorizo from pan with slotted spoon and place on platter covered with paper towels. Place second layer of paper towels on top and press gently to absorb excess fat.

3. Place flour, cornmeal, sugar, baking powder, and salt in large bowl and set aside. In another bowl, whisk eggs, milk, vegetable oil, and sour cream until smooth. Whisk egg mixture into dry ingredients until combined. Stir in chorizo, cheese, and green chilies. Place batter in prepared pan and bake 35 to 38 minutes, or until top is golden brown and tester inserted into middle comes out clean. Lift cornbread from pan with foil. Cut into 3-inch squares and serve warm with butter.

½ pound chorizo sausage

2 cups flour

1½ cups yellow cornmeal

⅓ cup sugar

2 tablespoons baking powder

1½ teaspoons salt

2 eggs

1 cup milk

½ cup vegetable oil

½ cup sour cream

6 ounces cheddar cheese, shredded (2¼ cups)

1 (4-ounce) can mild green chilies, drained and chopped

Tips & Touches

- Instead of chorizo, try pepperoni. You will not have to fry it.

Muffin pan, American, 1880s

Oma Geywitz's Stollen

MAKES 1 LOAF

{ *1930s* }

When we met Mike Ripley on a *train and fed him brownies, we never thought we'd find a recipe for a true German Christmas stollen. This recipe is from his grandmother, Oma Emma, who taught her daughter, Erika, to make her stollen. Mike is the 3rd generation to make the family stollen, and he is teaching his children to make it, too.*

1. To make sponge: Dissolve yeast in warm water. Stir in sugar. Set in warm place to proof, about 10 minutes.

2. To make dough: Mix sugar, butter, egg, salt, lemon juice, milk, cinnamon, nutmeg, and vanilla in bowl of standing mixer fitted with paddle attachment. Add proofed yeast. Add flour 1 cup at a time, beating until smooth after each addition. Change to dough hook and knead for 3 to 4 minutes, or until dough comes together and is smooth and shiny.

3. Coat medium bowl with vegetable spray or butter. Place dough in greased bowl. Coat piece of plastic wrap with vegetable spray (to prevent sticking) and place it loosely over dough. Allow dough to rise until double in size, about 1 hour. Punch down.

4. Coat 14-inch by 16-inch baking sheet with vegetable spray. Knead almonds and dried fruit into dough. On lightly floured work surface, flatten dough with rolling pin or with hands to 12-inch by 16-inch rectangle. Arrange dough rectangle with shorter side at bottom. Spread butter over bottom half of dough and fold over. Place stollen on prepared baking sheet. Cover with clean dish towel and allow to rise in warm place about 1 hour, or until double in size.

5. Set oven rack in middle position. Preheat oven to 350°F.

6. Bake stollen 30 minutes, or until golden brown. Remove from baking sheet, place on rack, and immediately brush with butter; butter will melt into the warm stollen. Sprinkle top with 2 tablespoons of the confectioners' sugar. Most of the sugar should melt into crust. Let cool to room temperature. Sprinkle with remaining 2 tablespoons confectioners' sugar. Slice and enjoy plain or with butter. Store loosely wrapped in wax paper at room temperature for 1 week.

FOR YEAST SPONGE

1 (¼-ounce) package dry yeast

¼ cup water, warmed to 115°F

1 teaspoon sugar

FOR DOUGH

¾ cup sugar

½ cup butter, softened to room temperature

1 egg

1 teaspoon salt

1 tablespoon lemon juice

¾ cup milk

1 teaspoon cinnamon

¼ teaspoon nutmeg

2 teaspoons vanilla

4½ cups flour

FOR FILLING

1 cup toasted slivered almonds

1½ cups mixed dried fruit, chopped, and raisins

2 tablespoons butter, softened

FOR TOPPING

2 tablespoons butter, softened to room temperature

¼ cup confectioners' sugar

Tips & Touches

- We used dried cherries, chopped dried apricots, and maraschino cherries, as well as golden raisins. Candied orange and lemon peel are also good.

Traditional Greek Easter Bread (*Lambropsomo*)

{ *1 9 4 0 s* }

FOR YEAST SPONGE

2 (¼-ounce) packages dry yeast

½ cup water, warmed to 115°F

½ cup milk, warmed to 115°F

1 teaspoon sugar

FOR DOUGH

½ cup butter, melted and cooled

3 eggs, beaten

¼ cup sugar

½ teaspoon salt

1½ teaspoons vanilla

¼ teaspoon ground masticha (optional)

4½ cups flour

FOR TOPPING

10 eggs, hard-cooked, shells dyed red or pastel colors

1 egg, beaten

1 tablespoon sesame seeds

THIS RECIPE COMES FROM THEODORA BENOS GUERAS, *of Winthrop, Massachusetts. Theodora was an accomplished artist as well as an excellent cook. Born in Maine, she learned her heirloom kitchen skills from her mother and grandmother, who were both born in Greece. Theodora was a treasured home cook for more than 80 years, and her family still remembers fondly the traditional loaves of bread she baked at Easter.*

1. To make sponge: Dissolve yeast in warm water. Stir in warm milk and sugar. Put in warm place to proof for about 10 minutes. Mixture will bubble when yeast has proofed.

2. To make dough: Mix melted butter, eggs, sugar, salt, vanilla, and masticha (if using) in bowl of standing mixer fitted with paddle attachment. Add proofed yeast and beat to blend thoroughly. Beat in flour 2 cups at a time. Continue to beat until soft dough forms, 1 to 2 minutes. Change to dough hook and knead for 5 minutes, or until dough is smooth and elastic; or turn dough out onto lightly floured board and knead 10 minutes.

3. Coat medium bowl with butter or vegetable spray. Place dough in greased bowl. Coat piece of plastic wrap with vegetable spray (to prevent sticking) and place it loosely over dough. Put dough in warm place and allow to rise for about 2 hours, or until double in bulk. Punch down dough and knead again until smooth.

4. For round loaves, coat two 14-inch by 16-inch baking sheets with vegetable spray. For braided loaf, coat 1 pan with spray.

5. To make 2 round loaves: Divide dough in half. On lightly floured surface, shape each piece of dough into round loaf. Make 5 depressions in each loaf for eggs. Place on prepared baking sheets.

6. To make 1 braided loaf: Divide dough into 3 equal pieces. On lightly floured surface, roll each piece into rope about 18 inches long. Pinch top ends together, braid ropes tightly, and pinch bottom ends together. Place on prepared baking sheet.

7. Cover loaves or braid with clean dish towels and allow to rise in warm place 1 to 1¹⁄₂ hours, or until double in size. For round loaves, place hard-cooked eggs in prepared depressions. For braid, nestle eggs in between ropes of braid. Cover loaves or braid with clean dish towels and allow to rise in warm place 1 to 1¹⁄₂ hours, or until double in size.

8. Set oven rack in middle position. Preheat oven to 350°F.

9. Brush top of each loaf with beaten egg (do not brush hard-cooked eggs) and sprinkle with sesame seeds. Bake 30 minutes, or until golden brown. (After baking, usually just tops of eggs will be visible.) Remove from baking sheet(s) and cool on rack. Store loosely wrapped in wax paper in refrigerator.

Tips & Touches

- Eggs are placed three down in the center of the loaf and one egg on each side of the center egg, making a cross. Traditionally, eggs are dyed a deep red, symbolizing the blood of Christ.

- A suitable red dye is available in Greek or Middle Eastern grocery stores. Conventional red food coloring may fade on the dough as it bakes. Pastel egg dye can be used instead of red dye.

- Masticha is a natural white resin. It is used to flavor breads, cookies, and beverages. It can be found in Middle Eastern grocery stores. Anise extract, vanilla extract, or orange zest can be substituted in Greek pastries.

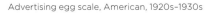

Advertising egg scale, American, 1920s–1930s

Bagels from Chicago

MAKES 12 BAGELS

{ *1940s* }

THIS BAGEL RECIPE WAS GIVEN TO US *by Sara Baser, the daughter of the founders of the Arfa Family Bakery in Chicago. Leon Arfa founded the bakery in 1948 and ran it with his wife, Dina, until 1974. Although the bakery closed several years ago, there are still those who fondly remember eating Arfa bagels. We adapted the original commercial recipe for baking in a home kitchen, and it produces a dozen large, chewy, yeasty bagels.*

1. For sponge: Dissolve yeast in warm water. Add sugar and set in warm place to proof, about 10 minutes.

2. For dough: Combine flour, salt, water, sugar, oil, and proofed yeast sponge in bowl of standing mixer fitted with paddle attachment. Beat for 1 to 2 minutes, or until combined. Change to dough hook and knead 3 to 4 minutes at low to medium speed.

3. Butter large bowl. Place dough in bowl and turn dough so all surfaces are lightly coated. Cover with clean dish towel and put in warm place to rise until double in size, about 1 hour.

4. Divide dough into 12 equal pieces. Roll each piece of dough into rope 9 to 10 inches long. Bring ends of each dough rope together to form ring and roll ends between fingers to secure. Place bagels on metal cooling rack and let rest for 15 minutes.

5. Bring large, covered pot of water to a boil. Reduce heat so that water simmers. Slide 3 bagels into simmering water and cook 30 seconds. Turn with large slotted spoon and cook another 30 seconds. Remove bagels to rack with slotted spoon. Repeat to boil remaining bagels. Let rest 15 minutes.

6. Set oven rack in middle position. Preheat oven to 450°F. Line 14-inch by 16-inch baking sheet with foil, shiny side up, and coat with vegetable spray, or use silicone liner.

7. Place 6 bagels on prepared baking pan. Brush tops with beaten egg. Bake 15 to 18 minutes, or until shiny and golden brown. Cool on clean metal rack. Repeat to bake and cool remaining bagels. Serve with butter, cream cheese, or jam. Store wrapped in wax paper at room temperature.

FOR YEAST SPONGE

2 (¼-ounce) packages dry yeast

½ cup water, warmed to 115°F

1 teaspoon sugar

FOR DOUGH

5 cups unbleached bread flour

2 tablespoons salt

1½ cups water

1 tablespoon sugar

2 tablespoons vegetable oil

1 egg, beaten

 TIPS & TOUCHES

- After kneading dough, add ½ cup raisins, if desired, and knead an additional 30 seconds.
- Bagels can be topped with poppy seeds, sesame seeds, onion flakes, or chopped onions fried in olive oil.

Homemade Croutons

{1940s}

MAKES 4 SERVINGS

4 slices good-quality white bread
or French bread

2 teaspoons flavored olive oil

2 teaspoons butter, melted

Pinch of kosher salt

⅛ teaspoon dried herbs (optional)

TIPS & TOUCHES

• Flavored oil and herbs give
croutons a more complex taste.

SEVERAL HEIRLOOM RECIPES SUGGEST *serving soup with croutons. Home cooks loved to use up pieces of leftover bread by making their own croutons. It's simple to make your own and worth the effort. Croutons cut in fancy shapes such as stars or hearts add a festive touch to a bowl of homemade soup.*

1. Set oven rack in middle position. Preheat oven to 350°F. Line 14-inch by 16-inch baking sheet with foil, shiny side up, and coat with vegetable spray, or use silicone liner.

2. Cut off crusts from bread slices and discard or save to make bread crumbs. Cut bread into 1-inch cubes.

3. Combine oil, melted butter, salt, and herbs (if using) in medium bowl. Add bread cubes and toss to coat. Place bread in single layer on prepared pan. Bake 7 minutes. Remove pan from oven, turn croutons, and bake another 7 minutes, or until golden brown. Serve immediately. Store cooled leftover croutons in plastic bag at room temperature.

Albany slip glazed pottery jug and mixing bowl, American, early 20th century

White Hall Crackers

MAKES 3 DOZEN

THIS NEW ENGLAND RECIPE CAME FROM A *manuscript cookbook inscribed "Mary C. Talbot, Special & Fine Recipes, Bread & Cakes." Mary filled the pages with yeast breads, quick breads, biscuits, and crackers. Many of the recipes were attributed to White Hall, Barberry Hill, and the Katydid Cottage Tea Room, places where ladies went for refreshment during World War I. Although there is a reference to Maine, the book also contains recipes for grits bread, Maryland beaten biscuits, and Southern spoon bread.*

1. To make crackers: Place sifted flour, salt, baking soda, and butter in large bowl. Work butter into dry ingredients with pastry blender or your fingers until it looks like cornmeal. Add milk, stir, and mix quickly with fingers until dough forms ball. Or place flour, salt, and baking soda in bowl of food processor fitted with metal blade. Pulse to mix. Add butter and pulse until crumbly. Add milk. Pulse until dough comes together.

2. Set oven rack in middle position. Preheat oven to 400°F. Line 14-inch by 16-inch baking sheet with foil, shiny side up, and coat with vegetable spray, or use silicone liner.

3. Roll dough between 2 sheets of wax paper to $\frac{1}{8}$-inch thickness. Cut into square crackers using $1\frac{1}{2}$-inch square cookie cutter dipped in flour. Prick each cracker 4 or 5 times with a fork. Place on prepared pan. Brush with butter or cream. Sprinkle with choice of toppings, pressing down gently with palm of hand. Bake 10 to 12 minutes, or until tops are pale brown. Remove to rack and let cool at least 10 minutes. Crackers will firm up as they cool. Serve crackers with butter. Store between sheets of wax paper in covered metal tin.

FOR CRACKERS

2 cups sifted flour

$\frac{1}{2}$ teaspoon salt (reduce salt to $\frac{1}{4}$ teaspoon if salt is also used as topping)

$\frac{1}{2}$ teaspoon baking soda

4 tablespoons cold butter, cut into $\frac{1}{2}$-inch dice

6 tablespoons milk

$\frac{1}{4}$ cup butter, melted, or $\frac{1}{4}$ cup heavy cream

OPTIONAL TOPPINGS

Kosher salt

Coarse sea salt

Coarsely ground black pepper

Black or white sesame seeds

$\frac{1}{4}$ cup finely grated cheddar cheese

Garam masala

Brownware milk pan, baking dish, American, early 20th century

Lizzie Goldberg's One-Bowl Babka

{ 1 9 2 0 s }

MAKES 12 SERVINGS

FOR YEAST SPONGE

2 (¼-ounce) packages dry yeast

½ cup milk, warmed to 115°F

FOR DOUGH

½ cup butter, softened to room
temperature

¼ cup sugar

3 egg yolks

1 teaspoon vanilla

¼ teaspoon salt

4 cups flour

½ cup sour cream

FOR FILLING

2 egg whites

⅔ cup sugar

¼ teaspoon cinnamon

½ cup sugar

½ cup toasted pecans, chopped

½ cup raisins

½ cup maraschino cherries,
drained and chopped

TIPS & TOUCHES

- Toasted chopped walnuts or
  toasted sliced almonds can
  be used in place of pecans.
- Lizzie's Babka is also good
  toasted and spread with butter.

BAKING THIS BABKA REMINDS HELAINE DAVIS OF *her childhood visits to her grandparents, Philip and Lizzie Goldberg, in Dorchester, Massachusetts. This babka was the one Grandmother Lizzie and Great Aunt Frieda Goldman used to make.*

1. To make sponge: Dissolve yeast in warm milk and set in warm place to proof for 10 minutes. Mixture will bubble when yeast has proofed.

2. To make dough: Cream butter and sugar in bowl of standing mixer fitted with paddle attachment until fluffy. Beat in yolks, one at a time. Add vanilla and salt.

3. Add flour in 4 additions, alternating with yeast mixture and sour cream. Beat well after each addition. Change to dough hook and knead for about 5 minutes, or until dough is satiny and comes away from sides of bowl.

4. Coat large bowl with vegetable spray or butter. Place dough in bowl, cover with paper towels and plastic wrap, and refrigerate overnight.

5. The next day, coat 10-inch by 4¼-inch tube pan with vegetable spray or butter. Beat egg whites with sugar in bowl of standing mixer fitted with whisk attachment until soft peaks form. Set aside. On sheet of parchment or wax paper, roll out dough to 14-inch square, approximately ¼-inch thick.

6. To make filling: Mix cinnamon and sugar in small bowl and set aside. Spread thin layer of meringue over dough, leaving 1-inch border on all 4 sides. Sprinkle meringue with cinnamon-sugar mixture, pecans, raisins, and maraschino cherries. Roll up dough tightly like jelly roll and slice into 6 equal pieces.

7. Arrange slices in prepared tube pan, placing cut sides of dough slices against side of pan. Cover with clean dish towel and allow to rise in warm place for 2 hours, or until double in size.

8. Set oven rack in middle position. Preheat oven to 350°F.

9. Bake babka for 1 hour to 1 hour and 15 minutes, or until top is golden brown and tester inserted into middle comes out clean. Cool in pan on rack for 20 minutes. Run knife around the inside of pan to loosen edges and turn out babka. Slice when cool. Store loosely wrapped in wax paper at room temperature.

Grandma Gaydos's Gum Boots
(Farina Dumplings)

{ *1920s—1930s* }

⅓ cup butter, softened to room temperature

1 cup fine bread crumbs (see "How to Make Fine Bread Crumbs" on page 204)

1 pound farmer's cheese or pot cheese

½ cup dry farina (Cream of Wheat cereal)

¼ cup flour

1 egg, lightly beaten

TIPS & TOUCHES

- Use homemade fine bread crumbs.
- Sour cream is a nice accompaniment.
- Farina is a milled grain meal, usually made with wheat. It is sold under the brand name Cream of Wheat. It is also used to make Middle Eastern sweets.

HELEN GAYDOS, A YOUNG SLOVAKIAN GIRL WHO *married a Greek Orthodox priest and raised 5 children during the Depression, fed her family these delicious hearty dumplings. Her children called them gum boots because they couldn't pronounce the Slovakian name. Helen traveled through the Midwest and the South with her husband, serving the needs of several congregations.*

1. Melt butter in medium frying pan over low heat. Add bread crumbs and cook, stirring with wooden spoon, until bread crumbs absorb butter and turn light brown, about 5 minutes. Set aside on platter in warm place.

2. Bring large pot of water to a boil. Mix cheese, farina, flour, and egg in large bowl until dough forms. Roll golf ball–size pieces of dough between palms of your hands to form dumplings. Drop dumplings into boiling water. Cover pot and cook 3 minutes. Remove cover and continue cooking until dumplings bob to top, 5 to 7 minutes total. Remove dumplings from pot with slotted spoon and transfer immediately to platter with bread crumbs, rolling to coat. Serve immediately. Store leftover dumplings in covered container in refrigerator. Reheat gently in frying pan with a little butter over low heat to warm through.

→→ DRY CURD, FARMER'S, AND POT CHEESES ←←

The original gum boots recipe called for dry curd cottage cheese, which contains less moisture than regular cottage cheese. It is sold in groceries catering to Eastern European cooks but is not always easy to find. Either farmer's cheese or pot cheese will make a fine substitution. Farmer's cheese is less moist than dry curd cottage cheese, and pot cheese is the least moist of the three.

Margaret's Scottish Baps

MAKES 12 BAPS

{ *1950s* }

MARGARET YARRANTON IS A BIT OF A *Renaissance woman. She is an antiques dealer, an artist, a mother, and a grandmother. She is known to make her own butter and bake her own bread. A native of the Isle of Wight, she often turns the dough for her baps into braided loaves for Thanksgiving.*

1. To make sponge: Dissolve yeast in warm water in large bowl. Let stand uncovered in warm place for 10 minutes to proof.

2. To make dough: Combine proofed yeast mixture, sugar, salt, butter, and 2 cups of the flour in bowl of standing mixer fitted with paddle attachment; mix until smooth. Beat in remaining 2 cups flour. Change to dough hook and knead for 5 minutes at medium speed until dough comes together and is smooth and elastic.

3. Coat medium bowl with vegetable spray or butter. Place dough in greased bowl. Coat piece of plastic wrap with vegetable spray (to prevent sticking) and place it loosely over dough. Put in warm place and allow dough to rise until double in size, 40 minutes to 1 hour.

4. Line two 14-inch by 16-inch baking sheets with foil, shiny side up, and coat with vegetable spray. Dust with cornmeal. Punch down dough and divide into 12 equal pieces. Shape into flat rounds or ovals, 1/2-inch thick, and place on prepared baking sheets. Cover baps with clean dish towel and let rise in warm place 1 hour, or until double in size.

5. Set oven rack in middle position. Preheat oven to 425°F.

6. To make topping: Mix beaten egg with water. Brush tops of baps with egg wash. Sprinkle with sesame seeds or poppy seeds, if desired. Bake 10 to 15 minutes, or until golden brown. Cool on racks. Store wrapped in wax paper at room temperature.

FOR YEAST SPONGE

2 (1/4-ounces) packages dry yeast

1 1/2 cups water, warmed to 115°F

FOR DOUGH

1/4 cup sugar

2 teaspoons salt

1/4 cup butter, softened

4 cups flour

Cornmeal, for pan

FOR TOPPING

1 egg, beaten

1 tablespoon water

Sesame seeds (optional)

Poppy seeds (optional)

TIPS & TOUCHES

- To make Margaret's Thanksgiving loaves, divide dough in half, then divide each half into 3 pieces, and braid. Bake at 375°F for 25 minutes, or until golden in color.

Winnie McCarthy's Irish Bread

{ *1925* }

3 cups flour

¼ cup sugar

4 teaspoons baking powder

2 cups milk

2 eggs

1 tablespoon vegetable shortening

½ cup raisins

½ cup currants

1 tablespoon butter, melted

Tips & Touches

- This bread is wonderful toasted and served with butter and orange marmalade.
- Winnie suggests adding 1 tablespoon of caraway seeds to the batter to give this bread a more authentic Irish taste.

WE FOUND THIS RECIPE HANDWRITTEN ON THE *endpapers of a well-used copy of the* Boston Cooking School Cookbook. *Winnie McCarthy was an Irish maid working for a Mrs. Powell, in North Scituate, Massachusetts, during the 1920s and 1930s. The owner of the book enjoyed Winnie's bread while visiting with Mrs. Powell and requested the recipe. This bread is not the traditional crumbly Irish soda bread but a firmer loaf. Winnie suggests testing for doneness with a silver knife.*

1. Set oven rack in middle position. Preheat oven to 350°F. Cut wax paper liner to fit bottom of 9-inch cake pan. Coat pan with vegetable spray, insert liner, and spray again to coat liner.

2. Sift together flour, sugar, and baking powder into bowl of standing mixer fitted with paddle attachment. Add milk gradually, beating to combine. Add eggs one at a time and shortening. Fold in raisins and currants.

3. Mix batter twice with folding motion before turning out into pan. Brush top of loaf with melted butter. Bake 55 to 60 minutes, or until top of loaf is crisp and golden brown and tester inserted into loaf comes out clean. Cool in pan on rack. Store loosely wrapped in wax paper at room temperature.

Enormous Popovers

MAKES 8 SERVINGS

THESE POPOVERS ARE REALLY "ENORMOUS." THEY REMIND *us of the popovers served in Boston restaurants in the 1960s and 1970s. They are buttery, crisp, and wonderful. We tried several different ways of making popovers, but we found that this recipe is the best. We also found that we were able to produce the lightest, tallest popovers using ovenproof china custard cups.*

1. Set oven rack in middle position. Preheat oven to 375°F. Coat eight 8-ounce ovenproof china custard cups with vegetable spray. Place custard cups on foil-lined jelly roll pan; foil should be shiny side up.

2. Whisk eggs in large bowl until frothy. Add milk and cooled, melted butter and whisk to combine. Whisk in flour and salt. There will be some lumps. Fill each custard cup with $3/4$ cup batter.

3. Bake popovers on jelly roll pan about 1 hour, or until tall and buttery brown. Do not open oven door while popovers are cooking.

4. Remove pan from oven; leave oven on. Puncture neck of each popover on 4 sides to allow steam to escape. Return pan to oven and bake popovers 10 minutes more. Remove popovers from oven and turn out of cups. Serve immediately with butter or jam.

6 eggs

2 cups milk

6 tablespoons butter, melted and cooled

2 cups flour, sifted

½ teaspoon salt

TIPS & TOUCHES

- Popovers are best eaten the day they are made, but leftovers may be stored in a plastic bag at room temperature and reheated the next day in the oven. They will be neither as light nor as crisp as the day they were fresh, but they will still be tasty.

New England Brown Bread

{ 1 8 7 0 s }

MAKES 10 TO 12 SLICES

1 cup raisins

1 cup whole wheat flour

1 cup cornmeal

1 cup graham flour

½ teaspoon salt

1 teaspoon baking soda

¾ cup molasses

2 cups buttermilk

THIS SIMPLE RECIPE IS MORE THAN 140 *years old, and it is as delicious today as it was in our great-grandmother's time. The graham flour can be replaced by more whole wheat flour. A more substantial version of this bread is sometimes made with a smaller proportion of rye flour. This is the steamed raisin-filled bread that is traditionally served with New England baked beans.*

1. Coat 2-quart pudding mold with vegetable spray or butter, dust with flour, and tap out excess. Prepare buttered parchment sheet to fit top of mold. Select covered pot large enough to accommodate mold with 2-inch clearance around sides. Set metal rack inside pot.

2. Toss raisins with 2 tablespoons of the whole wheat flour in small bowl. Set aside.

3. Mix remaining ¾ cup plus 2 tablespoons whole wheat flour, cornmeal, graham flour, salt, and baking soda in large bowl. Add molasses and stir. Add buttermilk and stir to combine. Fold in

➤➤ HOW TO STEAM BREAD ◄◄

Steaming a bread is very much like steaming a pudding. The cake pan or mold should be no more than two-thirds full. Place buttered parchment round on top of cake pan or mold, and cover mold. If pan or mold does not have cover, fold 2 sheets of foil over buttered parchment and tie securely with white cotton kitchen string.

Bread should be steamed on rack in deep, heavy pot in simmering, not boiling, water that comes about one-third of the way up sides of mold. To safely prepare steamer, set filled mold pan on rack in pot. Add enough water to come one-third of the way up sides of mold. Remove mold and bring water to a boil. Turn off heat and carefully return filled mold to rack. Cover pot, adjust heat so that water simmers, and steam bread for suggested time. It's very important to check the water level periodically to make sure it remains stable. *Do not let the water boil out because a tightly covered mold could explode.*

floured raisins. Spoon into prepared mold, making sure that it is no more than two-thirds full. Place buttered parchment round on top of mold and add cover.

4. Set filled mold on rack in pot. Add water to come about one-third of the way up side of mold. Remove mold. Cover pot and bring water to a boil. Turn off heat, lift pot cover, and carefully place filled mold on rack. Cover pot and adjust heat so that water simmers; do not let water boil.

5. Steam bread approximately 1 hour to 1 hour and 15 minutes, or until tester inserted into middle comes out clean. Check water level periodically during steaming and add water as needed. *Do not let water boil out because a tightly covered mold could explode.*

6. Turn off heat. Remove mold carefully from steamer and place on cooling rack. Carefully remove cover and parchment from top of mold. Let cool for 20 minutes. Invert mold on cooling rack and remove mold from bread. If mold does not release easily, run small knife around inside of mold, or let stand until bread begins to shrink away from sides of mold. Serve at room temperature with butter. Store loosely wrapped in wax paper in refrigerator.

Tips & Touches

- We found that 1 hour to 1 hour and 15 minutes was usually enough to steam the bread, not the traditional 3 to 4 hours.

Cheese Bread

{ 1 9 5 0 s }

FOR DOUGH

1 cup milk

½ cup butter, softened to room temperature

1½ teaspoons salt

¼ cup sugar

2 eggs, beaten

6 ounces extra-sharp cheddar cheese, shredded (2 cups)

4 cups flour

4 ounces extra-sharp cheddar cheese, cut into ½-inch dice (1½ cups or a bit more)

Melted butter, for brushing (optional)

FOR YEAST SPONGE

1 (¼-ounce) package dry yeast

¼ cup water, warmed to 115°F

1 teaspoon sugar

TIPS & TOUCHES

- Cheese Bread is great toasted in a sandwich with egg salad and bacon.

THE CHEDDAR CHEESE, BOTH SHREDDED AND DICED, *in this bread takes us back to those heavenly days when we ordered our egg salad sandwiches on cheese bread at Schraft's in the 1950s. To think that it was so simple to make this bread at home! The recipe, handwritten on an index card, was tucked into a manuscript cookbook from the Midwest.*

1. To make dough: Scald milk. Whisk in butter to melt. Add salt and sugar and mix well. Let cool to room temperature.
2. To make sponge: Dissolve yeast in warm water. Add sugar. Let stand uncovered in warm place to proof, about 10 minutes.
3. Combine milk-butter mixture, proofed yeast, eggs, and shredded cheese in bowl of standing mixer fitted with paddle attachment. Add 2 cups of the flour and mix well. Add remaining 2 cups flour and beat to make soft dough.
4. Coat medium bowl with butter or vegetable spray. Place dough in greased bowl. Coat piece of plastic wrap with vegetable spray (to prevent sticking) and place it loosely over dough. Refrigerate for at least 2 hours, or overnight.
5. Coat bottom and sides of two 9-inch by 5-inch by 3-inch loaf pans with vegetable spray. Turn dough out onto lightly floured work surface. Divide dough in half. Pat or roll 1 half gently to 11-inch by 11-inch square. Scatter half of the diced cheddar cheese over dough square. Fold in thirds to form loaf. Place seam side down in prepared pan. Repeat to make 2nd loaf. Allow to rise in warm place until double in size, 1 to 1½ hours.
6. Set oven rack in middle position. Preheat oven to 400°F.
7. Brush loaves with melted butter, if using, for a darker crust. Bake 20 to 25 minutes, or until golden brown. Remove pans from oven. Turn out of pans onto rack to cool. Store wrapped in wax paper at room temperature.

Mike's Mother's Spaetzle

{ *1930s* }

MAKES 8 CUPS

4 eggs

1 cup milk

3 cups flour, sifted

1½ teaspoons salt

⅛ teaspoon nutmeg

Butter, softened to room
    temperature

Buttered bread crumbs (optional)

Grated cheese (optional)

Salt

Coarsely ground black pepper

TIPS & TOUCHES

- It may take a few tries before
  you are satisfied with your
  spaetzle. After making this
  recipe several times, we still
  like to think of our spaetzle as a
  work in progress. Spaetzle can
  be substantial little dumplings
  when served with butter.

WE MET MIKE RIPLEY ON A TRAIN *and we ended up talking about the recipes his mother, Erika, and his grandmother, Emma, made in their native Germany. Mike generously shared his family's recipes for spaetzle and stollen (see Oma Geywitz's Stollen on page 167). Our interpretation of his mother's spaetzle produces more of a dumpling than a noodle—good for soaking up gravy.*

1. Fill large heavy-bottomed pot with water and bring to a boil.

2. Place eggs in large bowl and whisk until combined. Add milk and whisk. Add flour, salt, and nutmeg and whisk until blended and smooth. Let batter stand for at least 5 minutes.

3. Using a cup measure, fill spaetzle hopper with batter. Holding spaetzle maker over pot of boiling water, slide hopper across base so that batter falls through holes and into boiling water. When spaetzle rise to surface, cover and boil 5 to 8 minutes, or until spaetzle are cooked through, tender, and no longer taste of raw flour. (Scoop out a few spaetzle with slotted spoon and taste them to be sure.) Scoop out spaetzle into colander set in large bowl of hot water to prevent spaetzle from sticking together. Continue to cook remaining spaetzle.

4. Drain spaetzle and place in large bowl. Add butter and either buttered bread crumbs or grated cheese. Add salt and pepper to taste. Store leftovers in covered container in refrigerator.

➤➤ HOW TO CUT SPAETZLE ◄◄

Spaetzle are small handmade German noodles served with savory German dishes such as sauerbraten or in soup. Although experienced spaetzle makers cut spaetzle with a knife, from a wooden board into boiling water, beginners may prefer an inexpensive metal spaetzle maker, available in most kitchen stores. Some cooks push spaetzle dough through the holes of a metal colander, but this is time-consuming and tricky. There is an old German saying, *Die Spaetzle muessen schwimmen,* which translates, "There should always be oceans of gravy when serving spaetzle."

Souffléed Common Crackers

MAKES 28 CRACKERS

COMMON CRACKERS ARE DIRECT DESCENDANTS OF *hardtack, the seemingly indestructible biscuits carried on sea voyages or by soldiers during the 19th and early 20th centuries. Made of flour, water, and salt, these biscuits were so hard that they usually had to be soaked in liquid before being consumed. Today's common crackers, while substantial, can be enjoyed souffléed or broken into a bowl of soup. Even Fannie Farmer, the head of The Boston Cooking School, suggested preparing them this way to produce crisp, puffy crackers.*

1. Set oven rack in middle position. Preheat oven to 400°F. Line 14-inch by 16-inch baking sheet with foil, shiny side up, and coat with vegetable spray, or use silicone liner.

2. Split crackers in half and soak in ice water for 7 minutes. Remove crackers from water, place in single layer on prepared pan, and dot with butter. Bake 40 to 45 minutes, or until crackers are brown and crispy. Check crackers occasionally during baking and turn down heat if they brown too quickly. Serve hot with soup and chowders. Store between sheets of wax paper in tightly covered tin.

1 (8-ounce) package Vermont
  Common Crackers

Ice water

½ cup butter, cut into dice

TIPS & TOUCHES

- Broken crackers can be crushed with a rolling pin and used for breading chicken or fish, for stuffing, or for meatloaf.

Sheffield tray, English, early 20th century; silver napkin rings, American and English, late 19th, early 20th century

NDAY NIGHT SUPPERS

The
SUNDAY
NIGHT
SUPPERS
Cook Book

TE SUNDAY MENUS
RECIPES

REC

36
WAYS
to Serve
BACON

ARMOUR AND COMPANY
CHICAGO

5.00

OODS
of the Sea
PARE
THEM

CESTER, MASS.

250
POULTRY
Specialties

Bird lore: The "know how" of
selecting, preparing, cooking,
serving and garnishing—clearly
presented for year-round use.

A "HOOK-UP"
COOK BOO

CHAPTER 7

HOME PLATES

Some call them main dishes or entrees. We call them home plates because these are the recipes that represent what eating at home is all about. Not all meals come with soup or salad. Some might not even have dessert, but all meals have a course that seems to invite us to the table. Whether the table is set with a lace cloth and fine silver or it's just a worn enamel work surface, the steaming plate of food on top of it connects us to all that nourishes and comforts us in the home kitchen. • Of all the living recipes we've collected, we've never found one that tells us to start with a 5-pound fillet roast. It's usually the humble piece of chuck, the brisket, the shoulder of lamb—the less expensive cuts— that blossom into succulent home plates when treated to the tender loving care of the braising, stewing, hashing, or boiling of the home cook.

The rib roast, the turkey, or the goose is always saved for special occasions, those holidays or celebrations when family members and dear friends congregate.

When we embark on an heirloom adventure with fish or poultry, the fish might be canned; the poultry might be what's on sale. Thrifty and filling have always been the standards of heirloom cooking. If a home plate was simple to make, that was even better, but it wasn't until women started to work outside the home that they were more willing to use convenience foods such as garlic powder and canned tomato soup or buy appliances such as blenders, food processors, and electric mixers to replace the meat grinders, raisin seeders, and bean shredders they'd been using to shortcut their time at the stove.

Because so many of the creators of manuscript cookbooks had made the journey from old world to new, they often brought with them the legacy of recipes passed from mother to daughter in the old country. The recipes for Irish Lamb Stew, Sauerbraten, Swedish Meatballs, Stuffed Cabbage, and Welsh Rarebit were transported to new homes, treasured, and prepared again and again in home kitchens. The Asselin family's tourtière, Arline Ryan's Swedish Meatballs with Sour Cream Sauce, and Bunny Peluso Slobodzinski's Stuffed Cabbage with Salt Pork Gravy are just a few of these heirloom recipes we re-created in our own home kitchen.

Baster, American, 1920s–1930s

The originators of manuscript cookbooks, always mindful of their household budgets, constructed menus that often featured ground beef, pork, and veal, which once were inexpensive ingredients. Meatloaf was the pizza of the 1930s, and casseroles, with their formulaic compositions, were the mainstays of the home kitchen. Following the rules of combining a starch (such as rice, potatoes, or pasta) and a liquid (such as gravy, stock, or milk) with leftover meat, chicken, fish, or beans, the home cook could put together a tasty, satisfying dish in minutes, leave it in the oven for an hour or less, and serve a succulent home plate for supper.

For those who chose not to eat meat, fish, or poultry for philosophical, dietary, or monetary reasons, the casserole was often the answer to the vegetarian's question of what to serve. Clever tricks such as adding homemade bread crumbs to a frittata or combining onions and olives in a savory pie made vegetarian home plates tasty and appealing.

We salute the ingenious and loving home cooks whose home plates sustained their families during hard times and helped them to celebrate good times.

Katherine's Shepherd's Pie

{ *1920s* }

FOR CARAMELIZED ONIONS

2 tablespoons extra-virgin olive oil

2½ cups chopped onion

1 teaspoon salt

5 ounces (⅔ cup) water

FOR FILLING

2 tablespoons extra-virgin olive oil

2 pounds ground lamb

½ teaspoon dried thyme

1 teaspoon coarsely ground
   black pepper

½ teaspoon Worcestershire sauce

1 teaspoon chopped fresh parsley

¾ cup low-sodium beef stock, or
   as needed

1 tablespoon Wondra quick-mixing
   flour, or as needed

FOR POTATO TOPPING

4 large potatoes, peeled, cut in
   quarters, and cooked in boiling
   water until tender

1 teaspoon salt

2 eggs, beaten

⅛ teaspoon nutmeg

½ cup heavy cream

TIPS & TOUCHES

• Place the mashed potatoes in
   a sturdy plastic bag. Snip off a
   corner diagonally with scissors
   to pipe potatoes. Always discard
   a used pastry bag or plastic bag
   because of possible raw egg
   contamination.

WE FOUND THIS RECIPE IN A MANUSCRIPT *cookbook that contained several hearty "man-pleasing" recipes. Since the recipe book with its categorized sections was inscribed to "Katherine and Fred," this came as no surprise. The recipe for Corned Beef Hash (page 201) was in the same section. Shepherd's Pie has a British heritage, but a similar pie made with ground beef is known as cottage pie in England. You can substitute ground beef for the ground lamb in this recipe, and the resulting pies will both be wonderful!*

1. To make caramelized onions: Heat olive oil in large frying pan over medium heat. Add onion and salt and cook, stirring with wooden spoon, until translucent, 5 to 7 minutes. Reduce heat to low, add water, cover, and cook another 5 minutes, checking occasionally to be sure onion is not catching on bottom of pan. Remove cover, increase heat to medium, and stir with wooden spoon. Continue cooking until water is completely evaporated and onion is golden brown. Remove to a bowl and set aside.

2. Set oven rack in middle position. Preheat oven to 400°F. Coat 9-inch by 13-inch ovenproof glass baking dish with vegetable spray.

3. To make filling: Add olive oil to frying pan and heat over medium heat. Add lamb and cook until no longer pink. Add caramelized onions, thyme, pepper, Worcestershire sauce, parsley, and beef stock. Stir with wooden spoon to combine. Add flour, reduce heat to low, and cook, stirring, until flour is absorbed and mixture thickens, approximately 3 to 5 minutes. Adjust consistency of gravy to your taste, adding more stock or flour as needed. Scrape mixture into prepared dish.

4. For potato topping: Place potatoes in potato ricer or mash in bowl until smooth. Add salt, eggs, nutmeg, and cream and stir well. Spoon potato mixture into a disposable pastry bag fitted with a rosette tip. Pipe potatoes over top of pie until it is completely covered. Bake 25 minutes, or until potatoes are golden brown. Cover with foil if potatoes brown too quickly. Serve immediately. Cover leftovers with plastic wrap and store in refrigerator.

Eggplant Lasagna

MAKES 12 SERVINGS

1¼ to 1½ pounds eggplant

2 teaspoons salt (or 1½ teaspoons salt if not draining eggplant)

2 eggs

1 cup flour

6 tablespoons extra-virgin olive oil

¼ teaspoon coarsely ground black pepper

4 to 5 cups Mary Gualdelli's Tomato Sauce (page 197)

8 ounces provolone cheese, sliced

12 ounces mozzarella cheese, grated

SOMETIME IN THE 1950s, TWO WOMEN FROM *different cultures met—The Church Lady, from Mansfield, Ohio, and an Italian woman named Mary Gualdelli. The 2 women shared a common interest in cooking, and this recipe passed between them. Eggplant Lasagna was probably a little exotic for the Midwest, but The Church Lady, an accomplished home cook and baker, knew a good thing when she tasted it.*

1. Peel eggplant and cut crosswise into ³⁄₈-inch-thick slices. Sprinkle slices with salt, layer them in metal colander, and set colander in sink (see "Salting Eggplant before Frying"). Set heavy glass plate on top of eggplant and weight with heavy cans of food. Let drain for 30 minutes to 1 hour. Rinse eggplant slices under cold running water to wash off excess salt. Pat dry with paper towels.

2. Beat eggs in deep plate or shallow bowl. Place flour on another plate. Dip eggplant slices in egg, dip in flour to coat, and set aside. Heat 2 tablespoons of the olive oil in large frying pan over medium heat. Add layer of eggplant slices, sprinkle with pepper (and salt, if you have not drained eggplant), and cook until nicely browned, 3 to 4 minutes each side. Remove to platter. Continue

Wooden noodle rolling pins, American 20th century; wooden pie crimpers, American and English, 1890s–1900s

> ## ⇥ SALTING EGGPLANT BEFORE FRYING ⇤
>
> Some recipes suggest that sliced eggplant be salted and drained in a colander to remove excess liquid. Removing this liquid prevents the eggplant from soaking up excess oil when it is fried. When using this method, moderately salt the eggplant slices and place them in a colander in the sink or on a deep plate. Set another heavy glass plate on top of the eggplant and place cans of food on top to weight the eggplant. Allow the eggplant to drain for 30 minutes to 1 hour. Rinse the slices under running water to wash off excess salt, and pat dry with paper towels before frying. Some cooks believe that salting and draining eggplant will remove any bitter juices. The larger varieties of eggplant have more moisture than smaller varieties. Many home cooks do not salt and drain their eggplant.

to sauté remaining eggplant slices in batches, adding remaining olive oil to pan as needed.

3. Set oven rack in middle position. Preheat oven to 350°F. Coat 9-inch by 13-inch ovenproof glass baking dish with vegetable spray. Line baking sheet with foil.

4. Spread layer of tomato sauce over bottom of prepared baking dish. Arrange half of eggplant slices on top. Spread with another layer of tomato sauce. Cover with layer of provolone and sprinkle with grated mozzarella. Add remaining eggplant slices in second layer, spread with tomato sauce, cover with remaining provolone, and sprinkle with remaining mozzarella. Press down gently so that layers adhere.

5. Coat sheet of foil with vegetable spray and place it, oiled side down, over top of lasagna to cover. Set lasagna on prepared baking sheet to catch any sauce that drips. Bake 40 minutes. Uncover and continue baking until lasagna is bubbling and cheeses are melted. Serve lasagna hot. Allow leftovers to cool, cover with paper towels and then plastic wrap, and store in refrigerator.

Mary Gualdelli's Tomato Sauce

MAKES ABOUT 12 CUPS

{ 1 9 4 0 s }

WE DON'T KNOW JUST WHO MARY GUALDELLI *was, but we know that she and The Church Lady, from Mansfield, Ohio, met in the 1940s and exchanged this recipe for Mary's tomato sauce. This sauce was part of Mary's recipe for Eggplant Lasagna (page 194).*

1. Heat 2 tablespoons of the oil in frying pan over medium heat. Add onion and cook until translucent, 5 to 7 minutes. Remove onion to large Dutch oven or heavy-bottomed pot. Add beef, pork, and pancetta (if using) to frying pan, add more oil if needed, and cook until meat is still a little pink. Remove to Dutch oven. Add lamb to frying pan along with a little more oil, if needed, and cook until still slightly pink. Remove to Dutch oven.

2. Add tomato puree, tomato paste, and stock to Dutch oven and stir well. Add salt, black pepper, red pepper flakes, garlic, oregano, thyme, parsley, and brown sugar. Cover and bring to a boil over medium heat. Reduce heat and simmer, stirring occasionally, for 2 hours. Uncover and cook until sauce thickens, about 20 minutes more. Check frequently to make sure sauce doesn't burn. Pour sauce into containers and cool to room temperature. Store in covered containers in refrigerator or freezer.

4 to 6 tablespoons extra-virgin olive oil

3 cups chopped onion

½ pound ground beef

½ pound ground pork

3 ounces pancetta, chopped (optional)

½ pound ground lamb

2 (28-ounce) cans tomato puree

¼ cup tomato paste

2 cups low-sodium beef stock

1½ teaspoons salt

1 teaspoon coarsely ground black pepper

½ teaspoon red pepper flakes

3 cloves garlic, smashed

1 teaspoon dried oregano

½ teaspoon dried thyme

2 tablespoons chopped fresh parsley

4 teaspoons firmly packed brown sugar

TIPS & TOUCHES

* Beef, pork, and lamb do not have to be completely cooked before adding to sauce. As they continue cooking, they will add more flavor to the sauce.

Curry of Lamb with Saffron Rice

{ *1 9 3 0 s — 1 9 4 0 s* }   MAKES 4 SERVINGS

3 tablespoons extra-virgin olive oil

2 pounds lean lamb shoulder, cut
　　into 2-inch cubes

2 tablespoons butter, softened to
　　room temperature

2½ cups chopped onion

2 cups chopped celery

2¼ cups peeled and chopped
　　Granny Smith apple

2 cloves garlic, minced

¼ cup curry powder

¼ cup flour

1 teaspoon salt

½ teaspoon coarsely ground black
　　pepper

2 cups canned tomato puree

1 tablespoon lemon juice

1 teaspoon sugar

Saffron Rice

WE FOUND THIS RECIPE NEATLY TYPED ON *the letterhead of the Hotel Lexington in New York City. From the executive's name on the letterhead we were able to determine approximately when this recipe was passed on from one of the hotel's employees. An American interpretation of an Indian curry, this recipe uses only the basic curry powder available at the time. There are no exotic spice blends in this dish. The use of saffron in the rice was a very trendy touch.*

1. Set oven rack in middle position. Preheat oven to 350°F.

2. Heat olive oil in Dutch oven or heavy-bottomed pot over medium-high heat. Add lamb and cook until nicely browned. Remove to bowl. Add butter to Dutch oven and reduce heat to medium. Add onion, celery, apple, and garlic and cook until softened, 5 to 10 minutes. Return lamb to pot; add curry powder, flour, salt, and pepper; and cook 2 minutes more, stirring constantly with wooden spoon.

3. Add tomato puree, lemon juice, and sugar. Add enough water to cover lamb. Cover, set in oven, and bake 1 hour. Uncover and continue baking another 30 minutes, or until lamb is very tender. Serve on bed of Saffron Rice. Store leftover curry in covered container in refrigerator.

➤➤ CURRY POWDER ◄◄

Curry powder and garam masala are two popular Indian spice blends. In India, there was traditionally no such thing as a "curry" powder. Curries were dishes of meat or vegetables cooked in sauce, and every family had its own mix of spices for each particular dish. British colonials, homesick for the dishes that they had eaten in India, brought back a powdered version of these spice mixtures so they could replicate the curries they had enjoyed abroad. Commercial curry powder, available in most grocery stores, gets its signature yellow color from turmeric. Coriander, cumin, turmeric, fenugreek, cinnamon, clove, cardamom, and nutmeg are just a few of the spices used to prepare curry powder. It is suggested that curry powder be added to a dish at the beginning of cooking so that the raw flavor of the spices is cooked out.

✈ SAFFRON RICE ✈

Similar to the recipe for French Risotto (page 125), this rice dish is prepared with butter instead of olive oil. Saffron gives the rice a distinctive yellow color and an exotic taste.

⅛ teaspoon saffron

2 cups low-sodium chicken stock or water, divided

1 tablespoon butter, softened to room temperature

½ cup chopped onion

1 cup long grain white rice

½ teaspoon salt

½ teaspoon coarsely ground black pepper

1. Combine saffron and ½ cup of the stock or water and set aside.

2. Melt butter in heavy-bottomed saucepan over medium heat. Add onion and cook, stirring with wooden spoon, until translucent, 3 to 4 minutes.

3. Add rice, saffron mixture, salt, and pepper to pan and stir. Add remaining 1½ cups chicken stock or water, bring to a boil, reduce heat to low, and simmer, covered, until rice is tender, 18 minutes. Remove pan from heat and give rice a stir. Cover and let stand 2 minutes. Stir again before serving.

Makes 6 servings

Controversial Irish Lamb Stew

MAKES 6 SERVINGS

2 pounds (3 to 4 large) boiling
   potatoes, peeled

½ teaspoon salt

½ teaspoon coarsely ground
   black pepper

3 tablespoons chopped fresh
   parsley, plus extra for garnish

Leaves from 10 sprigs fresh thyme

2 pounds lamb shoulder chops,
   trimmed of excess fat

1 cup chopped (¼-inch) leeks,
   white part only

½ cup chopped onion

2½ cups low-sodium beef stock

6 medium carrots, peeled and cut
   into 1-inch chunks

TIPS & TOUCHES

* The thin potato slices dissolve during cooking to thicken the gravy.
* Lamb stew is better served
  the next day. Pour off cooking
  juices and allow to cool in the
  refrigerator so that excess fat can
  be skimmed from the surface.
  Reheat the stew with juices over
  gentle heat.
* You can also use lamb neck meat
  for the stew. It is more economical
  and has a good flavor.

WE FOUND THAT THERE ARE AS MANY *ways to make an Irish Stew as there are recipes. Some cooks vote for potatoes as a thickener. Some say that the carrots should be prepared separately or not used at all. Some cooks, like Dan Carey, of Belmont, Massachusetts, even use beef instead of lamb but call it an Irish Stew. Whether you use leeks or thyme or onions, a big bowl of this stew topped with chopped fresh parsley will warm and fortify you.*

1. Cut 1 of the potatoes into ¼-inch-thick slices. Cut remaining potatoes into large chunks. Layer sliced potato over bottom of large Dutch oven or large heavy pot. Sprinkle with some salt, pepper, parsley, and thyme. Add layer of lamb chops and sprinkle with more salt, pepper, parsley, and thyme. Add layer of leeks and layer of onion, sprinkling each layer with salt, pepper, parsley, and thyme. Repeat layers, using potato chunks instead of slices and seasoning each layer as before, to use all of the potatoes and lamb chops.

2. Add stock, pouring it down the inside of pot. Cover pot and bring stew to a boil. Reduce heat and simmer until lamb and vegetables are tender, at least 1½ hours.

3. Steam carrot chunks in covered steamer basket set over simmer-ing water until tender, about 20 minutes. Add to pot with fin-ished stew and stir gently to combine. Serve stew in heated, deep soup bowls, garnished with chopped fresh parsley.

Corned Beef Hash

MAKES 4 MODERATE SERVINGS

{ 1920s }

Hᴀꜱʜ ᴡᴀꜱ ᴀɴᴏᴛʜᴇʀ ᴡᴀʏ ᴛᴏ ᴜꜱᴇ ʟᴇꜰᴛᴏᴠᴇʀꜱ *in a creative way. Home cooks always made extra corned beef so that they could serve their families a hot plate of crispy hash. We found several handwritten recipes for corned beef hash, but this is the one that seemed the best to us, simple and tasty. We didn't go in for the fancy flipping; we just turned the hash in the pan when the bottom got crusty. This recipe is easily doubled for larger portions. It is very nice served with a poached egg and ketchup.*

1. Place corned beef, potato, onion, salt, and pepper in bowl. Add beef stock, cream, or water. Mix gently with wooden spoon to combine and set aside.

2. Heat butter and oil in 10-inch frying pan over low heat and swirl to coat bottom of pan. Add corned beef mixture and flatten with spatula. Cook until bottom of hash is crispy. Cut hash into sections to make flipping easier. Flip over with spatula. Press down gently with spatula and cook until bottom is crispy. Turn out hash onto a serving dish and sprinkle with parsley.

2 cups chopped corned beef

1 cup chopped cooked potato

¼ cup minced onion

½ teaspoon salt

¼ teaspoon coarsely ground black pepper

¼ cup low-sodium beef stock, heavy cream, or water

1 tablespoon butter, softened to room temperature

1 tablespoon extra-virgin olive oil or vegetable oil

1 tablespoon chopped fresh parsley

Tips & Touches

- This recipe is just a starting point. You can add more potatoes or different herbs. You can chop the corned beef and vegetables fine or in slightly larger pieces.

Copper saucepan, American, early 1900s

Glazed Corned Beef from Michigan

MAKES 8 SERVINGS

{ 1 9 3 0 s }

We found this handwritten recipe on an *index card from Michigan. This is the type of dish we could prepare in minutes, stick in a pot, let cook, and serve, while looking as if we spent the afternoon eating bonbons. Although the original called for glazing with white corn syrup, being New Englanders, we decided to use a maple syrup—mustard glaze. No one has complained.*

1. To make corned beef: Coat ovenproof baking dish with vegetable spray. Rinse corned beef under cold running water and pat dry with paper towels. Place corned beef in large heavy pot. Add cold water to cover. Add orange slices, onions, celery, garlic, dill seeds, rosemary, cloves, bay leaf, and cinnamon. Add cold water to cover. Stir until spices are evenly distributed. Cover pot and bring to simmer over medium heat; do not boil. Simmer, covered, stirring occasionally, until fork penetrates meat easily, approximately 3 to 4 hours (about 1 hour per pound of meat). Remove corned beef from pot and place, fatty side up, in prepared baking dish. Set aside.

2. To make glaze: Place maple syrup, mustard, and pepper in heavy-bottomed saucepan and whisk to combine. Cook over medium heat, stirring with wooden spoon, until glaze comes to a boil. Reduce heat and continue stirring until glaze reduces and thickens, approximately 3 minutes.

3. Preheat oven to 375°F. Brush half of glaze over corned beef. Bake 8 minutes. Turn corned beef fatty side down, brush with remaining glaze, and return to oven to bake 8 minutes more. Remove to serving platter and allow to rest 10 minutes before slicing. Cut against grain to prevent slices from falling apart. Cover leftovers with plastic wrap and store in refrigerator.

FOR CORNED BEEF

3 to 4 pounds corned beef brisket

1 orange, sliced

2 large onions, quartered

3 stalks celery, cut into
  1-inch pieces

2 cloves garlic, quartered

1 teaspoon dill seeds

3 sprigs fresh rosemary, or
  $1/2$ teaspoon dried rosemary

6 whole cloves

1 bay leaf

3-inch stick cinnamon, or
  $1/2$ teaspoon cinnamon

FOR GLAZE

$3/4$ cup maple syrup

3 tablespoons prepared mustard

$1/2$ teaspoon coarsely ground
  black pepper

Easter Meatloaf

{ 1 9 2 0 s — 1 9 7 0 s }

MAKES 10 SLICES

FOR MEATLOAF

1 medium boiling potato, grated

1 cup fine bread crumbs

2 tablespoons dried parsley

1 teaspoon paprika

1 teaspoon garlic powder

1 teaspoon salt

½ teaspoon coarsely ground
    black pepper

1 cup red wine

1½ pounds ground beef

½ cup chopped onion

2 eggs, beaten

⅓ cup ketchup

3 tablespoons Dijon mustard

4 eggs, hard-cooked

FOR TOPPING

2 teaspoons dried parsley

¼ teaspoon garlic powder

ALTHOUGH WE FOUND SEVERAL REFERENCES TO THIS *particular meatloaf while reading our collection of manuscript cookbooks, this recipe has special significance for us. This is the meatloaf Marilynn made for friends at Easter in the early 1970s. Most of the guests were students away from home. Money was tight and kitchen resources were few, but she volunteered to make the holiday dinner, which featured slices of this appealing meatloaf. The hard-cooked eggs in each slice make a nice presentation.*

1. To make meatloaf: Set oven rack in middle position. Preheat oven to 350°F. Line bottom and narrow ends of 9-inch by 5-inch by 3-inch loaf pan with single strip of parchment, allowing 1- to 2-inch overhang at each end. Coat pan and liner with vegetable spray.

HOW TO MAKE
➤➤ FINE BREAD CRUMBS ◀◀

There is nothing like the flavor of homemade bread crumbs. They are essential to heirloom recipes for meatloaves, frittatas, and some pastries.

Set oven for 300°F. Place slices of dry white bread or brioche on jelly roll pans and set on middle and lower racks of oven. Bake 1 hour. Turn slices, and bake until bread is very dry, about 1 hour longer. Break bread into pieces and place in the bowl of a food processor fitted with the metal blade. Pulse to form fine crumbs. Put crumbs through a strainer to remove hard pieces. Store bread crumbs in a plastic bag in the refrigerator or freezer. Label and date the contents of the bag. Dry bread crumbs can also be made using a grater or by crumbing in a blender.

2. Squeeze grated potato in clean white dish towel to remove excess liquid. Place grated potato, bread crumbs, parsley, paprika, garlic powder, salt, pepper, and wine in bowl and stir with wooden spoon. Add ground beef, onion, eggs, ketchup, and mustard and mix thoroughly with your hands. Do not overmix or meatloaf will be tough.

3. Place half of meatloaf mixture in prepared pan and smooth the top. Arrange shelled hard-cooked eggs in line on top of meatloaf and gently press down on eggs to anchor them. Place remaining meatloaf mixture on top of eggs. Smooth the top.

4. To make topping: Mix parsley with garlic powder and sprinkle over meatloaf. Bake about 1 hour and 30 minutes, or until meatloaf pulls away from sides of pan and bubbles around edges, and instant-read thermometer inserted in center of meatloaf registers 160°F. Grasp both ends of parchment liner and lift meatloaf from pan. Let stand for 5 minutes. Cut into slices and serve.

Wire egg holder, American, 1890s–1900s

Dale's Meatloaf

{ 1 9 6 0 s }

MAKES 10 SLICES

1 pound ground beef

6 ounces loose sausage meat

1¼ cups chopped onion

1 cup fine bread crumbs (see "How to Make Fine Bread Crumbs" on page 204)

1 cup milk

3 eggs

1 teaspoon salt

½ teaspoon coarsely ground black pepper

⅛ teaspoon poultry seasoning

1 (10¾-ounce) can tomato soup, divided

2½ strips bacon

4 strips green bell pepper (½-inch wide, cut vertically)

We asked a lady in Maine for *her meatloaf recipe after hearing her son reminisce about the meatloaf she made for him when he was growing up in Connecticut. This is a dense meatloaf, more like a paté. It should be cooled before being cut, but in a pinch it can be served hot after it rests for 10 minutes. The sausage mixed with the ground beef, and the touch of poultry seasoning, make all the difference.*

1. Set oven rack in middle position. Preheat oven to 400°F. Line bottom and narrow ends of 9-inch by 5-inch by 3-inch loaf pan with single strip of parchment, allowing 1- to 2-inch overhang at each end. Coat pan and liner with vegetable spray.

2. Combine ground beef and sausage meat in large bowl. Set aside.

3. In smaller bowl, combine onion, bread crumbs, milk, eggs, salt, pepper, and poultry seasoning.

4. Working quickly with your hands, add bread crumb mixture to meat and mix to combine. Do not overwork or meatloaf will be tough. Add half of the tomato soup and quickly combine.

5. Place meatloaf in prepared pan. Spread remaining tomato soup over top. Cut strips of bacon in half and arrange alternating strips of bacon and green pepper over top of meatloaf. Bake 1 hour. Turn off oven and let meatloaf stand in oven another 30 minutes, or until instant-read thermometer inserted in center of meatloaf registers 160°F.

6. Remove meatloaf from oven and cool in pan on rack for 30 minutes. Grasp both ends of parchment liner and lift meatloaf from pan. To serve, cut meatloaf into slices, place in baking pan, cover with foil, and set in 350°F oven until heated through, 5 to 10 minutes.

Tips & Touches

*   Meatloaf is better the day after it is made. Leftover cold meatloaf makes wonderful sandwiches.
*   To tell if a meatloaf is properly seasoned, fry a small patty of raw meatloaf mix to sample. Never taste food containing uncooked egg, poultry, meat, or fish.

Sauerbraten

MAKES 8 SERVINGS

FOR BRINING

4- to 5-pound beef chuck roast

2 cups white vinegar

2 cups water

3 bay leaves

1 onion, cut in quarters

2 carrots, cut into ½-inch rounds

1 cup chopped celery leaves
    or celery

1 large clove garlic, minced

1 teaspoon cinnamon

1 teaspoon whole cloves

1 teaspoon whole allspice, or
    ½ teaspoon ground allspice

1½ teaspoons salt

½ teaspoon coarsely ground
    black pepper

1 lemon, sliced, with seeds removed

FOR BRAISING

1 slice bacon

2 tablespoons extra-virgin olive
    oil, or as needed

1 cup chopped celery

Reserved onion and carrots
    from brine

1½ cups reserved strained brine

1 slice (½-inch) rye or
    pumpernickel bread

FOR GRAVY

7½ cups low-sodium beef stock

¼ cup flour

3 tablespoons firmly packed
    brown sugar

We found this recipe handwritten on an *index card from Ohio. Making sauerbraten can seem daunting at first; dividing the recipe into three steps—brining, braising, and making gravy—renders the recipe more doable. We learned from our friend Mike Ripley that his aunt, Ruth Geywitz, who lives in Stuttgart, Germany, has been making sauerbraten for 60 years from an almost identical recipe. Ruth adds the bacon when she braises her sauerbraten. This dish is wonderful served on a bed of Mike's Mother's Spaetzle (page 186) to soak up the rich gravy.*

1. To brine sauerbraten: Rinse beef chuck under cold running water and pat dry with paper towels. Poke holes all over meat with small sharp knife. Place in nonreactive glass or stainless steel bowl. Combine vinegar and water in large pot and bring to a boil. Lower heat and add bay leaves, onion, carrots, celery, garlic, cinnamon, cloves, allspice, salt, pepper, and lemon slices and stir to combine. Bring to a boil again and boil an additional 5 minutes. Pour brine over meat. Turn meat once, cover with plastic wrap, and refrigerate for 3 to 4 days, turning at least twice a day.

2. Remove meat from brine, pat dry with paper towels, and set aside. Strain and reserve brine, onion, and carrots. Discard lemon, spices, celery or celery tops, and garlic.

3. To braise sauerbraten: Fry bacon in large Dutch oven or heavy-bottomed pot over medium heat until it starts to give off fat. Add olive oil and meat and cook until nicely browned and crusty all over, about 5 minutes each side. Add more oil if necessary. Remove meat to platter. Add celery to Dutch oven and cook, stirring with wooden spoon, until softened, about 7 minutes.

4. Return meat to Dutch oven, fatty side down. Add reserved onion and carrots from brine. Add water to come about one-third of the way up the side of the meat. Add the reserved brine. Break bread slice into pieces and add to Dutch oven.

5. Bring to a boil, reduce heat, and simmer, covered, turning sauerbraten every hour, until tender, 2½ to 3 hours. Remove to

serving platter and allow to cool for at least 20 minutes while you make gravy.

6. To make gravy: Strain and reserve braising liquid. Discard vegetables. Bring beef stock to a simmer in large saucepan. Measure $\frac{1}{2}$ cup braising liquid into small bowl and refrigerate until chilled. Add flour to cooled braising liquid and whisk to combine. Whisk flour mixture and brown sugar into simmering stock and cook until it thickens to the consistency of gravy.

7. Cut sauerbraten into slices against grain and serve with gravy and Mike's Mother's Spaetzle (page 186). Sauerbraten is even better the next day. Refrigerate meat and gravy separately. Place plastic wrap directly on surface of gravy to prevent skin from forming.

TIPS & TOUCHES

- We tried this recipe with top round roast and chuck roast. We prefer using chuck. If you use top round, braise for at least 3 hours and cut slices against the grain.
- Mike's Aunt Ruth uses a mixture of $\frac{1}{2}$ cup sour cream, 3 tablespoons flour, and $\frac{1}{4}$ cup water in lieu of our mixture of chilled braising liquid and flour to make her gravy; add the mixture to the simmering stock and cook the gravy exactly the same way.

Sauerbraten

4.- pound round steak
2 cups vinegar
2 cups water
3 bay leaves
1 teasp. whole cloves
1 teasp. whole allspice
1 1/2 teasp. salt
1/2 teasp. pepper
1 lemon sliced

1 kernel garlic
1 cup. onions, sliced
Celery tops
2 carrots sliced
Crust of rye bread
6 tblsp. butter
1 cup flour
2 teasp. salt
5 cups stock (?)
1/4 cup sugar

1.- Heat the vinegar & water to the boiling point. Then add the cloves, allspice, the 1 1/2 teasp salt, the 1/2 teasp.

Romanian Stuffed Cabbage

{ *1930s* }

2½- to 3-pound cabbage

FOR SAUCE

1½ cups tomato sauce

2 tablespoons ketchup

½ cup lemon juice

¾ cup firmly packed brown sugar

1 cup golden raisins

FOR FILLING

2 eggs

½ cup fine bread crumbs (see "How to Make Fine Bread Crumbs" on page 204)

1 teaspoon firmly packed brown sugar

1 teaspoon salt

½ teaspoon coarsely ground black pepper

½ teaspoon paprika

1½ pounds ground beef

1 cup finely chopped onion

2 cloves garlic, minced, or 1 teaspoon garlic powder

2 tablespoons fresh parsley, chopped, or 1 tablespoon dried parsley

¼ cup tomato sauce

¼ cup ketchup

THIS IS THE RECIPE FOR STUFFED CABBAGE *we grew up with. Our mother, Dorothy, made the true Romanian version, which uses tomatoes, brown sugar, and raisins. Preparation took several hours, but we all felt it was worth it. Because Sheila did not eat raisins then, our mother went into "restaurant mode" and made a separate pot of stuffed cabbage without raisins just for her. The recipe uses one 15-ounce can of tomato sauce, which is divided between the sauce (1½ cups) and the filling (¼ cup).*

1. To prepare cabbage: Remove 3 or 4 outer leaves from cabbage head, chop coarsely, and set aside. Cut out core of cabbage in cone-shaped section and discard. Bring water to a boil in large heavy pot. Add head of cabbage until fully immersed and let stand off heat for 4 minutes. Remove cabbage head to platter. Using long-handled fork, carefully remove leaves from head, keeping them whole. They should be pliable enough to come off easily. If not, return cabbage head to pot and let stand in hot water until leaves come away easily.

2. Cut out hard center spine from each leaf and discard. Cut any very large leaves in half. Dry leaves on paper towels and set aside. Coarsely chop any leaves that are too small to stuff and set aside with the rest of chopped cabbage.

3. Set oven rack in middle position. Preheat oven to 350°F. Coat 9-inch by 13-inch ovenproof glass baking dish with vegetable spray.

4. To make sauce: Combine tomato sauce, ketchup, lemon juice, brown sugar, and golden raisins in saucepan. Bring to a boil, reduce heat, and simmer 15 minutes to blend flavors. Remove from heat and set aside.

5. To make filling: Beat eggs in large bowl. Add bread crumbs, brown sugar, salt, pepper, and paprika and stir to combine. Add ground beef, onion, garlic or garlic powder, parsley, tomato sauce, and ketchup and mix well with hands.

6. To stuff cabbage: Place each cabbage leaf on flat surface and spoon ¼ cup of filling in center. Fold edges of cabbage leaf in toward center to enclose meat in a neat package. If a cabbage leaf is too

IN PRAISE OF KETCHUP

Ketchup has a long and respectable history dating back to the Romans, who enjoyed a sauce called *garum* made from fermented fish. Ketchup, as we know it, is usually made from tomatoes, sugar, spices, and vinegar. We add it to sauces, stews, and soups to enhance their flavor. We've even been known to use it when making gravy. Ketchup is also a condiment that is enjoyed on foods such as hamburgers and hot dogs. Victorians enjoyed tomato ketchup, but history tells us they also made ketchup from plums, mushrooms, and walnuts.

small to contain meat filling, overlap it with another halved leaf or overlap 2 smaller leaves.

7. Spread about half of sauce over bottom of prepared baking dish. Add stuffed cabbage leaves, seams down, in single layer. Pour remaining sauce over stuffed leaves. Bake about 1 hour, or until filling is cooked through and sauce is bubbling.

Tips & Touches

- If you have extra meat mixture, shape into meatballs and place in the pan between stuffed cabbage leaves. Bake as directed in the recipe.

Toy cast-iron stove, American, early 1900s; toy tin saucepan, 1890s–1900s

Alice McGinty's London Broil

MAKES 4 SERVINGS   {1960s}

ALICE MCGINTY GAVE MARILYNN HER RECIPE FOR *a London broil marinade more than 40 years ago, when they were both working at a research and development laboratory in Cambridge, Massachusetts. Her marinade uses gin and brown sugar, and there is no doubt this recipe will go down in history. Alice McGinty's London Broil can be either broiled or grilled.*

1. Rinse steak under running water, pat dry with paper towels, and set aside.

2. To make marinade: Combine olive oil, garlic, brown sugar, wine vinegar, lemon juice, soy sauce, gin, and pepper in large nonreactive stainless steel or glass bowl. Place steak in heavy-duty plastic bag, add marinade, and close securely. Place sealed bag in nonreactive glass dish in refrigerator for 8 hours or overnight. Shake and turn bag at least 3 times while steak is marinating.

3. Set oven rack 6 inches from broiler. Set oven temperature to broil. Line metal baking pan with foil. If using outdoor grill, follow manufacturer's instructions for heating.

4. Remove steak from plastic bag and place on prepared pan or grill. Brush steak on both sides with marinade and discard remaining marinade. Broil or grill for 4 minutes on each side for medium-rare. Remove steak from oven or grill and allow to rest 10 to 15 minutes. Carve against grain into thin slices and serve. Cover leftovers with plastic wrap and store in refrigerator.

1½- to 2-pound flank steak, 1-inch thick

FOR MARINADE

½ cup extra-virgin olive oil

3 cloves garlic, smashed and peeled

¾ cup firmly packed brown sugar

½ cup red wine vinegar

Juice of 2 lemons

⅓ cup soy sauce

3 tablespoons gin

1 teaspoon coarsely ground black pepper

TIPS & TOUCHES

- London Broil should not be cooked to well-done. It will be too dry.
- Carving against the grain means carving on the diagonal.
- London Broil does not refer to a cut of beef. It refers to a method of cooking beef.

Brisket

4- to 5-pound brisket

⅓ cup firmly packed brown sugar

2 teaspoons paprika

2 teaspoons kosher salt

1 teaspoon coarsely ground
    black pepper

2 tablespoons extra-virgin olive oil

2½ cups coarsely chopped onion

2 cups chopped carrots

2½ cups low-sodium beef stock

1½ cups red wine or sherry

¾ cup apricot jam

¼ cup ginger jam

½ cup ketchup

3 tablespoons tomato paste

½ teaspoon chopped hot chilies

1 teaspoon prepared mustard

3 to 4 cloves garlic, peeled
    and minced

6 medium boiling potatoes, peeled
    and quartered (optional)

MAKES 8 SERVINGS

BRISKET HAS ALWAYS BEEN A FAVORITE CHOICE *for holiday meals. It pretty much cooks itself in its braising liquid, and it's better the next day, so we recommend preparing it ahead and reheating it. Brisket used to be an inexpensive cut that served several people and provided a respectable amount of leftovers. There are as many brisket recipes as there are home cooks. We've reviewed multiple brisket recipes and found the common denominator to be a mix of sweet and sour ingredients, the aromatics—onions, carrots, and garlic—and a tomato-based braising liquid.*

1. Set oven rack in middle position. Preheat oven to 375°F. Line large roasting pan with foil and coat with vegetable spray.

2. Rinse brisket under cold running water and pat dry with paper towels. Place brisket in prepared pan, lean side up.

3. Combine brown sugar, paprika, salt, and pepper in small bowl. Rub half of seasoning mixture over top of brisket. Bake, uncovered, for 15 minutes. Remove pan from oven and turn brisket fatty side up. Carefully spread remaining seasoning mixture over brisket with back of tablespoon. Return to oven and bake, uncovered, another 15 minutes.

4. Meanwhile, heat oil in large frying pan over medium heat. Add onion and carrots and cook until slightly limp, about 5 minutes. Remove from heat, cover, and set aside.

5. Whisk beef stock, wine or sherry, apricot jam, ginger jam, ketchup, tomato paste, chilies, and mustard in large bowl until blended.

6. Remove roasting pan from oven. Pour stock mixture into pan. Lift brisket with tongs to allow liquid to flow underneath. Scatter some of cooked onion and carrots on bottom of pan and set brisket on top. Sprinkle brisket with half of garlic and remaining onion and carrots. Add rest of garlic to pan. Cover pan tightly with foil. Reduce oven temperature to 325°F, return brisket to oven, and bake until fork tender, about 4 hours. Add potatoes, if using, 3 hours into cooking, lifting foil carefully.

ALL ABOUT BRISKET

Brisket is a cut that comes from the breast section of the cow. It is usually cut into two sections: the flat cut, which is leaner, and the point cut, which contains more fat. The additional fat gives the point cut more flavor than the flat cut. Brisket responds well to long, hot, moist braising, which causes tough fibers to disintegrate into meltingly delicious meat. There are many ways to prepare brisket. Some recipes suggest a dry rub and a sear before braising. Others add carrots, potatoes, and onions. Some add tomato or chili sauce, coupled with a packet of instant onion soup, while others use prepared cranberry sauce or kosher wine. Some home cooks even marinate and baste their brisket with Coca-Cola. Brisket at its best is a succulent cut of beef with glorious gravy.

7. Remove pan from oven. Transfer brisket to platter, set platter on rack, and cool to room temperature, about 25 minutes. Remove potatoes, if used, to another platter.

8. Strain braising liquid into clean bowl, reserving carrots and onion. Place carrots and onion in bowl of food processor fitted with metal blade. Pulse to puree. Add pureed vegetables to braising liquid and whisk to blend; pureed vegetables will thicken gravy. Store cooled gravy in covered container in refrigerator. When brisket is completely cooled, cut into slices against grain and cover with plastic wrap and then with foil. Cover potatoes with plastic wrap. Refrigerate gravy, brisket, and potatoes overnight.

9. The next day, place gravy, brisket slices, and potatoes in large frying pan, cover, and cook over low heat until heated through, 5 to 7 minutes.

TIPS & TOUCHES

- For the best flavor, always cook a brisket the day before you plan to serve it.
- Remove any fat that rises to the top of the gravy after refrigerating it.

Creole Veal Chops

MAKES 4 TO 6 SERVINGS

6 tablespoons extra-virgin olive oil, divided

1½ cups coarsely chopped onion

3 pounds veal shoulder chops

1 cup flour

½ teaspoon paprika

¼ teaspoon salt

¼ teaspoon coarsely ground black pepper

3 eggs

2 cups ketchup

2 cups water

3 tablespoons lemon juice

2 teaspoons sugar

TIPS & TOUCHES

• If using a Dutch oven, you might have to add a little chicken stock to cover the chops.

• For a more pronounced tomato flavor, add ¼ cup tomato paste to the sauce.

BOTH GRANDMA KATZIFF AND OUR MOTHER USED *this recipe for Creole Veal Chops. Since Mama and Grandma Katziff shared a kitchen for 5 years, the recipe went back and forth between them, with each one adding her own touch. In our family, "Creole" meant using tomato ketchup as a sauce. No one ever traveled to Louisiana, as far as we knew, so we invented our own version of "Creole" cooking. You will have to use 2 frying pans or a large Dutch oven for this recipe.*

1. Heat 2 tablespoons of the olive oil in 10-inch frying pan over medium heat. Add onion and cook until brown around edges, 3 to 5 minutes. Remove onion to bowl, reserving frying pan.

2. Rinse veal chops under cold running water and pat dry with paper towels. Place flour, paprika, salt, pepper, and veal chops in large plastic bag, seal, and shake until veal is evenly coated with flour. Remove veal from bag and shake in strainer over sink to remove excess flour.

3. Beat eggs with fork on deep plate or shallow bowl. Heat 2 table-spoons olive oil in reserved frying pan over medium heat. Dip chops in beaten egg to coat, add to pan, and cook until crispy, about 5 minutes on each side. Do not crowd veal chops. Heat remaining 2 tablespoons olive oil in another frying pan of same size and fry remaining veal chops in same way.

4. Add reserved onion to pans. Whisk together ketchup and water in large glass measuring cup until smooth. Add lemon juice and sugar and whisk to blend. Divide sauce between both pans and simmer, uncovered, 15 minutes. Cover pans, reduce heat to low, and simmer very gently for another 30 minutes. Pieces of egg crust will break off from chops and thicken sauce. Serve alongside rice or noodles. Store leftover veal chops in covered container in refrigerator.

Arline Ryan's Swedish Meatballs with Sour Cream Sauce

{ 1 9 2 0 s }

THIS HEIRLOOM RECIPE WAS FOUND HANDWRITTEN ON *an index card from Indiana. These delicate meatballs in a sour cream sauce are a wonderful home plate served with wide noodles or rice to make the most of the gravy. This lady knew how to cook one of the best examples of Midwestern heirloom cooking. Serve this dish with a salad of torn greens dressed with oil and vinegar.*

1. Place veal and pork in bowl of food processor fitted with metal blade. Process until smooth. Add onion, cream or half-and-half, flour, cracker crumbs, nutmeg, salt, pepper, and summer savory (if using). Pulse until texture is almost as smooth as a paste. Remove mixture from food processor and shape into balls, using about 2 tablespoons of meat mixture for each meatball.

2. Heat 1 tablespoon of the butter and 1 tablespoon of the oil in each of 2 large frying pans over medium heat. Add meatballs and cook, turning with tongs, until evenly browned, 5 to 7 minutes. Add ¼ cup white wine and ½ can of chicken stock to each pan and simmer 5 minutes.

3. Remove pans from heat. Remove meatballs to platter and set aside. Consolidate all of cooking juices in 1 pan. Whisk ¼ cup of warm pan juices with flour in small bowl, return to pan, and whisk to blend. Set pan over low heat and bring to a bare simmer; do not allow sauce to boil. Whisk in sour cream a few tablespoons at a time. Return meatballs to pan and turn in sauce until completely heated through. Place in serving dish and garnish with chopped fresh parsley.

1½ pounds ground veal

¾ pound ground pork

1 cup finely chopped onion

¾ cup light cream or half-and-half

2 tablespoons flour

¾ cup soda cracker crumbs

¾ teaspoon nutmeg

½ teaspoon salt

½ teaspoon coarsely ground black pepper

Pinch of summer savory (optional)

2 tablespoons butter, softened to room temperature

2 tablespoons vegetable oil

½ cup white wine

1 (14½-ounce) can low-sodium chicken stock

2 tablespoons flour

1 pint sour cream

2 tablespoons chopped fresh parsley, for garnish

TIPS & TOUCHES

- Veal and pork should be ground twice if not using a food processor.
- Check sauce for lumps before adding sour cream and strain if necessary.

Wisconsin Beer-Baked Beans with Short Ribs

MAKES 8 CUPS

{ *1950s* }

2 cups dried navy beans

¾ cup firmly packed brown sugar

1 cup ketchup

1 tablespoon salt

½ teaspoon coarsely ground black pepper

2½ cups chopped onion

1 pound pork short ribs with bones, sliced between bone to separate

6 ounces beer

TIPS & TOUCHES

- We found that 4 hours, including the boiling time, produced succulent beans with a rich, sweet tomato sauce. These beans keep their shape. For a softer texture, bake the beans 1 hour longer.
- We suggest that you count the ribs before cooking and retrieve the same number of bones before serving.
- To make this recipe in a slow cooker, follow the manufacturer's instructions and adjust the cooking time.

THIS RECIPE COMES FROM OUR AGENT KAREN *Johnson's grandmother, Eva Viola Johnson. The dish is a hearty mass of beans, sweeter than the New England recipe, but spicy and rich. Pork short ribs make it more of a main dish than a side. Onions and beer intensify the flavor of the sauce. This recipe is just as appealing as its no-nonsense New England cousin, Boston baked beans.*

1. Place beans in strainer and pick over for gravel or husks. Rinse under cold water. Place beans in large nonreactive bowl, add cold water to cover, and let soak overnight. The next day, drain beans and discard soaking water. Rinse beans under cold running water.

2. Transfer beans to Dutch oven or heavy-bottomed pot. Add fresh water to cover by about 2 inches. Cover and bring to a boil. Reduce heat slightly so that water continues to boil and cook, stirring occasionally, 1 hour. Drain beans, reserving 1½ cups of the cooking liquid. Return beans to clean pot and set aside.

3. Set oven rack in middle position. Preheat oven to 350°F.

4. Place bean cooking liquid in small saucepan. Add brown sugar, ketchup, salt, and pepper. Whisk to combine. Bring mixture to a boil, reduce heat, and simmer 5 minutes. Add sauce to pot with beans and stir. Add onion. Add short ribs, burying them below surface of beans and distributing them evenly throughout.

5. Cover pot, place beans in oven, and bake 2 hours, stirring once every hour. Add beer to beans, mix gently, and bake 1 hour more, or until beans are tender and succulent and sauce is sweet and reduced. Remove pot from oven carefully. Remove ribs from beans with tongs. Remove meat from ribs and return meat to pot. Serve immediately. Store leftover beans in covered glass or plastic container in refrigerator.

Bunny Slobodzinski's Stuffed Cabbage with Salt Pork Gravy

{ *1960s* }

2½- to 3-pound cabbage

1 (4-inch square) piece salt pork, or 5-ounce piece pancetta (optional)

4 tablespoons extra-virgin olive oil, divided

2 pounds "fresh cut" or uncured boneless pork butt, trimmed of fat and cut into ½-inch pieces, or 2 pounds ground pork

1 cup coarsely chopped onion

2 cups cooked long grain rice

2 tablespoons dried parsley

½ teaspoon coarsely ground black pepper

2 cups low-sodium chicken stock

BUNNY PELUSO SLOBODZINSKI MARRIED *her husband, Edwin, when she was just 21. Bunny had been brought up in a Neapolitan-American household, but with advice from her mother-in-law, Rosalie, and armed with a copy of a Polish cookbook and a lot of ingenuity, she learned to prepare traditional Polish meals, relying on her new husband to critique the dishes she placed before him. This recipe is based on one Bunny makes. The use of rendered salt pork fat or pancetta for the gravy is optional.*

1. To prepare cabbage: Remove 3 or 4 outer leaves from cabbage head, chop coarsely, and set aside. Cut out core of cabbage in cone-shaped section and discard. Bring water to a boil in large heavy pot. Add head of cabbage until fully immersed and let stand off heat for 4 minutes. Remove cabbage head to platter. Using long-handled fork, carefully remove leaves from head, keeping them whole. They should be pliable enough to come off easily. If not, return cabbage head to pot and let stand in hot water until leaves come away easily.

2. Cut out hard center spine from each leaf and discard. Cut any very large leaves in half. Dry leaves on paper towels and set aside. Coarsely chop any leaves that are too small to stuff. Sprinkle all chopped cabbage over bottom of large Dutch oven or large heavy-bottomed pot and set aside.

3. If using salt pork, cut off thick skin and discard. Cut salt pork (or pancetta) into strips or cubes and place in saucepan. Cook over low heat until fat is rendered, 8 to 10 minutes. Pour off fat carefully into bowl, leaving salt that has collected at the bottom of pan, and set aside.

4. To make filling: Heat 2 tablespoons of the olive oil in large heavy frying pan over medium heat. Add half of pork and cook until no longer pink. Remove to large bowl. Add remaining 2 tablespoons oil and onion and cook over medium heat until onion is brown around edges, 5 to 7 minutes. Add rest of pork and cook until no

longer pink. Remove to bowl with rest of cooked pork. Add cooked rice, parsley, and pepper and combine.

5. To stuff cabbage: Place each cabbage leaf on flat surface and spoon $1/4$ cup of filling in center. Fold edges of cabbage leaf in toward center to enclose meat in neat package. If cabbage leaf is too small to contain meat filling, overlap it with another halved leaf or overlap 2 smaller leaves.

6. Place stuffed cabbage, seams down, on top of chopped cabbage leaves in Dutch oven or large pot. Pour chicken stock into pot and add enough water to just cover stuffed cabbage. Bring to a simmer, cover, and cook over medium heat for $1^{1}/_{2}$ hours.

7. Remove stuffed cabbage to platter. Cut 2 slits in each stuffed leaf. Drizzle bit of rendered fat from salt pork (or pancetta) over stuffed leaves. Serve stuffed cabbage hot. Place leftovers seam side down in container, cover with plastic wrap, and refrigerate. Stuffed cabbage can be frozen for up to 6 months. Thoroughly defrost in refrigerator overnight before serving. Then reheat in frying pan with olive oil or butter.

TIPS & TOUCHES

- We substituted the pancetta for the salt pork because it's a little less salty.
- Add $1/2$ teaspoon of salt to the filling if you do not use the salt pork or pancetta.

Silver napkin rings, American, early 20th century

Germain Asselin's Stuffing Pie
(*Tourtière*)

MAKES 6 TO 8 SERVINGS

{ 1 9 3 0 s }

THIS RECIPE CAME FROM THE FAMILY OF *Germain Asselin, who passed it on to his daughter Bonnie. Germain Asselin's Stuffing Pie is very similar to the French-Canadian tourtière, or meat pie. His version used more beef to pork, but we changed the proportions to make a heartier version. The Asselins use poultry seasoning, while other versions use a touch of thyme and savory. Bonnie grinds her crackers, but we found that pulsing them in a food processor is as good. French-Canadians serve tourtière at Reveillon celebrations on Christmas Eve and New Year's Eve, but this savory meat pie is especially comforting on cold wintry days.*

1. To prepare crust: For detailed instructions, see Sheila's Savory Pie Crust on page 306. Coat 9-inch ovenproof glass pie plate with vegetable spray. Roll out pastry dough. Fit half of dough into bottom of pie plate and trim off excess. Chill pastry for top and bottom crust in refrigerator while you make filling.

2. Heat olive oil in large frying pan over medium heat. Add onion and shallot and cook, stirring with wooden spoon, until translucent, 5 to 7 minutes. Do not brown. Add ground pork and beef and sauté, breaking up clumps of meat with wooden spoon, until meat is no longer pink. Remove mixture to large bowl. Add poultry seasoning, salt, pepper, and cloves. Add cracker flakes and combine. Set mixture aside until cool.

3. Set oven rack in middle position. Preheat oven to 450°F. Line 14-inch by 16-inch baking sheet with foil, shiny side up, and coat with vegetable spray, or use silicone liner.

4. Add cooled filling to pie shell. Brush edges of pastry shell with beaten egg. Add top crust and seal and crimp edges. Make 2 slits in center of pie to allow steam to escape. Brush top crust and edges with beaten egg.

5. Place pie on foil-lined baking sheet and bake 30 minutes, or until top is golden brown. Check for browning after 20 minutes. If crust is browning too quickly, cover loosely with foil. Remove pie to rack and cool slightly. Serve while still hot. Cover cooled leftover pie with paper towel and plastic wrap and store in refrigerator.

Pastry for double-crust pie, divided in half and chilled (see Sheila's Savory Pie Crust on page 306)

2 tablespoons extra-virgin olive oil

¼ cup chopped onion

2 tablespoons chopped shallot

1 pound ground pork

½ pound ground beef

1 teaspoon poultry seasoning

1 teaspoon salt

½ teaspoon coarsely ground black pepper

¼ teaspoon ground cloves

1 cup crushed soda crackers, pulsed to large flakes in the bowl of a food processor fitted with the metal blade

1 egg, beaten

TIPS & TOUCHES

- Reheat leftover tourtière uncovered in a 300°F oven for 20 minutes, or until warmed through.
- Serve slices of tourtière with Dijon mustard or horseradish sauce.
- *Reveillon* means "waking." In French-speaking countries, guests stay up most of the night celebrating Christmas or the New Year.

Deviled Ham and Cheese Strata

{ 1 9 3 0 s }

MAKES 12 SERVINGS

FOR DEVILED HAM

1 pound cooked ham

1 cup minced sweet gherkins

$\frac{1}{2}$ cup minced onion

$\frac{1}{2}$ cup mayonnaise

1 tablespoon dried parsley

1 teaspoon paprika

$\frac{1}{2}$ teaspoon chopped, brined hot peppers

1 teaspoon salt

1 teaspoon coarsely ground black pepper

3 cups whole milk ricotta cheese

FOR BREAD LAYERS

15 to 16 ($\frac{1}{2}$-inch-thick) slices white bread

$\frac{1}{2}$ cup butter, melted

FOR CUSTARD

$1\frac{1}{2}$ cups milk

$1\frac{1}{2}$ cups half-and-half

8 eggs, beaten

8 ounces provolone or cheddar cheese, sliced and cut in strips

FOR TOPPING

2 tablespoons butter, melted

1 cup Ritz cracker crumbs

1 cup grated parmesan cheese

THIS IS A LARGE STRATA WITH SEVERAL *layers, but it's worth the effort. The sour-sweet flavor of the gherkins and the salty ham are tamed by the addition of creamy ricotta cheese. We found the recipe for this old-fashioned dish handwritten on an index card. This is really just a savory bread pudding, but it can become the star of breakfast, lunch, or brunch. We serve it with a green salad to balance the richness.*

1. To make deviled ham: Place ham in bowl of food processor fitted with metal blade. Pulse until finely chopped. Remove ham to bowl. Add gherkins, onion, mayonnaise, parsley, paprika, hot peppers, salt, and black pepper and combine. Fold in ricotta and set aside.

2. To prepare bread: Trim off and discard crusts. Cut bread slices in half. Brush each piece on both sides with melted butter and set aside.

3. To make custard: Coat 9-inch by 13-inch ovenproof glass baking dish with vegetable spray. Combine milk and half-and-half in large bowl. Add eggs and whisk to combine. Pour small amount of custard in bottom of baking dish. Tilt and swirl dish until bottom is covered.

4. Spread deviled ham generously on piece of bread and place it, ham side up, on bottom of baking dish. Continue with several more pieces of bread, spreading with ham and cutting them as needed to fit, until bottom of dish is completely covered. Cover ham with second layer of bread. Pour over half of the custard and layer half of the cheese on top. (The bread will start to absorb custard.) Use a spatula to spread remaining deviled ham generously over top. Layer remaining cheese on top of ham and pour over remaining custard. If there isn't room for all of the custard, refrigerate it; you'll be able to add the rest of it later as custard in baking dish is absorbed by bread.

5. Use a knife to cut 8 slits through the layers of the strata to allow custard to soak through. Place baking dish on tray to catch drips. Cover the top of strata with plastic wrap and press down firmly

with your palm all over until custard rises to top. Let stand
10 minutes, pushing down gently on top of pudding 2 more times.

6. Refrigerate strata on tray overnight. Add any leftover custard to
strata as it becomes possible. The next day, remove strata from
refrigerator and allow to sit at room temperature at least 1 hour.

7. To add topping: Toss melted butter with crumbs and cheese.
Spread topping over top of strata.

8. Set oven rack in middle position. Preheat oven to 350°F. Place
baking dish with strata on rack in large metal pan. Pour hot water
from glass measuring cup into pan until water comes halfway up
sides of baking dish. Place carefully in oven. Bake approximately
1 hour, or until topping is golden brown, strata bubbles along
sides, and tester inserted into middle comes out clean. *Do not let water
bath evaporate.* Check strata periodically during baking to be sure
topping is not burning; cover loosely with foil if topping seems to
be drying out.

9. Remove baking dish carefully from oven and water bath. Cool on
a rack slightly before serving to prevent strata from falling apart.
Store leftover strata covered with plastic wrap in the refrigerator.

Tips & Touches

- It's going to take some time
for the bread to absorb the
custard, but when you take
this puffy strata out of the
oven, your patience will be
rewarded.
- Use soft white bread for
the strata because it absorbs
the custard faster than a
firmer bread.

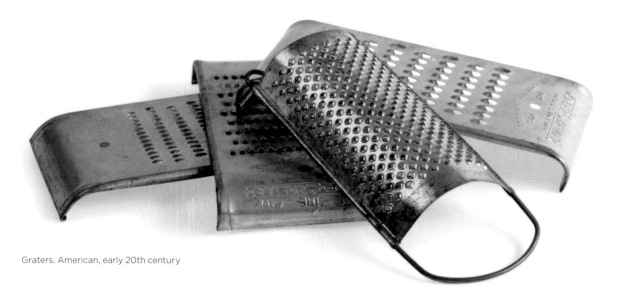

Graters, American, early 20th century

Ham Loaf

{ 1 9 3 0 s }

FOR HAM LOAF

1 (20-ounce) can sliced pineapple

1 cup milk

1 cup fine bread crumbs (see "How to Make Fine Bread Crumbs" on page 204)

¾ pound baked or boiled ham, cut into chunks

1 medium onion, quartered

¾ pound ground pork

3 eggs, beaten

¼ teaspoon coarsely ground black pepper

¼ teaspoon ground cloves

1 tablespoon firmly packed brown sugar

FOR SAUCE

Reserved pineapple juice (see step 2)

1 tablespoon sherry (optional)

1 tablespoon prepared mustard

¼ cup firmly packed brown sugar

TIPS & TOUCHES

* Place a foil-lined pan on an oven rack below the ham loaf to catch any drips.

THIS SAVORY LOAF IS MADE WITH BOTH *ground ham and ground pork. A touch of cloves along with pineapple and brown sugar makes it a festive dish for Sunday night suppers. We found this recipe in the manuscript cookbook of a woman who loved entertaining but who also clearly understood the words* economical *and* delicious. *Served cold with a dab of sharp mustard, this ham loaf tastes like paté.*

1. Set oven rack in middle position. Preheat oven to 350°F. Coat 9-inch by 5-inch by 3-inch loaf pan with vegetable spray.

2. To make ham loaf: Drain pineapple, reserving fruit and juice separately. Combine milk and bread crumbs in large bowl and stir. Set aside for 5 minutes.

3. Place ham in bowl of food processor fitted with metal blade. Pulse until ham is the texture of ground pork. Remove to bowl with bread crumbs. Add onion to bowl of food processor and pulse until finely chopped. Scrape into bowl with ham. Add pork to bowl and mix to combine. Add eggs, pepper, and cloves. Mix all ham loaf ingredients with your hands (wear disposable gloves if desired) until just combined. Place in prepared loaf pan.

4. To make sauce: Combine reserved pineapple juice, sherry (if using), mustard, and ¼ cup brown sugar in small bowl and whisk to combine.

5. Pour half of sauce over ham loaf, place in oven, and bake 1 hour. Remove ham loaf from oven and arrange about half of the pineapple rings on top. Pour as much of remaining sauce as will fit on top of loaf, sprinkle with 1 tablespoon brown sugar, and return to oven for 30 minutes, or until an instant-read thermometer inserted into middle of loaf reads 160°F. Cool in pan on rack for 15 minutes. Turn out loaf onto serving platter and surround with remaining pineapple slices.

Salmon Squares

{ 1920s }

THIS IS ONE OF THOSE UNIVERSAL HANDWRITTEN *recipes that we find frequently in our collection of manuscript cookbooks. It seems that canned salmon was one of those standbys that every home cook relied on. However, canned salmon was never an inexpensive staple. It was just convenient. We've updated our version of Salmon Squares by using canned wild salmon, fresh parsley, fresh dill, and more cream. Using regular canned salmon is also fine.*

1. Set oven rack in middle position. Preheat oven to 350°F. Coat 2-quart, 8-inch by 11-inch rectangular ovenproof glass baking dish with vegetable spray or butter. Make water bath: Set rack in metal pan large enough to hold glass baking dish.

2. To make salmon squares: Place bread crumbs in bowl. Heat milk in saucepan until small bubbles form around edges; do not boil. Pour hot milk over bread crumbs. Add egg yolks, mix to combine, and set aside.

3. In another bowl, combine rice, cream, salmon, onion, 4 tablespoons of the melted butter, the dill, parsley, salt, pepper, and paprika. Add bread crumb mixture and stir to combine.

4. Beat egg whites in bowl of standing mixer fitted with whisk attachment until soft peaks form. Fold egg whites into salmon mixture and transfer to prepared baking dish. Smooth the top. Mix remaining 2 tablespoons melted butter with cracker crumbs and sprinkle over top.

5. Bring water to a boil for water bath. Place dish in water bath. Use glass measuring cup to pour hot water into pan to come about halfway up sides of glass dish. Cover water bath with foil. Place carefully in oven and bake 30 minutes, checking water level periodically and replenishing as needed. *Do not let the water evaporate.* Remove foil and bake another 30 minutes, or until tester inserted into salmon comes out clean.

6. Carefully remove salmon from oven. Cool in baking dish on rack for 10 minutes. Cut into squares and serve with dill mayonnaise. Store leftover squares wrapped in wax paper in the refrigerator.

7. To make dill mayonnaise: Stir together mayonnaise, dill, lemon juice, sugar, and salt in small bowl and refrigerate.

FOR SALMON SQUARES

2 cups fine bread crumbs (see "How to Make Fine Bread Crumbs" on page 204)

1 cup milk

2 eggs, separated

1 cup cooked rice

1 cup heavy cream

1 (14.75-ounce) can wild salmon, skin and bones removed

1/4 cup finely chopped onion

6 tablespoons butter, melted, divided

1 1/2 tablespoons finely chopped fresh dill

1 tablespoon finely chopped fresh parsley

1 teaspoon kosher salt

1/2 teaspoon coarsely ground black pepper

1/4 teaspoon paprika

20 Ritz crackers, crushed (about 1 cup)

FOR DILL MAYONNAISE

1 cup mayonnaise

3 tablespoons finely chopped fresh dill

2 teaspoons lemon juice

1/2 teaspoon sugar

Pinch of salt

Daddy's Fried Lox

{ 1 9 5 0 s }

½ pound lox bits

¼ cup flour

2 tablespoons solid vegetable
   shortening

1½ cups sliced onion

TIPS & TOUCHES

- Lox is salt-cured salmon. Do not use smoked salmon.
- Red onion looks nice with fried lox.

MAKES 4 SMALL SERVINGS

THIS IS ONE OF THE WONDERFUL BREAKFAST *dishes our father, Harry, made for our Sunday breakfasts when we were growing up. We bought our lox and white fish at Revere Smoked Fish, which was located in Chelsea, Massachusetts. We suggest that you use the less expensive lox bits, rather than the fancy cuts of lox. We always ate Daddy's Fried Lox with scrambled eggs and a salad of lettuce, tomato, and cucumber.*

1. Rinse lox bits under cold running water. Place in glass bowl and add cold water to cover. Cover with plastic wrap and refrigerate at least 8 hours or overnight. Change water at least twice during soaking to remove extra salt.

2. Rinse lox again and pat dry with paper towels. Toss with flour. Place in strainer and shake to remove excess flour. Set aside.

3. Melt shortening in frying pan over medium heat. Add onion slices and sauté until they are just browned around edges. Remove onion or push to one side of frying pan. Add lox to pan and fry until coating is a pale brown. Turn and fry the other side until crust is browned and crispy. Serve lox with onions and a salad. Store leftovers wrapped in wax paper in refrigerator. Fried lox is also good served cold the next day.

Elinor's Shrimp Creole

{ *1940s* }

MAKES 4 SERVINGS

2 tablespoons extra-virgin olive oil

1½ cups chopped onion

1½ cups chopped green
bell pepper

1½ cups chopped celery

⅓ cup chopped pimentos

3 cloves garlic, chopped

1 teaspoon salt

½ teaspoon coarsely ground
black pepper

1 teaspoon dried thyme

2 bay leaves

¼ teaspoon chopped, brined
hot peppers

1 (28-ounce) can whole plum
tomatoes in juice

1 (15½-ounce) can tomato sauce

1 tablespoon firmly packed
brown sugar

1 pound cooked shrimp

2 cups cooked rice

THIS IS ANOTHER RECIPE FROM ELINOR JENNINGS, *with whom Marilynn worked in the late 1960s. A true Southern lady, Elinor loved the combination of the shrimp and spices. She recommended simmering the sauce for at least 45 minutes to enjoy the true flavor of this dish. Elinor was proud of the fact that she timed her dishes to the minute. Once again, this is a home cook's interpretation of a popular restaurant dish.*

1. Heat olive oil in large heavy-bottomed pot over medium heat. Add onion, bell pepper, and celery and cook until onion just begins to brown. Add pimentos, garlic, salt, black pepper, thyme, bay leaves, and hot peppers and stir to combine.

2. Add tomatoes with juice and break up with wooden spoon. Add tomato sauce and brown sugar and stir to combine. Bring to a boil, reduce heat, and simmer, covered, 15 minutes, stirring occasionally. Uncover pot and continue cooking another 45 minutes, or until sauce thickens. Stir occasionally to prevent sauce from catching on bottom of pot. Remove from heat.

3. Add shrimp and let stand in sauce 10 minutes to absorb flavor. Reheat gently. Serve shrimp on bed of rice. Store leftovers in covered container in refrigerator.

TIPS & TOUCHES

* Chop garlic in large pieces so it can be removed before serving.
* Mounding rice in custard cups and unmolding on plates makes a festive presentation.

Curried Shrimp

{ 1 9 6 0 s }

MAKES 6 TO 8 SERVINGS

THIS IS A RECIPE FOR CURRIED SHRIMP *that an American home cook would have prepared in her kitchen in the 1960s. It carries the rather contradictory notation "for sudden planned party." It's an easy recipe presenting a Westernized version of an exotic dish. Curry powder and canned coconut milk can usually be found at your local grocery store. The sweetened coconut balances the flavor of the curry.*

1. Heat oil in large frying pan over medium heat. Add onion and sauté until translucent, stirring with wooden spoon, about 5 to 7 minutes. Remove to large bowl and set aside.

2. In another bowl, combine curry powder, salt, cayenne pepper, flour, and coconut milk. Whisk to form a paste. Add milk and Worcestershire sauce and whisk until smooth. Add to bowl with onion and stir to mix well. Add shrimp and shredded coconut.

3. Place curry mixture in large heavy-bottomed pot over low heat. Simmer very gently 10 to 15 minutes. Do not overcook or shrimp will be tough. Do not allow curry to boil. Serve on bed of hot cooked rice. Store leftovers in covered container in refrigerator.

3 tablespoons extra-virgin olive oil

5 cups coarsely chopped onion

2 teaspoons curry powder

1 teaspoon salt

1/8 teaspoon cayenne pepper

3 tablespoons flour

1/2 cup coconut milk

1/2 cup milk

1 tablespoon Worcestershire sauce

3 cups cooked shrimp

1/3 cup shredded sweetened coconut

Cooked rice

Silver salt and spoon, American, early 20th century

Dot's Tuna Crescents

{ *1950s* }

MAKES 4 TO 6 SERVINGS

FOR DOUGH

3 cups flour

2 teaspoons baking powder

1 teaspoon salt

½ cup vegetable oil

⅔ cup milk

1 egg, beaten (for egg wash)

FOR FILLING

2 (6-ounce) cans tuna, drained
   and flaked

1 cup finely chopped celery

¼ cup mayonnaise

1 egg, beaten

THIS RECIPE GAVE US AN ALTERNATIVE TO *eating tuna in sandwiches or salads. Our mother usually made these on winter nights when a hot meal was welcome. The celery and tuna unite to form an almost Asian flavor, and the crescents are very good with the Ginger–Lime Mayonnaise. Smaller versions are nice as appetizers.*

1. To make dough: Combine flour, baking powder, and salt in bowl of food processor fitted with metal blade. Pulse for 3 seconds. Pour in oil and milk. Process until dough comes away from sides of bowl. Process another 20 seconds. Remove dough from bowl of processor and divide in half.

2. To make filling: Mix tuna, celery, mayonnaise, and egg in small bowl.

3. Set oven rack in middle position. Preheat oven to 450°F. Line 14-inch by 16-inch baking sheet with foil, shiny side up, and coat with vegetable spray, or use silicone liner.

4. Place half of dough between two 12-inch squares of wax paper. Roll out dough until it reaches edges of wax paper. Remove top sheet of paper. Cut dough into 6 rectangles, 6 inches by 4 inches.

GINGER-LIME MAYONNAISE

This is a quick mayonnaise based on several of the recipes we found. It's wonderful with Tuna Crescents or as a salad dressing. Fresh ginger brings out the flavor of the mayonnaise. Scrape the skin from the root with the edge of a spoon. If the skin is tough, use a vegetable peeler. Grate the ginger on a Microplane zester/grater. If you don't have ginger jam on your pantry shelf, apricot jam is a good substitute for adding a bit of sweetness.

1 cup mayonnaise

2 tablespoons grated fresh ginger

5 tablespoons fresh lime juice

2 teaspoons grated lime zest

2 tablespoons ginger jam

Whisk mayonnaise, ginger, and lime juice and zest in small bowl. Add ginger jam and whisk to combine. **Makes 1¼ cups**

5. Divide half of filling evenly among dough rectangles, placing it horizontally in center third of each rectangle. Flour your hands and fold top third of dough rectangles over filling, then roll toward you to make cylinders. Roll cylinders 2 or 3 times toward you with the palm of your hand until they look very neat and even (like a mini egg roll). Press dough together at both ends and seal using tines of salad fork. Bend both ends in toward the center to form crescents. Place crescents on prepared pan and brush with beaten egg. Bake 10 to 15 minutes, or until crust is golden brown. Repeat with remaining dough and filling to make 6 more crescents; bake 1 pan at a time unless you have a double-oven. Serve immediately. Store leftover crescents wrapped in wax paper in refrigerator. Reheat in low oven.

Danish Roast Goose Stuffed with Apples and Prunes (*Stegt Gås*)

{ 1 9 6 0 s }

MAKES 6 SERVINGS

2 cups pitted prunes

4 cups boiling water

Young goose, about 10 pounds

1 lemon, cut in half

1½ teaspoons salt, divided

1 teaspoon coarsely ground black pepper

2 cups peeled, cored, and chopped apples

1 large onion, peeled and quartered

Gravy (see "How to Make Gravy for Your Goose" on page 239)

GOOSE, WITH ITS MOIST DARK MEAT AND *glistening skin, is the traditional heart of the Danish Christmas feast. This recipe is from Ed Steenberg, of Minneapolis, Minnesota. Ed helped his mother, Erma, raise geese and ducks in Minnesota during the 1940s, and he has been cooking geese for Christmas for 50 years. His recipe is challenging, but if you follow the instructions, you will be rewarded with a picture-perfect roast goose. Ed suggests serving roast goose with Red Cabbage (Rødkål) (page 122) and Caramelized Potatoes (Brunede Kartofler) (page 107). The slightly sour, pungent taste of the red cabbage and the crispy texture of the potatoes balance the rich flavor of the goose. This recipe does not boil the goose before roasting.*

1. Place prunes in saucepan and pour boiling water over them. Let stand 20 to 30 minutes, or until prunes absorb water and become plump and soft. Drain prunes and let cool until easy to handle.

2. Wash goose under cold running water and pat dry with paper towels. Remove any loose fat from around cavities. Cut off wing tips. Rub goose, inside and out, with lemon halves. Sprinkle inside and out with 1 teaspoon of the salt and the pepper. Stuff body cavity with prunes, apples, and onion. Close body cavity with metal skewers and lace with wet cotton kitchen string. Close neck cavity

---

➤➤ THE VALUABLE GOOSE ◄◄

The goose has always been prized by heirloom cooks for its dark, flavorful meat and crispy skin. Its fine down and feathers were used for stuffing coverlets and pillows, and its quills were formed into pens. Goose fat was doubly valuable; it was an excellent choice for frying potatoes and other foods and was thought to have medicinal benefits when rubbed on the chests of those suffering from congestive colds. We don't recommend the latter.

⇥ **HOW TO ROAST A GOOSE** ⇤

Roasting a goose should be done cautiously because you are working with hot fat and boiling water. Follow these steps to have a safer, easier experience with your goose.

1. Read the recipe through at least twice.

2. Clear off the counter and have utensils and ingredients within easy reach.

3. Place the goose on a roasting rack in pan.

4. Stuff the cavity with prunes, apples, and onions. Be careful when placing your hand in the cavity because sharp bones can scratch.

5. Use *metal* skewers and *wet* cotton kitchen string to truss the goose. Do not use string made from plastic. It will melt.

6. Use a heavy pot to boil water for basting.

7. Have another heavy pot at hand when draining fat from the goose. Empty this pot periodically to another container so that fat will not remain on the stove while the goose is roasting.

8. Be careful when turning the goose in the pan. Any fat that spills in the oven can cause a fire. The safe way is to remove the roasting pan from the oven, place it on a flat surface, and then turn the goose.

9. Be sure that the goose reaches the correct temperature before serving.

with skewer. Truss bird securely with wet cotton kitchen string. Prick skin around thighs, back, and lower breast with fork so fat will drain during roasting.

3. Place oven rack in middle position. Preheat oven to 425°F. Line large roasting pan with foil, shiny side up. Set rack over foil.

4. Place goose, breast side up, on rack in prepared pan. Roast 15 minutes, to brown lightly. Reduce oven temperature to 350°F. Turn goose on one side and roast 1 hour, basting every 15 to 20 minutes with boiling water to help dissolve fat. Carefully remove fat from pan periodically with bulb baster. The bulb may be hot to handle.

5. Turn goose onto its other side. Continue roasting until juices run clear when thigh is pierced with small knife and instant-read thermometer inserted into thigh registers 165°F, about 2 hours and 45 minutes total. If juice is rosy-colored, roast another

5 minutes or so, or until juice runs clear yellow. Continue to drain fat and baste goose every 15 minutes. After bird has roasted 2 hours and 30 minutes, salt goose with remaining $\frac{1}{2}$ teaspoon salt and turn breast side up. Salting will help to crisp skin.

6. When goose is fully cooked, remove from oven. Remove goose to platter. Scoop out and discard apples, prunes, and onion. Strain pan juices into medium saucepan. Skim fat. Reserve fat and pan juices separately to make gravy.

7. Let goose rest in warm place for 15 minutes. Carve and serve with gravy. Wrap leftover goose in wax paper and store in refrigerator.

HOW TO MAKE GRAVY FOR YOUR GOOSE

2 tablespoons goose fat
2 tablespoons Wondra quick-mixing flour
2 cups strained goose pan juices or low-sodium chicken stock
Salt and coarsely ground black pepper

Melt goose fat in heavy-bottomed frying pan over low heat. Add flour and whisk until combined. Cook for about 1 minute, stirring with wooden spoon. Gravy is usually made with a roux (a mixture of flour and fat) and is thicker than a pan sauce. For thicker gravy, use 3 tablespoons flour rather than 2 tablespoons. Gradually pour in pan juices or chicken stock, stirring constantly, and cook until gravy begins to thicken. Chicken stock can be added to juices from goose or substituted for them. Increase heat to medium and continue cooking until gravy reaches desired consistency. If there are any lumps or bits, put gravy through strainer. Adjust seasonings. Store leftover gravy in covered container in refrigerator. **Makes 2 cups**

Libby's Curried Turkey Pie

{ *1950s* }

FOR CRUST

2½ to 3 cups soft bread crumbs (see "How to Make Soft Bread Crumbs")

¼ cup butter, melted

2 to 4 tablespoons water

¼ cup finely chopped onion

¼ cup finely chopped celery

¼ cup finely chopped fresh parsley, or 2 teaspoons dried

2 teaspoons poultry seasoning

½ teaspoon coarsely ground black pepper

¼ teaspoon salt

FOR FILLING

¼ cup raisins

1½ cups boiling water

2 tablespoons butter, softened to room temperature

¼ cup chopped white mushrooms

1 (10½-ounce) can cream of mushroom soup, or 1 recipe Homemade "Canned" Cream of Mushroom Soup (page 259)

½ cup milk

2 cups chopped (¾-inch) cooked turkey

½ cup frozen peas, thawed

1 tablespoon finely chopped onion

2 teaspoons curry powder

¼ teaspoon salt

THIS IS A GREAT WAY TO SERVE *leftover turkey. It's quick and easy and was a little exotic in the 1950s because of the curry powder. The homemade bread crumbs make a big difference in this dish. We treasure Libby's living recipes, which were found at a yard sale in her hometown of Groton, Massachusetts.*

1. Set oven rack in middle position. Preheat oven to 375°F. Coat 9-inch ovenproof glass pie plate with vegetable spray. Line 14-inch by 16-inch baking sheet with foil, shiny side up, and coat with vegetable spray, or use silicone liner.

2. To make crust: Place bread crumbs and melted butter in large bowl and mix thoroughly. Add 2 tablespoons water and stir. Add up to 2 more tablespoons water, as needed, until bread crumbs are completely moistened. Add onion, celery, parsley, poultry seasoning, pepper, and salt and combine with hands. Reserve one-third of the mixture. Press remaining mixture over bottom and up

BRINGING AN ORIGINAL
›› INTO THE ‹‹
21ST CENTURY

The original recipe for Libby's Curried Turkey Pie called for cream of mushroom soup. But we've provided a substitute white sauce and butter-fried mushrooms (see Basic White Sauce on page 259). Frozen peas and fresh mushrooms replace canned ones, while a mixture made from fresh bread crumbs is used for the pie's crust.

HOW TO MAKE SOFT BREAD CRUMBS

Heirloom recipes for breading and for pastries often require soft bread crumbs. Making your own soft bread crumbs ensures that they are flavorful and fresh. Remove and discard the crusts from slightly dry bread. Tear the bread into pieces and place in the bowl of a food processor fitted with the metal blade. Pulse a few times. Crumbs should be larger and softer than fine bread crumbs. Commercially prepared Japanese bread crumbs (called panko) are a good substitute for homemade soft bread crumbs. Panko can be found in most grocery stores as well as those specializing in international foods.

sides of prepared pie plate to form crust. Place pie plate on prepared baking sheet and set aside.

3. To make filling: Place raisins in small bowl and pour boiling water over. Let stand 5 minutes. Drain and set aside.

4. Melt butter in saucepan over medium heat. Add mushrooms and cook until softened and lightly browned, 5 to 7 minutes. Set aside.

5. Place canned mushroom soup in large bowl. Add milk and whisk. Add raisins, mushrooms, turkey, peas, onion, curry powder, and salt. Stir with wooden spoon until combined.

6. Pour mixture into prepared crust. Sprinkle reserved crust mixture over top. Bake, uncovered, 30 to 35 minutes, or until pie starts to bubble and topping is crunchy. Cover pie with foil if crust browns too quickly. Serve immediately. Cover cooled leftover pie with paper towel and plastic wrap and store in refrigerator.

TIPS & TOUCHES

- Chicken can be substituted for turkey.
- Add a little more butter if the crust mixture seems dry.
- Packaged herbed stuffing mix can also be used.
- Do not add milk when using homemade Mushroom Soup.

Turkey Divan

{1930s}

MAKES 4 SERVINGS

FOR TURKEY CASSEROLE

1 pound frozen broccoli

3 cups thinly sliced cooked turkey

3 tablespoons butter, softened to room temperature

3 tablespoons flour

3/4 teaspoon salt

1/8 teaspoon coarsely ground black pepper

1/8 teaspoon paprika

1 cup milk

1/2 cup half-and-half

1 cup grated cheddar cheese

FOR TOPPING

2 cups soft bread crumbs (see "How to Make Soft Bread Crumbs" on page 241)

3 tablespoons butter, melted

Tips & Touches

* You can use fresh broccoli instead of frozen.

THIS RECIPE IS AN OLD ONE AND *came from our friend Elinor Jennings. When we mentioned this delicious recipe to a young woman we met in a spice shop, her eyes misted with memories of long-ago servings of chicken divan. This is another imaginative way to serve leftover turkey. The combination of broccoli and cheese turns simple ingredients into a party dish. As our friend Nellie Carey would say, "You could serve this!"*

1. Set oven rack in middle position. Preheat oven to 350°F. Coat 9-inch by 13-inch ovenproof glass baking dish with vegetable spray.

2. To make casserole: Cook broccoli in boiling water according to package directions until just tender, still bright green, and firm. Drain well. Cut stalks in half lengthwise. Arrange broccoli over bottom of prepared baking dish. Cover with turkey slices and set aside.

3. Melt butter in saucepan over low heat. Add flour, salt, pepper, and paprika and stir with wooden spoon to combine. Gradually add milk and half-and-half, raise heat to medium, and cook, stirring, until sauce is thickened and smooth, about 5 minutes. Add cheese and stir to melt. Pour cheese sauce over turkey and cooked broccoli.

4. To make topping: Mix bread crumbs with melted butter. Sprinkle topping over casserole. Bake about 40 minutes, or until sauce bubbles around edges. Cover casserole with foil if topping browns too quickly. Store leftovers in covered container in refrigerator.

Miniature tin roasting pans, American, early 20th century

Hot Chicken Salad

MAKES 4 TO 6 SERVINGS

THIS DISH ISN'T WHAT IT SOUNDS LIKE. *It's more of a chicken casserole than a salad. It's very colorful with its chopped green pepper and pimento and is very representative of a dish that a home cook would serve to her family in the 1950s, the Golden Age of the Casserole. This is a treasured Southern recipe from a manuscript cookbook from North Carolina.*

1. Set oven rack in middle position. Preheat oven to 450°F. Coat 9-inch by 13-inch ovenproof glass baking dish with vegetable spray.

2. To make casserole: Heat butter and olive oil in large frying pan over medium heat. Add celery, onion, mushrooms, pimentos, and green bell pepper and cook until vegetables are softened but only partially cooked, 5 to 7 minutes. Add almonds and stir to coat with butter and oil. Stir in salt and black pepper. Remove to large bowl. Add chicken and mayonnaise and stir to coat ingredients with mayonnaise. Spoon into prepared baking dish and smooth the top. Set aside.

3. To make topping: Heat butter and oil in frying pan over medium heat. Add bread crumbs and cook, stirring, until they turn a light brown color, being careful not to burn them. Remove from heat and stir in cream.

4. Spread topping over casserole and bake about 15 minutes, or until top is golden brown and bubbly. Serve hot. Store leftovers covered with wax paper in refrigerator.

FOR CASSEROLE

2 tablespoons butter, softened to room temperature

2 tablespoons extra-virgin olive oil

1 cup chopped celery

½ cup chopped onion

1 cup sliced white mushrooms

½ cup chopped pimentos

⅔ cup chopped green bell pepper

1 cup slivered almonds

1 teaspoon salt

½ teaspoon coarsely ground black pepper

4 cups chopped cooked chicken

1 cup mayonnaise

FOR TOPPING

1 tablespoon butter, softened to room temperature

1 tablespoon extra-virgin olive oil

1 cup fine bread crumbs (see "How to Make Fine Bread Crumbs" on page 204) or panko

½ cup heavy cream

Miniature au gratin dish, American, 1920s–1930s

TIPS & TOUCHES

- It might be necessary to brown bread crumbs in two batches.
- Bread crumbs should be fried to a light brown, not dark brown.
- Use a combination of butter and olive oil to sauté vegetables and brown bread crumbs to prevent burning.
- Wild mushrooms can be substituted.

Chicken Pot Pie

{ 1 9 5 0 s }

Pastry for 9-inch single-crust pie, chilled (see Sheila's Savory Pie Crust on page 306)

1 egg, beaten

FOR FILLING

1/4 cup butter, softened to room temperature

1/4 cup flour

1 cup low-sodium chicken stock

1/2 cup half-and-half

1/2 teaspoon salt

1/2 teaspoon paprika

1/8 teaspoon coarsely ground black pepper

1 tablespoon grated onion

1 tablespoon extra-virgin olive oil

1 cup sliced white mushrooms

1 cup sliced (1/4-inch thick) carrots

2 cups diced (1/2-inch) cooked chicken

1 cup fresh or frozen peas

THIS RECIPE CAME FROM THE MANUSCRIPT COOKBOOK *of The Pie Lady from North Carolina. An expert on making cakes and sweet pies, she also excelled in making this old-fashioned savory Chicken Pot Pie. She wrote this recipe on an invoice for Remco Supply, located on Wendover Avenue in Greensboro, North Carolina. Remco sold fasteners, tools, shelving, shop equipment, and storage racks.*

1. To make pastry for top of pie: For detailed instructions, see Sheila's Savory Pie Crust on page 306.

2. To make filling: Melt butter over low heat in 2-quart saucepan. Add flour and whisk to blend. Turn heat to medium and cook, stirring with wooden spoon, for 1 minute. Add stock and half-and-half and continue cooking, stirring constantly, until sauce begins to thicken, 4 to 6 minutes. Remove sauce from heat and stir in salt, paprika, black pepper, and grated onion. Pour into large bowl and cool to room temperature.

3. Heat olive oil in frying pan over medium heat. Add mushrooms and cook until softened and lightly browned, 5 to 7 minutes. Cook carrots in boiling water about 10 minutes, or until tender; drain. For filling, fold chicken, mushrooms, carrots, and peas into reserved sauce.

4. Set oven rack in middle position. Preheat oven to 400°F. Line 14-inch by 16-inch baking sheet with foil, shiny side up.

5. Add filling to 9-inch ovenproof glass pie plate. Add crust on top and crimp edges. Cut 6 decorative slits. Brush crust and edges with beaten egg.

6. Place pie on prepared baking sheet and bake 30 minutes, or until crust is golden brown and filling is bubbling. Cover pie with foil if crust browns too quickly. Cut into wedges and serve immediately. Cover leftovers with wax paper and store in refrigerator.

Anna Morse's Lemon Chicken

ANNA MORSE WAS A MEMBER OF A *group of women who commuted daily from their Marblehead and Swampscott homes to Boston during the 1950s and 1960s. The friends enjoyed chatting and exchanging recipes during their train rides and referred to themselves as The Railroad Club. Eventually they formed an investment club. Anne Kemelman, who was one of the club's members, gave us the background for this recipe.*

1. Coat bottom and sides of 9-inch by 13-inch ovenproof glass baking dish with vegetable spray. If using metal baking pan, line it with foil, shiny side up, and coat with vegetable spray. Rinse chicken under cold running water and pat dry with paper towels. Place lemon juice in shallow bowl. Dip chicken in lemon juice, place on platter, and set aside. Pour leftover lemon juice into prepared pan.

2. Place flour, salt, and paprika in plastic bag. Add chicken, seal, and shake to coat with flour. Place chicken in strainer and tap over sink to remove excess flour. Set aside.

3. Set oven rack in middle position. Preheat oven to 375°F.

4. Melt olive oil and butter in large heavy frying pan over medium heat. Add chicken and cook until both sides are golden brown. Remove chicken to prepared baking dish and scatter lemon slices over. Sprinkle with brown sugar.

5. Pour chicken stock into frying pan set over medium heat and simmer, scraping with wooden spoon to retrieve all of the browned bits clinging to bottom of pan. Cook until slightly thickened. Pour sauce into corner of baking pan, being careful not to disrupt lemon slices and brown sugar topping. Gently shake pan to distribute sauce over bottom. Cover pan with foil and bake until chicken is cooked through, about 30 minutes for boneless, skinless chicken breasts, 40 to 45 minutes for bone-in pieces of chicken. Baste with pan juices at least once during cooking. Serve Lemon Chicken on a bed of Saffron Rice (page 199).

6 to 8 bone-in chicken pieces, or 4 large boneless, skinless chicken breasts

5 tablespoons lemon juice

1/3 cup flour

1 1/2 teaspoons salt

1/2 teaspoon paprika

3 tablespoons extra-virgin olive oil

2 tablespoons butter, softened to room temperature

2 lemons, sliced 1/8- to 1/4-inch thick

3 tablespoons firmly packed brown sugar

1 cup low-sodium chicken stock

Reta Corbett's Wild Rice and Chicken Casserole

{ 1 9 4 0 s }

MAKES 4 SERVINGS

1 cup wild rice

3 cups cubed (½-inch cubes) cooked chicken

1 teaspoon salt

½ teaspoon coarsely ground black pepper

½ cup butter, softened to room temperature

½ cup flour

2 cups milk

2 cups low-sodium chicken stock

1½ cups toasted slivered almonds

ELINOR JENNINGS GAVE US RETA'S RECIPE FOR *Wild Rice and Chicken Casserole 40 years ago. It is a very fancy-sounding dish that's easy to make and looks as if you've been in the kitchen all afternoon. Wild rice is now more available than it used to be, and it's a nice ingredient to have on your pantry shelf.*

1. Cook wild rice in boiling water according to package directions, undercooking it slightly.
2. Season chicken with salt and pepper.
3. Melt butter in saucepan over low heat. Add flour and whisk until blended. Cook, stirring, 1 minute. Add milk and chicken stock. Increase heat to medium and cook, stirring constantly, until sauce starts to thicken and small bubbles form around edges, 4 to 6 minutes. Season to taste with salt and pepper.
4. Set oven rack in middle position. Preheat oven to 400°F. Coat 9-inch by 13-inch ovenproof glass baking dish with vegetable spray.
5. To assemble casserole: Spread one-third of wild rice over bottom of prepared baking dish. Cover with one-third of chicken and one-third of sauce. Repeat twice more to use all of the rice, chicken, and sauce. Sprinkle with almonds. Bake, uncovered, 30 to 35 minutes, or until bubbling. Cover with foil if almonds brown too quickly. Serve immediately. Store leftovers in covered container in refrigerator.

Miniature enamelware bucket and bowl, German, late 19th century

Rose Howard's Cheese Frittata

MAKES 4 SERVINGS

{ *1950s* }

This recipe was originally called Cheese Fondue, *but we found we couldn't dip anything in it. Not light enough to be a soufflé, it was almost a crustless quiche. This is actually a substantial baked luncheon dish, similar to an omelet, closer to a frittata, and great served with a touch of sour cream and some chopped fresh tarragon. You'll need your whisk for this recipe. Another suggestion from the file of The Church Lady from Mansfield, Ohio.*

1 cup milk

4 ounces sharp cheddar cheese, grated

1 tablespoon butter, softened to room temperature

1 cup soft bread crumbs (see "How to Make Soft Bread Crumbs" on page 241)

3 eggs, separated

½ teaspoon salt

1. Set oven rack in middle position. Preheat oven to 350°F. Butter 1½-quart ovenproof glass or ceramic baking dish or coat with vegetable spray.

2. Scald milk in heavy saucepan over medium heat, stirring with wooden spoon, until small bubbles form around edges. Remove saucepan from heat, add cheese and butter, and whisk until smooth. Place over low heat and whisk in bread crumbs. Remove pan from heat.

3. Whisk egg yolks in small bowl. Pour small amount of cheese mixture into bowl with yolks and whisk quickly to temper. Return yolks to pan with cheese mixture and whisk until thoroughly combined. Add salt and remove from heat.

4. Beat egg whites in bowl of standing mixer fitted with whisk attachment until soft peaks form. Do not overbeat. Add about one-fourth of beaten whites to cheese mixture and stir gently to combine. Fold in remaining whites. Pour batter into prepared dish and bake 40 minutes, or until tester inserted in middle comes out clean. Serve immediately. Store leftovers wrapped in wax paper in refrigerator. Reheat in low oven.

TIPS & TOUCHES

- Mixing a small amount of the egg whites into the batter and then folding in the rest of the egg whites makes the combining easier.

Miniature enamelware pot, American, early 1900s

Mama's Pie Crust Pizza with Mushroom Tomato Sauce

{ 1950s }

FOR MUSHROOM TOMATO SAUCE

3 tablespoons extra-virgin olive oil, divided

1 cup thinly sliced onion

1½ cups diced green bell pepper

2 cloves garlic, minced

1 tablespoon butter, softened

12 ounces white mushrooms

1 (29-ounce) can tomato puree

2 tablespoons tomato paste

½ cup water

2 tablespoons red wine vinegar

¼ cup firmly packed brown sugar

¼ teaspoon coarsely ground black pepper

¼ teaspoon dried oregano

¼ teaspoon dried thyme

½ teaspoon salt

FOR CRUST

2½ cups flour

½ teaspoon salt

½ teaspoon dried oregano

½ cup butter, softened

½ cup solid vegetable shortening, chilled

¼ cup ice water

FOR TOPPING

Mushroom Tomato Sauce

6 ounces American or cheddar cheese, shredded

1 teaspoon dried oregano

BECAUSE WE KEPT A KOSHER HOME, OUR *mother tried to reproduce commercial pizza without using any meat. Her dough was the one she used for her pie crust. The topping was simply canned tomato soup, shredded American cheese, and a dusting of Italian seasoning. We've added a quick Mushroom Tomato Sauce.*

1. To make sauce: Heat 2 tablespoons of the oil in Dutch oven over medium heat. Add onion and bell pepper and cook 5 to 7 minutes. Add garlic and cook 1 minute. Remove vegetables to bowl. Add remaining 1 tablespoon oil and butter to pot and sauté mushrooms until softened, 5 to 7 minutes. Drain mushrooms and add to bowl with other vegetables.

2. Add tomato purée, tomato paste, and water to pot and stir over medium heat to combine. Stir in vinegar, brown sugar, black pepper, oregano, thyme, and salt. Add vegetables and cook, stirring, until sauce just starts to boil. Reduce heat to low and simmer until sauce thickens, at least 15 minutes. Let cool before using.

3. To make crust: Place flour, salt, and oregano in bowl of food processor fitted with metal blade. Pulse 3 times to mix. Add butter and shortening and pulse until crumbly. Add ice water. Pulse until mixture comes together. Remove dough from food processor and divide into quarters.

4. Set oven rack in middle position. Heat oven to 400°F. Line bottom and sides of 14-inch by 17-inch baking sheet or 17-inch by 11-inch jelly roll pan with foil, shiny side up, and coat with vegetable spray. Working with one quarter at a time, pat dough into pan, making sure dough reaches into edges and corners. Crimp edges of dough with tines of salad fork.

5. To add topping: Spoon sauce, a few tablespoons at a time, onto dough, and spread evenly with spatula. A small amount of sauce may be left over. Distribute cheese evenly over top. Sprinkle with oregano. Bake 25 to 30 minutes, or until edges of crust are light brown and cheese is bubbling.

Onion and Olive Tart

MAKES 4 MAIN-COURSE SERVINGS;
6 TO 8 FIRST-COURSE SERVINGS

THIS RECIPE MADE US REWRITE THAT OLD *saying to "Good things come in big packages." The original recipe made enough Onion and Olive Tart for an army, so we reduced the ingredients until we came up with a delightful little tart, just enough for a small gathering of family and very good friends. Smaller slices are wonderful for appetizers, and large slices make a good main course for lunch with a salad of crisp greens. Manuscript cookbooks of the 1950s often contained recipes suitable for quantity cooking.*

1. To prepare crust: Coat 8-inch round tart pan with vegetable spray. Roll out pastry dough. Fit dough into bottom of tart pan and trim, leaving $^3/_4$-inch overhang. Fold overhang inward and press against side of pan. Chill in refrigerator while you make filling.

2. To make filling: Heat butter and oil in frying pan over medium heat. Add onion and cook, stirring with wooden spoon, until translucent, 5 to 7 minutes. Remove pan from heat. Add garlic, salt, pepper, $^1/_2$ teaspoon of the thyme leaves, flour, olives, and cheese and stir to combine.

3. In separate bowl, beat 2 of the eggs. Add small amount of onion mixture and stir quickly to temper eggs. Add remaining onion mixture and stir to combine. Allow filling to cool.

4. Set oven rack in middle position. Preheat oven to 350°F. Line 14-inch by 16-inch baking sheet with foil, shiny side up.

5. Add cooled filling to tart pan. Beat remaining egg and brush onto edges of pastry shell. Place tart on prepared baking sheet and bake 35 to 40 minutes, or until top is set. Sprinkle with remaining $^1/_2$ teaspoon fresh thyme leaves, cut into wedges, and serve immediately. Store leftovers covered with wax paper in refrigerator. Reheat in low oven.

Pastry for single-crust pie, chilled
(see Sheila's Savory Pie Crust
on page 306)

FOR FILLING

2 tablespoons butter, softened to
room temperature

2 tablespoons extra-virgin olive oil

2 cups finely chopped onion

1 clove garlic, minced

$^1/_4$ teaspoon salt

$^1/_4$ teaspoon coarsely ground
black pepper

1 teaspoon fresh thyme
leaves, divided

2 tablespoons flour

$^1/_2$ cup black, brined calamata
olives, pitted, or pimento-
stuffed green olives, chopped

$^3/_4$ cup grated Parmesan cheese

3 eggs, divided

TIPS & TOUCHES

- You might want to choose a square or rectangular tart pan for a different presentation.

Susanne Simpson's Apple Puff-Pancake

{ *1960s* }

MAKES 6 SERVINGS

6 eggs

1½ cups milk

1 cup flour

¼ cup sugar

1 teaspoon vanilla

¾ teaspoon salt

½ teaspoon cinnamon

½ cup butter, softened to room temperature

2 Granny Smith apples, peeled, cored, and sliced

3 tablespoons firmly packed brown sugar

Tips & Touches

- Any firm baking apple can be used.
- Do not overbeat batter.
- Try serving with a little sour cream on the side.

THIS LIVING RECIPE PRODUCES AN INTRIGUING DISH *suitable for brunch or lunch. Although the puffy edges are very much like a popover, the center tastes like an omelet filled with cinnamon and baked apples. This recipe came to Massachusetts via Susanne's friends in Michigan and Pennsylvania. We used a 12-inch quiche dish, and we got wonderful results.*

1. Set oven rack in middle position. Preheat oven to 425°F. Coat 12-inch ovenproof fluted quiche dish with butter or vegetable spray.

2. Mix eggs, milk, flour, sugar, vanilla, salt, and cinnamon in large bowl with wooden spoon. Batter will be slightly lumpy. Set aside.

3. Melt butter in prepared quiche dish in oven. This should take about 3 minutes. Remove dish from oven and tilt pan to coat bottom with butter. Arrange apple slices over bottom of dish in spiral fashion. Return to oven and heat about 5 minutes, or until butter sizzles. (Do not let butter or apples brown.) Remove dish from oven and immediately pour in batter. Sprinkle with brown sugar. Bake 20 to 25 minutes, or until pancake is puffed and lightly browned. Serve immediately. Apple pancake is best served the day it is made. Store leftovers loosely covered with wax paper in refrigerator.

Toy kitchen utensils, American, early 20th century

Aunt Ida's Apple Cranberry Noodle Pudding

MAKES 8 TO 10 SERVINGS

{ *1940s* }

THIS RECIPE CAME FROM AUNT IDA KATZIFF'S *recipe file. It is actually a kugel, one of those Eastern European dishes that contain layers of noodles, fruit, and butter. There's no cheese in this pudding, which can be eaten as a main dish, a snack, or a dessert. The recipe is brief and to the point and was probably taken down over the telephone from one of Ida's four sisters, or from her good friend, Dorothy Lerman, who was a magnificent home cook into her 90s.*

1. Set oven rack in middle position. Preheat oven to 350°F. Coat 9-inch by 13-inch ovenproof glass baking dish with vegetable spray.

2. To make pudding: Cook noodles in large pot of boiling water for 7 to 10 minutes, or until just tender. Drain noodles and rinse under cold water. Place noodles in large bowl. Add melted butter, ¼ cup of the sugar, and 1 teaspoon of the cinnamon. Whisk eggs with pineapple juice to blend, add to noodles, and stir to combine. Set aside.

3. Mix remaining 1 teaspoon of cinnamon with remaining ¼ cup sugar and toss with apples in another bowl.

4. Spread half of noodles in prepared baking dish. Add all of the apples in an even layer. Spread cranberry sauce over apples. Sprinkle evenly with walnuts. Layer remaining noodles on top.

5. To make topping: Toss melted butter with walnuts to coat and scatter over top of pudding. Sprinkle with brown sugar. Bake 35 to 45 minutes, or until pudding is bubbling and top is golden brown. Serve warm or at room temperature. Store leftovers in clean dish covered with wax paper in refrigerator.

FOR PUDDING

1 (12-ounce) package egg noodles

¾ cup butter, melted

½ cup sugar, divided

2 teaspoons cinnamon, divided

4 eggs

1½ cups pineapple juice

3 apples (about 1½ pounds total), peeled, cored, and sliced ¼-inch thick

1 (16-ounce) can whole cranberry sauce

¾ cup toasted walnuts, chopped

FOR TOPPING

2 tablespoons butter, melted

½ cup toasted walnuts, finely chopped

¼ cup firmly packed brown sugar

Billionaire's Macaroni and Cheese

{ *1 9 5 0 s* }

1 pound elbow macaroni

¼ cup butter, softened to room temperature

¼ cup flour

2 cups milk

8 ounces extra-sharp cheddar cheese, grated (2¼ cups)

1 teaspoon salt

1 teaspoon coarsely ground black pepper

1 teaspoon paprika

2 tablespoons grated onion

3 eggs, beaten

1 cup whole milk ricotta

1 cup half-and-half

8 ounces provolone cheese, cut in strips

FOR TOPPING

¼ cup butter, melted

1½ cups soft bread crumbs (see "How to Make Soft Bread Crumbs" on page 241)

5 ounces Parmesan cheese, grated (1¾ cups)

TIPS & TOUCHES

- This dish can be made one day ahead and kept refrigerated before baking.
- This is a great buffet dish.

THIS RECIPE CAME FROM THE MOTHER OF *one of "The Girls," our first customers when we started buying and selling antiques more than 35 years ago. The Girls shared an apartment in a large ornate building in Cambridge, called The Lowell. They invited us to lunch and served us Millionaire's Macaroni and Cheese on unmatched plates at a card table. We had a wonderful time eating this rich, savory dish, but we've changed its name because of inflation.*

1. Cook macaroni in large pot of boiling water for 5 to 7 minutes, or until still slightly firm. Drain and rinse under cold water. Transfer to large bowl.

2. Melt butter in heavy-bottomed saucepan over low heat. Remove pan from heat, add flour, and stir with wooden spoon until completely combined to make a roux. Set pan over medium heat and cook roux until little bubbles form around edges, 1 to 2 minutes. Remove pan from heat and add milk, stirring to blend. Return pan to heat and cook, stirring constantly, until thickened. Off the heat, add cheddar cheese, salt, pepper, paprika, and onion. Stir until cheese melts and sauce is smooth. If cheese doesn't melt completely, stir gently over low heat until melted.

3. Fold cheese sauce into cooled macaroni with spatula. Whisk eggs with ricotta and add to bowl with macaroni. Add half-and-half and stir until combined.

4. Set oven rack in middle position. Preheat oven to 350°F. Coat 9-inch by 13-inch ovenproof glass baking dish with vegetable spray.

5. Place half of macaroni mixture in prepared baking dish and smooth the top. Cover with strips of provolone. Top with remaining macaroni and smooth.

6. To make topping: Mix melted butter, bread crumbs, and Parmesan cheese. Sprinkle topping evenly over macaroni. Cover dish with foil and bake 30 minutes. Remove foil and continue baking another 10 to 15 minutes, or until macaroni is bubbling and top is nicely browned. Serve at once. Store leftovers in covered container in refrigerator.

Welsh Rarebit

{ *1930s* }

2 tablespoons butter, softened to room temperature

2 tablespoons flour

2 cups milk

2 teaspoons dry mustard

¾ teaspoon salt

¼ teaspoon coarsely ground black pepper

⅛ teaspoon cayenne pepper

3 cups grated American or cheddar cheese

2 eggs, beaten

¼ teaspoon chopped, brined hot peppers (optional)

TIPS & TOUCHES

- You can substitute 1 teaspoon of prepared mustard for the dry mustard.
- Adjust seasonings to taste.

MAKES 4 CUPS

THIS IS ONE OF THE FIRST RECIPES *Marilynn learned to prepare in cooking class at Winthrop Jr. High. This version of Welsh Rarebit came from the manuscript cookbook of a lady who liked to entertain and who served roast lamb and blueberry pie to the minister. Welsh Rarebit (or Rabbit) is a tangy cheese sauce served over toast or crackers, perfect for a luncheon dish for the ladies or a snack for the gentlemen. Some rarebits call for beer or ale, but this one is made with milk. The only clue to the origin of our recipe is the word Proctors, which might be the name of the hostess who served it to the lady who transcribed it.*

1. Melt butter in heavy-bottomed 2-quart saucepan over low heat. Whisk flour into butter to combine. Increase heat to medium and cook mixture for 1 minute, stirring with wooden spoon, to make a roux. Add milk and cook, stirring constantly, until sauce begins to thicken and small bubbles form around edges, 4 to 6 minutes. Do not overcook.

2. Add mustard, salt, pepper, cayenne pepper, and cheese and stir briskly. Cook over low heat until cheese is completely melted. Remove from heat.

3. Whisk about ¼ cup of the sauce into beaten eggs to temper them. Return egg mixture to rarebit and whisk to combine. Set pan over low heat and continue cooking, whisking constantly, until eggs are cooked and rarebit is heated through, about 2 minutes. Do not boil. Add peppers if desired. Serve Welsh Rarebit on toast or Pilot crackers, a crunchy "Down East" favorite in New England.

Basic White Sauce

MAKES APPROXIMATELY 1¼ CUPS

{ 1 9 5 0 s }

WHITE SAUCE IS THE FIRST SAUCE STUDENTS *were taught how to make in the cooking classes of the 1950s. It is the base for several other sauces; we use a variation on it to prepare a cheese sauce, Welsh Rarebit, and our version of the ever-popular casserole standby, Mushroom Soup. Be sure to try this recipe if you prefer not to use canned mushroom soup in your cooking.*

1. Melt butter in heavy-bottomed 2-quart saucepan over low heat. Whisk flour into butter to combine. Increase heat to medium and cook mixture for 1 minute, stirring with wooden spoon or whisk.
2. Add milk and stir to combine. Add salt and pepper and cook, stirring constantly, until sauce starts to thicken and small bubbles form around edges, 4 to 6 minutes. Do not overcook.

2 tablespoons butter, softened to room temperature

2 tablespoons flour

1 cup milk

Salt and coarsely ground black pepper to taste

TIPS & TOUCHES

- Add a little more milk at the end for a thinner sauce.

➤➤ HOMEMADE "CANNED" ◄◄
CREAM OF MUSHROOM SOUP

2 tablespoons butter, softened to room temperature

3 tablespoons flour

1 cup milk

⅛ teaspoon salt

¼ teaspoon freshly ground white pepper

¼ teaspoon onion powder

½ cup white mushrooms, sliced and fried in butter

1. Melt butter in heavy-bottomed 2-quart saucepan over low heat. Whisk flour into butter to combine. Increase heat to medium and cook mixture for 1 minute, stirring with wooden spoon.
2. Add milk and stir to combine. Add salt, white pepper, and onion powder and cook, stirring constantly, until sauce starts to thicken and small bubbles form around edges, 4 to 6 minutes. Do not overcook. Add a little more milk at the end for thinner sauce.
3. Remove pan from heat and fold in mushrooms. **Makes approximately 1¾ cups**

CHAPTER 8

SWEET FINALES

We have to admit that we are partial to dessert. If we could have it three times a day, that would not be too often for us. We even confess to eating dessert for breakfast, especially after a party the night before. We relish tales of a restaurant in Pennsylvania that prides itself on serving dessert at the beginning of the meal, and we fondly remember a venerable chain of department stores that allowed male customers two desserts when they ate at its in-store tearoom. Dessert can be as simple as a plate of cookies or as elaborate as a Red Velvet Cake decorated with mounds of vanilla frosting and toasted pecans. It is the sweet conclusion to a meal—that sublime time when the table is cleared, the coffee is put on to perk, and another pitcher of sweet iced tea is passed around.

Sometimes dessert is served as a buffet, and guests circle the sweet spread, carefully considering each offering, or defying custom, as our Uncle Julius did, and sitting down at the buffet table to enjoy all that it displayed.

Baking has always been more precise than cooking when it comes to measurements, oven temperatures, and times, so it is no surprise that dessert is often more of a challenge than any other part of the meal. It also offers the opportunity for the home cook to express her creativity with that extra swirl of frosting, a rosette of whipped cream, or a sprinkle of toasted coconut. It does not surprise us that heirloom recipes are often referred to as "rules" because of the necessity to abide by the regulations of ingredients and instructions.

Dessert knows its place. It is an important part of the ritual of friends and family coming together for the comfort of a meal and spirited conversation, especially at the holidays. It is defined by the Coconut Pie with the flakey fluted crust, the tender crumb of a Milk Chocolate Pound Cake, or the soft and comforting layers of a Sweet Potato Pudding. The appetizer may stimulate; the soup may warm; the main dish may satisfy; but the dessert is what sweetly completes the meal.

As we made our culinary journey through our extensive collection of manuscript cookbooks, we were not surprised to find that the appeal of dessert is universal. Many of the same desserts appear in these handwritten recipes, but they are personally interpreted by home cooks. Some women have transcribed a whole catalog of desserts that are part of their repertoire. A woman from North Carolina showed herself to be an outstanding dessert maker with her recipes for Green Tomato Pie, Buttermilk Cake, and Shoofly Pie. Two well-loved women in service generously share their

Silverplate tea caddy, English, early 1900s; tea strainer, nut cup, and sugar tongs, American, early 20th century

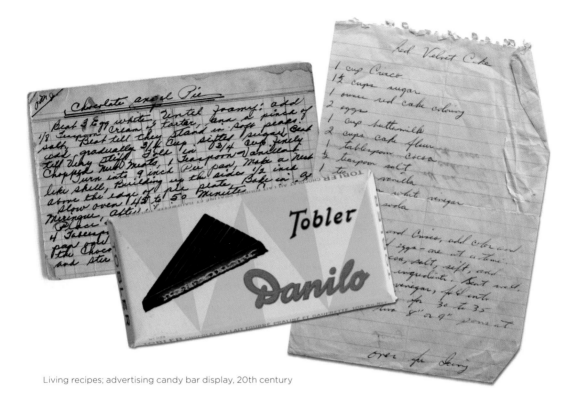

Living recipes; advertising candy bar display, 20th century

recipes for Chocolate Angel Pie and Lemon Angel Pie with the family and friends of their employers.

We learn the story of Gertrude Huerkamp Woods, the ingenious young woman who raised her five children on the family farm, sketched ladies' hats for her father's dry goods store, went to the St. Louis World's Fair on her honeymoon, and baked a wonderful steamed pecan cake, treasured for its abundance of nuts and raisins and its generous ration of bourbon. Mrs. Woods stored her cake in a black cast-iron pot, wrapped in a whiskey-soaked tea towel to mellow.

In this chapter, we salute those who bring forth the birthday cake glowing with candles; the creators of that architecturally faulty but delicious dessert, the Blueberry Buckle; and two enterprising women from Marblehead, Massachusetts, who capture forever the symbol of the maritime heritage of their Northeastern home with a captivating spicy molasses cookie in the shape of a whale.

Often, at the end of a gathering, guests who are comfortable with one another's company linger to relate stories that have been told many times before. As the remnants of dessert are quietly removed, there are some who stealthily palm a cookie, nibble a leftover morsel of cake, or munch a forgotten piece of crust. For them, the company and dessert are both sweet.

We encourage you to add some sweetness to your own lives by baking these desserts in your own kitchen.

Red Velvet Cake

{ *1930s* }

MAKES 8 SLICES

FOR CAKE

2 cups cake flour

½ teaspoon salt

1 tablespoon cocoa

1 cup solid vegetable shortening

1½ cups sugar

2 eggs

1 (1-ounce) bottle red food coloring

1 teaspoon vanilla

1 cup buttermilk

1 teaspoon baking soda

1 tablespoon vinegar

FOR ICING

1 cup milk

¼ cup cake flour

¼ teaspoon salt

1 cup butter, softened to room temperature

1 cup sugar

1 teaspoon vanilla

1½ cups toasted pecans, coarsely chopped (optional)

TIPS & TOUCHES

- Divide batter equally among or between prepared pans. Using a kitchen scale to weigh pans of batter is helpful.
- Wearing disposable gloves when adding red food coloring will keep hands clean.

THIS IS THE SOUTHERN DESSERT. *Versions of this cake have made their appearance in the boutique bakeries of New York and Boston. We use vegetable shortening and the bottle of red food coloring that were originally called for in this recipe from The Lady from North Carolina. You will not taste the red food coloring. We have heard that some bakers have turned to beets to color Red Velvet Cake.*

1. Set oven rack in middle position. Preheat oven to 350°F. Line the bottoms of three 7-inch cake pans or two 9-inch cake pans with parchment paper and coat with vegetable spray. Dust with flour and tap out excess.

2. To make cake: Sift together flour, salt, and cocoa and set aside.

3. Cream shortening and sugar in bowl of standing mixer fitted with paddle attachment until soft and fluffy. Add eggs one at a time. Add red food coloring. Add vanilla to buttermilk. Add sifted dry ingredients to batter alternately with buttermilk, beating after each addition. Add baking soda to vinegar and fold into batter.

4. Place batter in prepared pans and bake 30 to 35 minutes, or until tester inserted into middle comes out clean. Place on rack and allow to cool 20 minutes. Run butter knife gently around edges and invert cakes onto second rack. Let cool completely.

5. To make icing: Whisk milk, flour, and salt in heavy-bottomed saucepan until combined. Stir constantly with wooden spoon over medium heat until thickened, about 2 minutes. Transfer to bowl and allow to cool.

6. Cream butter and sugar in bowl of standing mixer fitted with paddle attachment until fluffy. Add vanilla. Add cooled milk and flour mixture and beat on highest speed for 5 minutes, or until thick and creamy.

7. Place bottom layer of cake on cake round lined with 4 small pieces of wax paper, and spread frosting over top of this cake layer with offset spatula. Set top cake layer in position and frost top and sides. (If using three 7-inch layers, ice top of bottom and middle layer only, add third layer, and frost top and sides.) Immediately cover sides of cake with chopped pecans, if using. Store under cake dome or loosely wrapped in wax paper at room temperature.

Milk Chocolate Pound Cake

MAKES 8 SLICES

{ 1 9 5 0 s }

THIS IS ANOTHER RECIPE FROM THE MANUSCRIPT *cookbook of The Lady from North Carolina. We substituted rum for the vanilla extract because we found this milky chocolate cake reminded us of the particular milk chocolate rum-flavored candy served at our mother's bridge parties. These candies came in star shapes, and we always managed to sneak a few before the ladies came to play bridge. Use 8-ounce milk chocolate candy bars for the cake and for the frosting.*

1. Set oven rack in middle position. Heat oven to 325°F. Line bottoms of three 7-inch cake pans with parchment paper and coat with vegetable spray. Dust with flour and tap out excess.

2. To make cake: Sift together flour and salt and set aside. Cream butter and sugar in bowl of standing mixer fitted with paddle attachment until fluffy. Add eggs one at a time, blending well after each addition. Add melted chocolate, chocolate syrup, and rum and beat to combine. Add dry ingredients alternately with buttermilk. Fold in pecans. Place batter in prepared pans and bake 45 minutes, or until tester inserted into cake comes out dry. Cool in pans on rack for 15 minutes before turning out of pans.

3. To make frosting: Place confectioners' sugar and salt in bowl of standing mixer fitted with paddle attachment. Add butter and shortening and cream until fluffy. Add rum and water or milk and beat until combined. Add melted chocolate and beat until fluffy. Thin with a little milk if necessary to achieve a better spreading consistency.

4. Place bottom layer of cake on cake round lined with 4 small pieces of wax paper to catch drips. Spread frosting over top of cake layer with offset spatula. Set middle cake layer in position and frost top. Top with top layer and frost top and sides. Store under cake dome or loosely wrapped in wax paper in refrigerator.

FOR CAKE

2½ cups flour

⅛ teaspoon salt

1 cup butter, softened to room temperature

1½ cups sugar

4 eggs

8 ounces milk chocolate, chopped and melted

½ cup plus 1 tablespoon chocolate syrup

2 teaspoons rum

1 cup buttermilk

1 cup toasted pecans, chopped

FOR FROSTING

4 cups confectioners' sugar, sifted

Pinch of salt

½ cup butter, softened to room temperature

½ cup solid vegetable shortening

2 teaspoons rum

2 tablespoons water or milk

8 ounces milk chocolate, chopped and melted

TIPS & TOUCHES

- Melt chocolate in a microwave at 10-second intervals or in a double boiler.
- Cake can also be baked in a 10-inch by 4¼-inch tube pan for 60 minutes and dusted with confectioners' sugar.

Mrs. Fleisher's Almond Cake

{ *1907* }

MAKES 8 TO 10 SLICES

FOR CAKE

8 ounces (1½ cups) whole almonds

1 cup sugar, divided

6 eggs, separated

1 teaspoon grated lemon zest

Pinch of ground cloves

FOR FILLING

¾ cup apricot jam

FOR CHOCOLATE GLAZE

½ cup plus 2 tablespoons sugar

½ cup water

4 ounces bittersweet
   chocolate, chopped

WE DISCOVERED THIS RECIPE IN THE MANUSCRIPT *cookbook of Mrs. Fleisher of Philadelphia, Pennsylvania. She wrote the recipe on the back of an invitation to introduce Miss Edna Weil to society. The party was scheduled for Saturday, January 19, 1907. Because of the quality of the paper used for the invitation, the recipe has been preserved.*

1. Set oven rack in middle position. Preheat oven to 350°F. Coat 9-inch springform pan with vegetable spray. Cut parchment paper or wax paper liner to fit bottom of pan. Insert liner and spray again. Dust pan with flour and tap out excess.

2. To make cake: Place almonds and ½ cup of the sugar in bowl of food processor fitted with metal blade. Grind until texture is fine.

3. Place egg whites in bowl of standing mixer fitted with whisk attachment. Beat until stiff but not dry.

4. Place egg yolks and remaining ½ cup sugar in bowl of standing mixer fitted with paddle attachment. Beat until light and fluffy. Add lemon zest and cloves. Add almond mixture. Pour one-fourth of beaten egg whites into almond batter and mix to lighten. Gently but thoroughly fold in remaining egg whites.

5. Pour mixture into springform pan. Smooth top gently with offset spatula. Bake 35 to 45 minutes, or until tester inserted in center of cake comes out clean. Cool on rack 15 minutes. Run butter knife gently around edges and remove sides of pan. Allow to cool another 30 minutes. Invert cake onto another rack, remove bottom of pan and paper liner, and invert back onto first rack. Allow to cool completely.

6. To make filling: Warm apricot jam in saucepan over low heat. Transfer jam to bowl of mini food processor fitted with metal blade, or put through mesh strainer. Process until smooth.

7. To make chocolate glaze: Combine sugar and water in heavy saucepan over medium heat and bring to a boil. Remove from heat. Add chocolate, stirring constantly until chocolate is melted. Return pan to medium heat and continue stirring until mixture

returns to a boil, thickens, and becomes shiny, about 3 minutes. Cool 10 minutes. The glaze will thicken further upon cooling.

8. Split cake into 2 horizontal layers using serrated knife. Place bottom layer on cake round. Place 4 strips of wax paper or parchment paper under edges of cake to protect plate. Spread filling on bottom cake layer with offset spatula. Set top cake layer in position. Pour glaze over top of cake and allow to run down sides. If sides are not adequately covered, spread glaze with offset spatula. Let glaze set. Place cake, uncovered, in refrigerator. About 15 minutes before serving, carefully remove strips of wax paper and bring to room temperature. Store loosely wrapped in wax paper in refrigerator.

Mrs. Chubb's Nut Cake

{ 1 9 2 0 s }

FOR CAKE

1 cup toasted whole almonds

1 cup sugar, divided

2 cups flour

1 teaspoon baking powder

1 teaspoon salt

1/4 teaspoon nutmeg

1/8 teaspoon cloves

1 cup butter

4 eggs, separated

3 teaspoons grated lemon zest

4 tablespoons lemon juice

1/2 teaspoon lemon oil or
   lemon extract

2 teaspoons vanilla

3/4 cup milk

FOR TOPPING

3 tablespoons untoasted
   slivered almonds

3 tablespoons clear sanding sugar

THIS RECIPE CAME FROM THE MANUSCRIPT COOKBOOK *of an artist living in Cambridge, Massachusetts. She did not specify what type of nut to use in the cake, but the lemon-clove flavoring and toasted almonds make it resonate. This is a rich, dense cake with a crisp macaroon-like topping. The nuts in the topping brown and meld with the sanding sugar during baking.*

1. Set oven rack in middle position. Preheat oven to 350°F. Cut parchment paper or wax paper liner to fit bottom of 10-inch tube pan. Coat pan with vegetable spray. Insert liner, spray again, and dust with flour.

2. To make cake: Place toasted almonds and 2 tablespoons of the sugar in bowl of food processor fitted with metal blade. Pulse until texture resembles coarse meal.

3. Sift together flour, baking powder, salt, nutmeg, and cloves.

4. Cream butter and remaining 7/8 cup sugar in bowl of standing mixer fitted with paddle attachment. Add egg yolks two at a time. Add lemon zest, lemon juice, lemon oil, and vanilla and mix to combine. Add sifted dry ingredients alternately with milk, mixing after each addition until completely blended. Fold in almond mixture.

5. Place egg whites in another bowl of standing mixer fitted with whisk attachment. Beat until egg whites hold a firm peak. Fold egg whites into batter.

6. To add topping: Place batter in tube pan. Sprinkle almonds and sanding sugar on top of batter. Bake 50 to 55 minutes, or until tester inserted into cake comes out dry. Cool on rack completely before turning out of pan. Store loosely wrapped in wax paper at room temperature.

Gertrude Woods's Steamed Pecan Cake

{ *1 9 1 5* }

MAKES 12 TO 14 SLICES

2 tablespoons Wondra

¾ cup raisins

1 cup toasted pecans,
  coarsely chopped

1½ cups flour, divided

¾ teaspoon baking powder

¼ teaspoon salt

¾ teaspoon nutmeg

½ cup butter, softened to room
  temperature

½ cup firmly packed brown sugar

2 eggs, separated

¼ cup molasses

½ cup whiskey or grape juice

TIPS & TOUCHES

- Use Wondra for dusting mold.
- This is a very substantial cake, best enjoyed in thin slices.
- The aroma of the whiskey is very prevalent when the cake is removed from the steamer. Some of the whiskey will evaporate on cooling, but this is a very potent cake.

WE BELIEVE THAT THIS STEAMED PECAN CAKE *should come with a warning because of its high alcohol content. It makes a wonderful confection for the holiday season or any time you feel like a sophisticated treat. This recipe was handed down through the Woods-Drain families and comes from Cynthiana, Kentucky. During Prohibition, Mrs. Woods replaced the whiskey with grape juice. You can do the same or compromise with half grape juice and half whiskey. We also like this cake when it's mellowed for at least 2 weeks in the refrigerator.*

1. Liberally butter 6-cup mold or coat with vegetable spray; dust with Wondra and tap out excess. Prepare buttered parchment sheet to fit top of mold. Select covered pot large enough to accommodate mold with 2-inch clearance around sides. Set metal rack inside pot.

2. Place raisins and pecans in small bowl. Add 1 tablespoon of the flour and toss to coat. Set aside.

3. Sift remaining flour, baking powder, salt, and nutmeg into large bowl and set aside. Cream butter and brown sugar in bowl of standing mixer fitted with paddle attachment until fluffy. Add egg yolks and then molasses.

4. Add dry ingredients in 3 parts, alternating with whiskey or grape juice. With mixer running, add raisins and pecans and beat 30 seconds, or until they are evenly distributed throughout batter. (Or fold them in.) Beat egg whites until they form soft peaks and fold into batter.

5. Pour batter into prepared mold until no more than two-thirds full. Place buttered parchment round on top of mold. Fold 2 sheets of foil over open top and tie securely with kitchen string.

6. Set filled mold on rack in pot. Add water to come one-third of the way up sides of mold. Remove mold. Cover pot and bring water to a boil. Turn off heat, lift pot cover, and carefully place filled mold on rack. Cover pot. Adjust heat so that water simmers; do not let water come to a boil. Steam pudding 40 minutes, or until tester

✈ FEEDING A FRUITCAKE ✈

Every heirloom cook had a favorite recipe for a substantial cake laden with raisins, nuts, and candied peels. But some fruitcakes assumed a more adventuresome role when they became a secret avenue for consuming spirits. Not only did the batters for fruitcake call for outrageous amounts of whiskey or brandy but the finished cake, when cool, was often wrapped in brandy-soaked cheesecloth and squirreled away in a cold, dark place to season. Some home cooks even poured brandy or whiskey into holes they'd poked into their fruitcakes. The cakes were inspected periodically and the cheesecloth refreshed with more whiskey. This was called "feeding the cake." Faced with the restrictions of Prohibition, resourceful heirloom cooks resorted to using a less potent means of flavoring their cakes—grape juice. It was never the same, because they couldn't mellow them with alcohol, but with the repeal of Prohibition, home cooks once again fed their fruitcakes with spirits. It must be said that these well-fed fruitcakes were served in very thin slices.

inserted in middle comes out clean. Check water level periodically during steaming and add water as needed. *Do not let water boil out because a tightly covered mold could explode.*

7. Turn off heat. Remove mold carefully from steamer and place on cooling rack. Carefully remove foil and parchment from top of mold. Allow to cool on rack for 20 minutes. Cake should release easily when mold is inverted. If mold does not release cake easily, run butter knife around edges or let sit until cake begins to shrink away from sides of mold. Store cake loosely wrapped in wax paper, or wrapped in cheesecloth soaked in whiskey, in refrigerator.

Miss Emma Smith's War Cake

{1914 – 1918}

MAKES 16 SLICES

3 cups flour, sifted

2 cups plus 1 teaspoon hot water

2 cups brown sugar

2 tablespoons lard (or butter)

1 cup raisins

1 teaspoon salt

1 teaspoon cinnamon

½ teaspoon cloves

½ teaspoon nutmeg

2 teaspoons cocoa

1 teaspoon baking soda

THIS RECIPE IS A WAR CAKE, BORN *out of necessity, since it includes no eggs, butter, or milk. It's also an example of a recipe giving the marital status of the originator. Miss Smith's contemporary, Mrs. William Eaton, apparently added the 2 teaspoons of cocoa to the recipe. Also noted by Miss Smith, "This cake is better at the end of a week or even longer. It ripens as does all fruitcakes."*

1. Set oven rack in middle position. Preheat oven to 300°F. Line bottom and ends of 9-inch by 5-inch by 3-inch loaf pan with single strip of wax paper. Coat pan and wax paper liner with vegetable spray.

2. Add flour to bowl of standing mixer fitted with paddle attachment.

3. Add 2 cups of the hot water, brown sugar, lard, raisins, salt, cinnamon, cloves, nutmeg, and cocoa to large heavy-bottomed saucepan. Cook over medium heat, stirring with wooden spoon, until mixture begins to bubble. Boil 5 minutes, stirring constantly. Remove from heat and cool thoroughly. Dissolve baking soda in remaining 1 teaspoon hot water and add to syrup. Allow mixture to cool.

4. Add mixture to flour and beat until thoroughly blended. Place in loaf pan. Bake 45 minutes, or until tester inserted into cake comes out clean. Cool on rack for 15 minutes before removing from pan. Cake should be eaten at room temperature. Store leftover cake covered with paper towel and wax paper in refrigerator.

Buttermilk Cake

MAKES 16 SLICES

{ *1 9 4 0 s* }

THIS ALL-OCCASION CAKE FROM NORTH CAROLINA IS *easy to make and delicious. It's equally good dusted with confectioners' sugar or drizzled with Vanilla Icing. It can be baked in a tube pan or in multiple cake pans, lending itself to layers sandwiched with generous amounts of frosting. A salutation piped on top makes this an ideal birthday cake.*

1. Set oven rack in middle position. Preheat oven to 350°F. Coat bottom and sides ofa 10-inch by $4^{1}/_{4}$-inch tube pan with vegetable spray. Cut parchment paper liner to fit bottom of pan. Add liner and coat with vegetable spray. Dust pan with flour and tap out excess.

2. To make cake: Sift flour, salt, baking powder, and baking soda and set aside.

3. Cream butter and sugar in bowl of standing mixer fitted with paddle attachment. Add eggs one at a time. Add vanilla to buttermilk. Add dry ingredients alternately with buttermilk, beginning and ending with dry ingredients.

4. Place batter in prepared pan and bake 60 minutes, or until tester inserted into cake comes out dry. Cool in pan on rack for 15 minutes before removing from pan.

5. To make icing: Sift confectioners' sugar and salt into bowl. Add vanilla and whisk to combine. Add water 1 teaspoon at a time and whisk until smooth. Drizzle icing over cake. Store leftover cake wrapped in wax paper at room temperature.

FOR CAKE

3 cups cake flour

½ teaspoon salt

½ teaspoon baking powder

½ teaspoon baking soda

1 cup butter, softened to room temperature

2 cups sugar

3 eggs

1½ teaspoons vanilla

1 cup buttermilk

FOR VANILLA ICING

1 cup confectioners' sugar

Pinch of salt

2 teaspoons vanilla

5 teaspoons water

 TIPS & TOUCHES

- Buttermilk Cake can be baked in three 8-inch round pans for 40 to 45 minutes. It can be iced with your favorite frosting.

Fluffy White Cake

{ 1 9 4 0 s }

FOR CAKE

1 tablespoon lemon juice

1 cup milk

2¼ cups flour

2½ teaspoons baking powder

1 teaspoon salt

½ cup butter

1½ cups sugar, sifted

2 eggs

1 teaspoon vanilla

FOR CARAMEL ICING

3 cups confectioners' sugar

½ cup butter

½ cup Soft Caramel Sauce
   (see recipe on page 335)

1 cup sliced almonds, toasted

TIPS & TOUCHES

- Buttermilk can be substituted for soured milk.
- This batter can also be baked in two 7-inch pans. Line the pans with parchment paper and coat with vegetable spray, dust with flour, and tap out the excess. Bake approximately 35 to 45 minutes.
- The cake layers may be split to make a four-layer cake. Add another cup of confectioners' sugar and water as needed to the icing.

THIS WAS THE CAKE OUR MOTHER BAKED *for special celebrations and during the holidays. She would divide the white frosted cake in half and decorate one side in red and green and the other in blue and yellow. Holly and Chanukah candles shared equal placement on the top of the cake. Little did we know our mother was baking the first politically correct cake of the time!*

1. Set oven rack in middle position. Preheat oven to 350°F. Coat 10-inch springform pan with vegetable spray. Cut parchment paper or wax paper liner to fit bottom of pan. Insert liner and spray again. Dust pan with flour and tap out excess.

2. To make cake: Add lemon juice to milk and stir to combine. Set aside to sour.

3. Sift together flour, baking powder, and salt.

4. Place butter and sugar in bowl of standing mixer fitted with paddle attachment. Cream together until soft and fluffy. Add eggs one at a time. Add vanilla to sour milk. Add dry ingredients alternately with sour milk, beating after each addition.

5. Place batter in springform pan. Bake 35 to 45 minutes, or until tester inserted into cake comes out clean. Place on rack and allow to cool 30 minutes. Run butter knife gently around edges and invert cake onto second rack. Let cool completely.

6. To make caramel icing: Combine confectioners' sugar, butter, and Soft Caramel Sauce in bowl of standing mixer fitted with paddle attachment (or place in small bowl and mix by hand). Thin with water if necessary, 1 teaspoon at a time, to desired spreading consistency. Frost top and sides of cake with offset spatula. Immediately cover top and sides with sliced almonds. Store under cake dome or loosely wrapped in wax paper at room temperature.

Esther Pullman and Mary Brinkman's Irish Sponge Cake

MAKES 10 SLICES

{ *1950s* }

THE RECIPE FOR THIS IRISH SPONGE CAKE *came from Esther Pullman, who grew up in Purchase, New York. It was given to her by Mary Brinkman, an inspired Irish baker who made special cakes for family parties. The sublime sugar crust makes this sponge cake extraordinary.*

1¼ cups sugar, divided

4 eggs, separated

1 teaspoon vanilla

1 cup cake flour

1. Set oven rack in middle position. Preheat oven to 350°F. Coat 8-inch Bundt pan with vegetable spray. Dust sides and bottom of pan with 3 tablespoons of the sugar.

2. Beat egg yolks in bowl of standing mixer fitted with paddle attachment. Add ½ cup of the sugar and beat until thick, about 5 minutes.

3. Place egg whites in another bowl of standing mixer fitted with whisk attachment. Beat until stiff. Add ½ cup of the sugar and beat again until sugar is incorporated

4. Add egg yolks to egg whites. Add vanilla and continue beating with paddle attachment at medium speed until combined. Fold in cake flour.

5. Pour batter into Bundt pan. Sprinkle remaining 1 tablespoon sugar on top of batter. Bake 30 minutes, or until tester inserted in middle comes out clean. Cake should have a nice yellow color. Place on rack to cool. When completely cool, invert cake onto plate. Slice with sawing motion. Store under cake dome or loosely wrapped in wax paper at room temperature.

Reverend Brown's Cake

{ *1890s* }

FOR CAKE

2 cups flour

1 teaspoon baking soda

¼ teaspoon salt

½ teaspoon cinnamon

½ teaspoon allspice

½ teaspoon nutmeg

¼ teaspoon cloves

½ cup butter

2 cups brown sugar

3 eggs

1 cup buttermilk, or
    ½ cup buttermilk and
    ½ cup heavy cream

FOR TOPPING

1½ cups Soft Caramel Sauce
    (page 335)

⅓ cup golden raisins

WE DON'T KNOW WHO REVEREND BROWN WAS, *but he lent his name to this cake. Handwritten on a yellowed index card, this recipe from the late 19th century is representative of the type of baking done when the minister came to dinner. We don't know if Reverend Brown made this cake himself or whether he inspired the baker. It's a simple festive cake, and we suggest you bake and serve it when someone special comes to dinner.*

1. Set oven rack in middle position. Preheat oven to 350°F. Coat 9-inch springform pan with vegetable spray. Cut parchment paper or wax paper liner to fit bottom of pan. Coat liner with vegetable spray and dust entire pan with flour. Tap pan to remove excess flour.
2. To make cake: Sift together flour, baking soda, salt, cinnamon, allspice, nutmeg, and cloves.
3. Cream butter and brown sugar in bowl of standing mixer fitted with paddle attachment. Add eggs one at a time. Add sifted dry ingredients alternately with buttermilk and beat to combine.
4. Pour batter into springform pan. Bake 55 to 60 minutes, or until edges of cake pull away from pan and tester inserted into cake comes out clean. Cool on rack to room temperature.
5. To add topping: Warm Soft Caramel Sauce in microwave on low for 30 seconds. Pour over cooled cake and smooth top and sides with offset spatula. Sprinkle raisins on top of cake. Store under cake dome or loosely covered with wax paper at room temperature.

Auntie Dot's Dutch Apple Cake

{ *1 8 9 0* }

FOR CAKE

2 cups flour

1 tablespoon plus 1 teaspoon baking powder

¼ teaspoon salt

½ cup vegetable shortening

½ cup sugar

2 eggs

1 tablespoon vanilla

¾ cup milk

FOR TOPPING

2 tablespoons sugar

1 teaspoon cinnamon

3 apples, peeled and sliced ¼-inch thick

1½ tablespoons butter, cut into dice

TIPS & TOUCHES

* This is a very moist cake; it is best served the day it is made. This cake can be frozen once it has completely cooled.

THIS WAS THE CAKE THAT OUR MOTHER *put together when relatives and friends unexpectedly crossed our threshold. It was quick to make because the ingredients could be found easily in our pantry. It baked in 40 minutes, and the apples made the cake moist, almost like a Danish. A slice of Auntie Dot's Dutch Apple Cake is wonderful in the fall with a cup of strong black coffee.*

1. Set oven rack in middle position. Preheat oven to 375°F. Cut wax paper liner to fit bottom of 9-inch cake pan. Coat pan and liner with vegetable spray and dust with flour.

2. To make cake: Sift together flour, baking powder, and salt into mixing bowl.

3. Cream shortening and sugar in bowl of standing mixer fitted with paddle attachment. Add eggs and vanilla. Add sifted dry ingredients alternately with milk, mixing well after each addition. Pour batter into pan and spread evenly.

4. To make topping: Mix sugar and cinnamon in bowl. Arrange apple slices in 2 circles on top of batter. Press apples into batter and sprinkle with cinnamon sugar. Dot with butter.

5. Bake approximately 40 minutes, or until tester inserted into cake comes out clean. Cool on rack. Serve cake slightly warm with vanilla ice cream or whipped cream. Store covered with paper towel and wrapped in wax paper in refrigerator.

Dorset Apple Cake

{ 1940s }

MAKES 9 3-INCH SQUARES

THIS RECIPE WAS CAREFULLY TYPED WITH A *manual typewriter on a small scrap of paper. We've interpreted this traditional English recipe from Dorset, where Jane Austin and Thomas Hardy were born. Almost a scone but a little lighter, the flavors of the apples, spices, and lemon zest come together in this English cake. It's wonderful with a cup of India tea or black coffee or, for the more adventuresome, a glass of port.*

1. Set oven rack in middle position. Heat oven to 350°F. Cover bottom and sides of 9-inch by 9-inch metal pan with foil, shiny side up. Coat foil with butter or vegetable spray.

2. Toss apples, sugar, raisins, and lemon zest in bowl and set aside.

3. Sift flour, baking soda, salt, cinnamon, and nutmeg into large bowl. Work in butter with your fingers. Add vanilla to cream; add to batter and mix in with wooden spoon. Add beaten eggs one half at a time. Fold in apple-raisin mixture with spatula.

4. Place dough in prepared pan and smooth top with offset spatula. Sprinkle sanding sugar over top and bake 40 minutes, or until tester inserted into cake comes out clean. Place cake on rack in pan to cool. Cut into squares and serve warm or at room temperature. Store leftovers covered with wax paper in refrigerator.

3½ cups peeled, cored, and diced (½-inch) Granny Smith apples

½ cup sugar

½ cup golden raisins

Grated zest of 1 lemon

2 cups flour

2 teaspoons baking soda

½ teaspoon salt

¼ teaspoon cinnamon

¼ teaspoon nutmeg

½ cup cold butter, cut into dice

1 teaspoon vanilla

⅓ cup heavy cream

2 eggs, beaten

2 tablespoons coarse sanding sugar

TIPS & TOUCHES

- Use any firm cooking apple.
- Treat this dough like a scone dough—do not overwork.
- This cake is wonderful with a little whipped cream on the side.

Cast-iron apple peeler, American, early 1900s

Pineapple Upside-Down Cake

MAKES 16 SLICES

{1920s}

THIS IS THE CLOSEST WE COULD COME *to replicating the Pineapple Upside-Down Cake Elinor Jennings made for Marilynn's birthday in 1971. It was a memorable cake with syrupy candied fruit on top and a macaroon-like crumb. Elinor made her cake in a cast-iron frying pan, and it was so heavy, she had to ask her husband to turn it onto a rack for her.*

1. Set oven rack in middle position. Preheat oven to 350°F. Swirl melted butter in 9-inch cake pan, coating sides but allowing most of butter to settle on bottom of pan. Sprinkle brown sugar over bottom of pan.

2. Wipe pineapple slices dry on both sides with paper towel. Also dry maraschino cherries, if using. Arrange pineapple and cherries in decorative pattern on bottom of cake pan.

3. Sift together cake flour, baking powder, and salt.

4. Beat egg yolks in large bowl. Add sugar, vanilla, and 5 tablespoons reserved pineapple juice. Mix well. Add sifted dry ingredients and combine.

5. Place egg whites in bowl of standing mixer fitted with whisk attachment. Beat until moderately stiff but not dry. Fold egg whites into batter.

6. Pour batter into cake pan. Bake 30 to 35 minutes, or until tester inserted into cake comes out clean. Cool on rack 2 to 3 minutes. Invert cake (it will still be very hot) onto second cooling rack. If bits of brown sugar or pieces of fruit remain in pan, retrieve and place them on top of cake. Serve warm or at room temperature with whipped cream. Store leftover cake loosely wrapped in wax paper at room temperature.

½ cup butter, melted

1 cup brown sugar

7 slices canned pineapple, drained, juice reserved

7 candied or maraschino cherries, drained (optional)

1 cup cake flour

1 teaspoon baking powder

½ teaspoon salt

3 eggs, separated

1 cup sugar

1 teaspoon vanilla

Tips & Touches

- This cake can also be made with canned peach or apricot halves. We used tiny cubes of candied citron with the pineapple and cherries to give the top of the cake a stained-glass effect.

Mrs. Justo's Orange Carrot Cake

{1930s}

1 juice orange, unpeeled

2 cups flour

2 teaspoons baking powder

2 teaspoons baking soda

2 teaspoons cinnamon

2 teaspoons nutmeg

1 teaspoon salt

1½ cups peanut oil

1 cup sugar

1 cup brown sugar

4 eggs

2 cups grated carrots

1 cup chopped toasted walnuts

¼ cup confectioners' sugar

Whipped cream

THIS IS ONE OF THE BEST CARROT *cakes we've ever eaten! A juicy whole orange, peel and all, is added to the crisp grated carrots and the toasted walnuts. This is a very sweet cake with a great texture. We think it really doesn't need embellishment because it forms its own sugar glaze, but if you like a glaze, try the one for Mrs. Tate's "Old and Tried" Orange Cake (page 289).*

1. Set oven rack in middle position. Preheat oven to 350°F. Coat 10-inch tube pan with vegetable spray. Cut parchment paper or wax paper liner to fit bottom of pan. Insert liner and coat with vegetable spray. Dust pan with flour and tap out excess.

2. Trim thin slice from each end of orange. Cut orange in half lengthwise. Make shallow V-shaped cut to remove center core. Cut into wedges, remove seeds, and cut into 1-inch pieces. Place orange pieces in bowl of food processor fitted with metal blade. Pulse 3 or 4 times, or until orange turns to "confetti."

3. Sift together flour, baking powder, baking soda, cinnamon, nutmeg, and salt.

4. Combine oil, orange confetti, sugar, and brown sugar in bowl of standing mixer fitted with paddle attachment. Add eggs one at a time, and combine thoroughly. Add sifted dry ingredients gradually. (Batter will be loose.) Fold in carrots and walnuts.

5. Pour batter into tube pan. Bake 60 minutes, or until tester inserted into cake comes out clean. Cool in pan on rack 10 to 25 minutes. Run butter knife gently around edges and invert cake onto second rack. Turn right side up and allow to cool completely. Dust top of cake with confectioners' sugar and serve with rosette of whipped cream. Store loosely covered with wax paper at room temperature.

Mrs. Tate's "Old and Tried" Orange Cake

MAKES 10 SLICES

{ *1 8 9 0* }

WE FOUND THIS RECIPE AS WE BROWSED *through a pile of cookbooks we had bought in central Massachusetts. It literally fell into our laps. We were intrigued by the simple little recipe and the reference to "old and tried." This delicate all-natural cake, flavored with the zest and juice of an orange, is very "Southern," and we still wonder how it made it all the way to New England. We'll never know.*

1. Set oven rack in middle position. Preheat oven to 350°F. Coat 8-cup tube pan with vegetable spray or butter. Cut piece of parchment paper or wax paper to line bottom of pan. Insert liner, coat it with vegetable spray, and dust pan with flour.

2. To make cake: Sift flour, baking powder, and salt.

3. Beat sugar and water in bowl of standing mixer fitted with paddle attachment. Beat in egg yolks one at a time. Add orange zest and juice. Add sifted dry ingredients and combine until mixture is smooth. Add butter. Transfer mixture to bowl.

4. Place egg whites in clean bowl of standing mixer fitted with whisk attachment. Beat until stiff. Fold egg whites into batter.

5. Pour batter into tube pan. Bake approximately 45 minutes, or until tester inserted into cake comes out clean. Cool on rack for 20 minutes before removing from pan. Cake will have pulled away from sides of pan.

6. To make orange glaze: Mix together confectioners' sugar, orange zest, orange juice, and salt to a glaze consistency. Slip sheet of wax paper under rack to catch drips. Poke tiny holes in top of cake with cake tester and liberally spoon glaze over cake. Let glaze harden before serving. Store under cake dome or loosely wrapped in wax paper at room temperature.

FOR CAKE

2 cups flour

2 teaspoons baking powder

1/4 teaspoon salt

2 cups sugar, sifted

1/2 cup water

5 egg yolks

2 teaspoons grated orange zest

1/4 cup orange juice

1/4 cup butter, melted

4 egg whites

FOR ORANGE GLAZE

1 1/2 cups confectioners' sugar, sifted

2 teaspoons grated orange zest

1/4 cup orange juice, as needed

1/8 teaspoon salt

Oklahoma Strawberry Shortcakes

{ 1 9 6 0 }

1 cup flour

2 teaspoons baking powder

¼ cup sugar

⅛ teaspoon salt

¼ cup cold lard, cut into
    ½-inch cubes

⅓ cup heavy cream

1 egg, beaten

Clear sanding sugar

1 cup heavy cream, whipped
    with 2 tablespoons
    confectioners' sugar

1½ cups strawberries, washed,
    hulled, drained, and sliced

8 whole strawberries

THIS RECIPE REPLICATES THE SHORTCAKE MADE BY *James "Tulsa" Stuart, a student from Oklahoma who worked at MIT in the late 1960s, for an employee gathering. More than 40 years later, his strawberry shortcake, made exclusively with lard as its shortening, is still unforgettable.*

1. Set oven rack in middle position. Preheat oven to 450°F. Cover 14-inch by 16-inch baking sheet with foil, shiny side up. Coat foil with vegetable spray, or use silicone liner.

2. Place flour, baking powder, sugar, and salt in bowl of food processor fitted with metal blade. Pulse 3 times to mix. Add lard and pulse 3 more times. Add heavy cream and pulse until dough comes together.

3. Place dough on lightly floured sheet of wax paper or parchment paper. Roll out or pat to ½-inch thickness. Cut 2½-inch circles using biscuit cutter dipped in flour. Press cutter straight down and lift up; do not twist cutter in dough or shortcakes will not rise. Use spatula to lift and transfer dough to baking sheet. Brush tops with beaten egg and sprinkle with sanding sugar. Gather up scraps and reroll to cut more shortcakes. Shortcakes made from scraps may not be as tender, but they will still be good. Bake 12 minutes, or until lightly browned. Place on rack to cool.

4. To serve, cut shortcakes in half. Place each bottom half on plate and cover generously with whipped cream and sliced strawberries. Replace top of shortcakes and garnish with more whipped cream and whole strawberry on the side. Store leftover shortcakes in sealed plastic bag at room temperature.

Double Lemon Shortcakes

{ *1940s—1950s* }

FOR SHORTCAKES

2 cups flour

2½ teaspoons baking powder

⅛ teaspoon salt

¼ cup sugar

¼ cup cold butter, cut into small dice

2 teaspoons grated lemon zest

½ teaspoon lemon oil or lemon extract

¾ cup heavy cream

1 egg, beaten

2 tablespoons clear sanding sugar

FOR LEMON CURD

1 egg

4 egg yolks

¾ cup sugar

Pinch of salt

2 teaspoons grated lemon zest

½ cup lemon juice

¼ cup butter, cut into small dice

1 cup heavy cream, whipped

Raspberries or blueberries, for garnish

TIPS & TOUCHES

- Do not handle dough too much or shortcakes will be tough.
- Brushing unbaked shortcakes with beaten egg gives them a brown color.

THIS IS A VERY UNUSUAL SHORTCAKE RECIPE *because there is no fruit involved other than a garnish of summer berries. The shortcake is just what it is—a little cake that is very short and flaky with the richness of its butter and cream. This is not a biscuit masquerading as a shortcake.*

1. Set oven rack in middle position. Preheat oven to 450°F. Cover 14-inch by 16-inch baking sheet with foil, shiny side up. Coat foil with vegetable spray, or use silicone liner.

2. To make shortcakes: Place flour, baking powder, salt, and sugar in bowl of food processor fitted with metal blade. Pulse 3 times. Add butter and pulse 3 more times. Add lemon zest, lemon oil or extract, and heavy cream and pulse until dough forms.

3. Place dough on lightly floured sheet of wax paper or parchment paper. Roll out or pat to ½-inch thickness. Cut 2-inch circles using biscuit cutter dipped in flour. Press cutter straight down and up when cutting; do not twist cutter in dough or shortcakes will not rise. Use spatula to lift and transfer dough to baking sheet. Gather up scraps and reroll to cut more shortcakes. Shortcakes made from scraps may not be as tender, but they will still be good. Brush shortcakes with beaten egg. Sprinkle with sanding sugar. Bake 12 minutes, or until tops are lightly browned. Place on rack to cool.

4. To make lemon curd: Whisk egg and yolks in heavy-bottomed saucepan. Add sugar, salt, and lemon zest to mixture and combine. Whisk in lemon juice. Add butter and whisk over medium heat until butter is melted. Continue to whisk until curd thickens, about 5 minutes. If you prefer smooth curd, strain to remove lemon rind. Let curd cool completely. Refrigerate until ready to serve.

5. To serve, cut shortcakes in half. Place bottom half on plate, spoon generous amount of lemon curd on top, and add top half. Add dollop of whipped cream alongside. Garnish with fresh raspberries or blueberries. Store unused shortcakes in sealed plastic bag in refrigerator.

Evalyn's Lightly Lemon Cake

MAKES 8 SLICES

WE FOUND THIS RECIPE IN A GREEN metal binder full of recipes spanning the 1890s to the 1940s. Evalyn's name appeared with this spelling on the handwritten recipe we found for simple lemon cake. Nothing fancy here, it's just an old-fashioned light cake, good with a little sweetened whipped cream.

1. Set oven rack in middle position. Preheat oven to 350°F. Coat 9-inch cake pan or springform pan with butter or vegetable spray. Cut wax paper or parchment paper liner to fit bottom of pan. Insert liner and coat with butter or vegetable spray. Dust pan with flour and tap out excess.

2. To make cake: Sift together flour, salt, and baking powder into medium bowl.

3. Beat eggs in bowl of standing mixer fitted with paddle attachment. Gradually beat in sugar. Add butter and combine.

4. Add vanilla and lemon oil or extract to milk. Add sifted dry ingredients alternately with liquid ingredients to egg mixture, ending with sifted dry ingredients. Pour batter into cake pan or springform pan.

5. Bake 35 minutes, or until tester inserted into middle comes out clean. Cover loosely with foil if top of cake browns too quickly. Place on rack to cool for 20 minutes. Run knife around edges of pan to loosen cake, flip it onto second rack or flat plate, and remove paper lining. Flip cake back onto first rack and allow to cool completely.

6. To make lemon glaze: Mix together confectioners' sugar, salt, lemon juice, and lemon zest. Slip sheet of wax paper under rack to catch drips. Drizzle glaze from teaspoon or fork over top of cake and allow to set before cutting. Store completely cooled cake loosely covered with wax paper at room temperature.

FOR CAKE

2¼ cups flour

½ teaspoon salt

2 teaspoons baking powder

2 eggs, beaten

1½ cups sugar

½ cup butter, melted

1 teaspoon vanilla

½ teaspoon lemon oil, or
    1 teaspoon lemon extract

1 cup milk

FOR GLAZE

1 cup confectioners' sugar

Pinch of salt

2 tablespoons lemon juice

2 teaspoons grated lemon zest

TIPS & TOUCHES

- If you don't have time to glaze the cake, sprinkle with confectioners' sugar.
- This cake is best served the day it is baked.

Lemon Cheesecake with Lemon Curd Topping

{ 1 9 3 0 s }

MAKES 16 SLICES

FOR CRUST

13 graham crackers, 2½ inches by 5 inches each (1 sleeve from a 3-sleeve box)

¼ cup butter, melted

½ cup sugar

FOR CHEESECAKE

2 (8-ounce) packages cream cheese, at room temperature

1½ cups sugar

½ teaspoon vanilla

3 tablespoons lemon juice

2 teaspoons grated lemon zest

1½ cups heavy cream

6 eggs

¼ cup plus 2 tablespoons flour

⅛ teaspoon salt

FOR TOPPING

1 egg

4 egg yolks

¾ cup sugar

Pinch of salt

2 teaspoons grated lemon zest

½ cup lemon juice

¼ cup butter, cut into large dice

THIS RECIPE CAME FROM A WELL-LOVED MANUSCRIPT *cookbook with a very Austrian flavor. Most of the wonderful desserts in this collection were for tortes, tarts, and delectable flaky cookies. The woman who wrote these recipes used loads of cream, butter, and sugar in her sweets. There is evidence that some-one annotated these recipes at some later date, slightly modifying ingredients and instructions.*

1. Set oven rack in middle position. Preheat oven to 350°F. Coat bottom and sides of 9-inch springform pan with vegetable spray. Cut wax paper liner to fit bottom of pan. Insert liner and coat with vegetable spray.

2. To make crust: Place graham crackers in bowl of food processor fitted with metal blade. Pulse to make crumbs the size of corn-meal (about 1½ cups). Add butter and sugar and pulse to com-bine. Press crumbs on bottom and 2 inches up sides of pan. Wrap outside bottom of pan with foil.

3. To make cheesecake: Place cream cheese in bowl of standing mixer fitted with paddle attachment and beat until smooth. Add sugar and mix well. Add vanilla, lemon juice, and lemon zest. Add heavy cream and mix in. Add eggs two at a time, mixing well after each addition. Add flour and salt and combine.

4. Pour batter into springform pan. Bake 1 hour and 15 minutes. Turn off oven and leave door ajar by inserting wooden spoon between oven and door. Remove cheesecake from oven after 45 minutes and allow to cool thoroughly on rack. Cover baking pan with plastic wrap and refrigerate overnight.

5. To make topping: Whisk egg and yolks in heavy-bottomed sauce-pan. Add sugar, salt, and lemon zest and whisk to combine. Whisk in lemon juice. Add butter and whisk over medium heat until butter is melted. Continue to whisk until curd thickens, about 5 minutes. If you prefer smooth curd, strain to remove lemon rind. Let curd cool completely. Remove cheesecake from

refrigerator. Spoon lemon curd gently onto top of cheesecake. Allow 15 minutes for lemon curd to set. Refrigerate until ready to serve. Remove cheesecake from refrigerator 10 minutes before serving. Run butter knife around edges and remove sides. To store leftover cheesecake, place sides back on pan, cover with plastic wrap, and refrigerate.

TIPS & TOUCHES

- You can use 1½ cups of cookie crumbs instead of graham cracker crumbs for the crust.
- We also made the cheesecake with artisanal or loose ricotta cheese purchased at an Italian grocery. If you have access to handmade ricotta, you can substitute 18 ounces for the cream cheese. The flavor will be slightly more tangy. Commercial ricotta also works well, but the texture will be lighter.

Mrs. Charles Barker's Blue Ribbon Blueberry Cake

{ *1890s* }

MAKES 16 SQUARES

1½ cups sifted cake flour

1 teaspoon cream of tartar

½ teaspoon baking soda

½ cup milk

¼ cup butter

¾ cup sugar, sifted, plus
   2 tablespoons for topping

1 teaspoon vanilla

1 egg, beaten

1 pint fresh blueberries, washed
   and dried

TIPS & TOUCHES

* Do not roll the blueberries in flour before adding them to batter if you want to create the blue ribbon effect.

THIS RECIPE WAS CALLED MRS. CHARLES BARKER'S *Blueberry Cake* in the manuscript cookbook in which it was recorded. *Our documentation is at least the third recorded version of this recipe. The second was attributed to Miss Elizabeth G. Barker in 1933. She referred to it as Mrs. Charles Barker's "rule."*

1. Set oven rack in middle position. Preheat oven to 350°F. Line bottom and sides of 8-inch by 8-inch pan with foil, shiny side up, and coat with vegetable spray.

2. Combine flour and cream of tartar in small bowl. Dissolve baking soda in milk.

3. Cream butter, ¾ cup of the sugar, and vanilla in bowl of standing mixer fitted with paddle attachment. Add egg and beat to combine.

4. Add dry ingredients to mixer in thirds, alternating with milk, and beat until blended. Fold in half of blueberries. Spoon half of batter into pan. Level top with spatula. Sprinkle remaining blueberries on top of batter. Spoon remaining batter over blueberries and smooth. Dust top with remaining 2 tablespoons sugar. Bake 35 minutes, or until tester inserted into middle comes out clean. Cool on rack. Remove from pan and cut into 2-inch squares. Serve with vanilla ice cream. Store under cake dome or loosely covered with wax paper at room temperature.

Blueberry Buckle

MAKES 16 SQUARES

{ 1 8 7 0 s }

BUCKLES ARE FRUIT DESSERTS COVERED WITH A *sweet crumb top-*
ping that buckles in the middle after baking. We make our buckles during spring
and summer to enjoy the best of seasonal fruit. Buckles are a little like coffee cakes
with a crunchy praline topping. We like to cut ours while they're still in the pan.
We used several similar heirloom recipes to come up with this delicious treat.

1. Set oven rack in middle position. Preheat oven to 375°F. Line
   bottom and sides of 8-inch by 8-inch pan with foil, shiny side up.
   Coat foil with butter or vegetable spray.

2. To make streusel: Place sugar, flour, salt, cinnamon, and nutmeg
   in bowl. Work in butter with fingers (wear disposable gloves if
   desired) until mixture looks like irregular crumbs. Add pecans to
   mixture and combine. Set aside.

3. To make buckle: Sift 1¾ cups of the flour in bowl. In another
   bowl, mix remaining 2 tablespoons of sifted flour with blueberries and set aside. Sift baking powder, salt, cinnamon, and nutmeg into remaining flour.

4. Cream butter and sugar in bowl of standing mixer fitted with
   paddle attachment until fluffy. Add egg and beat to combine. In
   glass measuring cup, stir vanilla into milk. Add dry ingredients
   and milk alternately to batter in thirds. Fold in blueberries. Pour
   batter into prepared pan. Sprinkle streusel over top. Bake 45 to
   50 minutes, or until tester inserted in middle comes out clean.
   After 30 minutes, cover buckle loosely with foil to prevent crumbs
   from browning too quickly.

5. Remove buckle from oven and cool on rack until still slightly
   warm. Cut into squares and serve with whipped cream or vanilla
   ice cream. Buckle is good served warm or at room temperature.
   Store loosely covered with wax paper in refrigerator.

FOR STREUSEL

½ cup firmly packed brown sugar

2 tablespoons sifted flour

⅛ teaspoon salt

½ teaspoon cinnamon

⅛ teaspoon nutmeg

3 tablespoons cold butter, cut into
  ½-inch dice

½ cup toasted pecans,
  coarsely chopped

FOR BUCKLE

1¾ cups plus 2 tablespoons
  sifted flour

2 cups fresh blueberries

2 teaspoons baking powder

½ teaspoon salt

¼ teaspoon cinnamon

¼ teaspoon nutmeg

½ cup butter, softened to room
  temperature

¾ cup sugar

1 large egg

1 teaspoon vanilla

½ cup milk

 TIPS & TOUCHES

- Warm leftover buckle slightly
  in a low oven for a few minutes
  before serving.

Esther Pullman's Plum Torte

MAKES 8 TO 10 SLICES

{ 1 9 6 0 s }

THIS IS A VERSATILE RECIPE THAT OUR *friend Esther Pullman, a talented baker and artist, has been making since she began exchanging recipes in the 1960s. Esther included her version of this torte in an elegant little book of recipes she and her husband, Chris, designed and illustrated in the 1970s. A gift to family and friends at the holidays, this personal collection of living recipes continues to be cherished by its recipients.*

1. Set oven rack in middle position. Preheat oven to 350°F. Coat 9-inch springform pan with vegetable spray and dust with flour. Cut parchment paper or wax paper liner to fit bottom of pan. Insert liner and coat with vegetable spray. Dust pan with flour and tap out excess.
2. Sift together flour, baking powder, and salt into mixing bowl.
3. Cream butter and 1 cup of the sugar in bowl of standing mixer fitted with paddle attachment. Beat in eggs. Add sifted dry ingredients. Add vanilla.
4. Pour batter into springform pan and smooth top with offset spatula. Arrange plums, skin side down, on top of batter, leaving a ½-inch border around edge of pastry. Sprinkle top with lemon juice. Combine cinnamon and remaining ⅓ cup of sugar in small bowl and sprinkle over top. Bake 55 to 60 minutes, or until fruit bubbles and tester inserted into cake areas of torte comes out clean. Cool on rack for 15 minutes. Run butter knife around edges while torte is still warm to loosen. Serve slightly warm with puff of whipped cream. Store when completely cool under cake dome or loosely covered with wax paper, at room temperature.

1 cup flour

1 teaspoon baking powder

⅛ teaspoon salt

½ cup butter

1⅓ cups sugar, divided

2 eggs

1 teaspoon vanilla

12 Italian plums, pitted and halved, or 3 large plums, pitted and cut into eighths

2 tablespoons lemon juice

¼ teaspoon cinnamon

Whipped cream (optional)

TIPS & TOUCHES

*   A little whipped cream is very good with this torte, but a little whipped cream flavored with brandy is even better!

Mary Melly's Chocolate Angel Pie

{ *1930s* }

MAKES 8 SLICES

1 pound semisweet or bittersweet
chocolate, chopped

¼ cup milk

2 tablespoons sugar

⅛ teaspoon salt

4 egg yolks, at room temperature

1 cup heavy cream

1 teaspoon vanilla

9-inch Meringue Pie Shell, baked
and cooled

Whipped cream, for garnish

Chocolate shavings, for garnish

MARY MELLY WAS THE BELOVED HOUSEKEEPER OF *Bob and Ethel Wise, of Brookline, Massachusetts. Bob and his brother Jack owned Supertaste Ice Cream. Mary was always considered one of the family, and she generously gave her recipes to members of the Wise family and their friends. Angel Pie is a first cousin to the Australian Pavlova—a meringue shell filled with fruit and topped with whipped cream.*

1. Place chocolate, milk, sugar, and salt in top of double boiler over simmering water. Heat, stirring occasionally with wooden spoon, until chocolate is melted. Remove top of double boiler and let mixture cool for about 5 minutes. Whisk in egg yolks one at a time. Return mixture to simmering water and heat, stirring, until mixture registers 160°F on thermometer. Remove from heat

Metal candy-shop scoops, English, early 1900s

→→ MERINGUE PIE SHELL ←←

4 egg whites

½ teaspoon cream of tartar

1 cup sugar

1 teaspoon vanilla

1. Place oven rack in middle position. Preheat oven to 300°F. Coat 9-inch ovenproof glass pie plate with vegetable spray or butter, making sure to coat rim, and set aside.

2. Place egg whites in bowl of standing mixer fitted with whisk attachment. Whip on low speed. With motor running, add cream of tartar. Gradually increase speed to medium and whip until soft peaks form. Gradually add sugar. Add vanilla. Increase speed to high and beat to form glossy, firm peaks. Sugar should be completely absorbed into meringue.

3. Gently spoon egg whites into prepared pan. Use back of tablespoon to even the bottom and build up sides of pie shell. Bake 50 minutes. Turn off oven and leave pie shell in oven for 1 hour to dry out. Remove from oven, place on rack, and allow to cool completely. Store at room temperature, tightly wrapped in wax paper or in covered tin, until ready to fill. Make sure prepared filling is completely cool before mounding in pie shell. **Makes one 9-inch pie shell**

and transfer to bowl. Let cool to room temperature. To speed cooling, place bowl with chocolate mixture into larger bowl of ice water.

2. Whip cream in bowl of standing mixer fitted with whisk attachment to form soft peaks. Add vanilla and beat until stiff. Add cooled chocolate mixture in 2 batches, beating after each addition. Spoon into prepared meringue shell. Place toothpicks at intervals in topping and cover pie gently with tent of plastic wrap. Refrigerate at least 3 hours to set. Remove toothpicks and decorate with swirls of whipped cream and shaved chocolate and serve. Store leftover pie loosely covered with plastic wrap in refrigerator.

Tips & Touches

* Filling can also be spooned into custard cups and served as chocolate mousse.

Mrs. Naka's Lemon Angel Pie

MAKES 8 SLICES

{ 1 9 5 0 s }

WE LEARNED ABOUT THIS LIVING RECIPE FROM *Holly Tarson, whose husband's grandparents, the Peppers, lived in Berkeley, California. A Japanese couple named Mr. and Mrs. Naka worked for the Peppers as gardeners, and Mrs. Naka used the Meyer lemons from the Peppers' yard to make a creamy lemon pie in a meringue crust. Years later, after Dr. and Mrs. Pepper had passed away, Holly's husband, Geoff, and his parents continued to visit the Nakas, who served them cashews and 7-Up and their favorite lemon pie. The generous Mrs. Naka always kept an extra pie in her freezer for them to take home.*

4 egg yolks

½ cup sugar

3 tablespoons lemon juice

1 teaspoon grated lemon zest

Pinch of salt

1 cup heavy cream

9-inch Meringue Pie Shell, baked and cooled (page 301)

1. Place egg yolks, sugar, lemon juice, lemon zest, and salt in heavy-bottomed saucepan. Whisk until combined. Cook over medium heat, stirring continuously, until mixture thickens and looks like custard, 5 to 7 minutes. Remove from heat, transfer to 1-quart bowl, and place plastic wrap directly on surface of custard to keep skin from forming. Let cool completely.

2. Whip cream until soft peaks form. Break up cooled lemon custard with whisk. Stir in small amount of whipped cream. Fold custard into whipped cream. Add mixture to pie shell and gently smooth the top. Stick several toothpicks into filling, cover loosely with wax paper, and refrigerate at least 24 hours before serving. Decorate pie with additional swirls of whipped cream. Store leftover pie loosely wrapped in wax paper in refrigerator and eat on same day for best taste. Mrs. Naka's pie can also be frozen.

TIPS & TOUCHES

- Meyer lemons are slightly sweeter than conventional lemons. They are available for a short season in grocery stores. Substituting a conventional lime for part of the zest and juice brings the flavor of this pie closer to that of the original.

Dorothy Brass's Pineapple Pie

{ *1 9 4 0 s* }

MAKES 10 GENEROUS SLICES

FOR CRUST

Pastry for double-crust pie, divided in half and chilled (see Sheila's Sweet Pie Crust on page 306)

1 tablespoon flour

1 egg, beaten

FOR FILLING

2 (20-ounce) cans unsweetened crushed pineapple

2½ tablespoons plus ½ cup juice from canned pineapple

2½ tablespoons cornstarch

¾ cup sugar

2 teaspoons grated lemon zest

1 tablespoon lemon juice

1 teaspoon vanilla

⅛ teaspoon salt

TIPS & TOUCHES

* Make your decorations on the top pie crust after rolling it out and before placing it over the pie filling.

THIS IS THE PIE MAMA MADE DURING *those sunny summer months when our entire family ate communally at the kitchen table. Mama always used canned pineapple and glazed the top crust with a beaten whole egg to give it a shine. She always made a daisy design on the top crust with her favorite tool, her pie crimper. We still have her crimper and use it when we bake pies.*

1. Set oven rack in middle position. Preheat oven to 400°F. Coat 9-inch ovenproof glass pie plate with vegetable spray. Cover 14-inch by 16-inch baking sheet with foil, shiny side up. Coat foil with vegetable spray, or use silicone liner.

2. To make crust: Roll out pastry dough. Fit half of dough into bottom of pie plate and trim off excess. Sprinkle bottom of pastry with flour. Chill in refrigerator. (For detailed instructions, see "To make a double-crust pie," steps 2 and 3, page 306.)

3. To make filling: Place pineapple in sieve set over bowl. Drain 30 minutes, pressing gently with palm of your hand to remove as much of juice as possible. Reserve and measure juice.

4. Place 2½ tablespoons of the reserved pineapple juice in large bowl. Whisk in cornstarch until dissolved. Add remaining ½ cup pineapple juice, sugar, lemon zest, lemon juice, vanilla, and salt. Whisk until thoroughly combined. Add pineapple and stir until evenly coated.

5. Add pineapple mixture to pie shell. Add top crust, seal and crimp edges, and cut decorative slits. Brush top crust and edges with beaten egg. (For detailed instructions, see "To make a double-crust pie," step 4, page 306.)

6. Place pie on baking sheet. Bake 30 minutes and check crust for browning. If crust is browning too quickly, cover loosely with foil. Bake another 15 minutes, or until top crust is evenly browned. Bottom crust should be light brown when completely baked. Cool pie on rack at least 2 hours before serving. Store pie loosely covered with wax paper at room temperature.

Sheila's Sweet or Savory Pie Crust

{ *1950* }

MAKES DOUGH FOR: 1 DOUBLE-CRUST 9-INCH PIE OR
2 SINGLE-CRUST 9-INCH PIES OR
2 8-INCH OR 9-INCH TARTS

SWEET PIE CRUST

2½ cups flour

⅓ cup sugar

¼ teaspoon salt

1 cup cold butter, cut into 16 slices

¼ cup ice water

1 egg, beaten (optional; for double-crust pie)

SAVORY PIE CRUST

2½ cups flour

¼ teaspoon salt

½ teaspoon chopped fresh herbs, or ⅛ teaspoon dried herbs (optional)

½ cup cold butter, cut into 8 slices

½ cup chilled vegetable shortening

¼ cup ice water

1 egg, beaten (optional; for double-crust pie)

WE'VE USED THIS EASY-TO-MAKE CRUST FOR MORE *than 50 years. It is like the ones we've found in our manuscript cookbooks. We've provided both a sweet and a savory version.*

TO MAKE PASTRY

1. Place dry ingredients in bowl of food processor fitted with metal blade. Pulse 3 times to mix. Add butter (or butter and shortening) and pulse until crumbly. Add ice water. Pulse until mixture comes together.
2. Remove dough from bowl of processor, divide in half, and shape each half into disk. Unless your kitchen is very warm, you don't have to chill dough before rolling out.

TO MAKE DOUBLE-CRUST PIE

1. Coat 9-inch ovenproof glass pie plate with vegetable spray.
2. Roll out each disk of dough between 2 sheets of floured wax paper or parchment paper until 2 inches wider than diameter across top of pie plate.
3. Fold 1 rolled disk in half and then in quarters. Place folded dough into bottom quarter of pie plate. Carefully unfold dough and let it relax into pie plate. Trim excess dough from rim. Chill bottom crust while preparing filling.
4. Brush edges of bottom crust with beaten egg. Fill pie and flip second crust over top of pie. Trim excess dough around rim, leaving just enough dough to make crimped edge. Press edges of dough together gently with your fingers. Crimp edges with tines of salad fork or pie crimper. Cut six 1-inch decorative slits in center of top crust to allow steam to escape. Brush top crust and edges with beaten egg. Bake as directed in recipe.

To make single-crust pie

1. Coat 9-inch ovenproof glass pie plate with vegetable spray.

2. Roll out 1 disk of dough between 2 sheets of floured wax paper or parchment paper until 2 inches wider than diameter across top of pie plate.

3. Fold rolled disk in half and then in quarters. Place folded dough into bottom quarter of pie plate. Carefully unfold dough and let it relax into pie plate. Trim excess dough around rim, leaving enough to form a decorative edge. Flute edge or shape as desired.

4. Chill crust while preparing filling. Fill and bake pie as directed in recipe.

To prebake pie shell

1. Place oven rack in middle position. Preheat oven to 400°F.

2. Prick pie shell pastry with fork. Cut piece of foil slightly larger than pie shell and coat it with vegetable spray. Place foil, greased side down, in pie shell, fitting it loosely into bottom and sides. Fill foil with uncooked rice or beans to prevent crust from bubbling during baking. Bake 18 minutes.

3. Remove foil and rice or bean filling carefully. Prick any existing bubbles in dough. Return shell to oven and continue baking, checking every 5 minutes for browning. If edge of crust appears to be browning too quickly, cover loosely with foil. Remove pie shell from oven when it is golden brown. Cool on rack before adding pie filling, unless otherwise directed. The rice or beans can be cooled, sealed in plastic bag, and reused several times to prebake pie shells.

Wood and china rolling pin, English, late 19th–early 20th century

Mama's Blueberry Pie

{ *1 9 4 0 s* }

MAKES 10 SLICES

FOR CRUST

Pastry for double-crust pie,
   divided in half and chilled
   (see Sheila's Sweet Pie Crust
   on page 306)

1 egg, beaten

FOR FILLING

4 cups blueberries

½ cup sugar

¼ cup flour

⅛ teaspoon salt

2 teaspoons grated lemon zest

3 tablespoons lemon juice

1½ tablespoons butter, cut
   into dice

THIS IS ANOTHER ONE OF OUR FAMILY *recipes that we had to recon-struct from memory. Mama never used cornstarch, tapioca, or cinnamon in her blueberry pies; just the juice and zest from a lemon and a little sugar so the true taste of the blueberries would be enhanced by the heat of the oven.*

1. Set oven rack in middle position. Preheat oven to 400°F. Coat 9-inch ovenproof glass pie plate with vegetable spray. Line 14-inch by 16-inch baking sheet with foil, shiny side up, and coat with vegetable spray.

2. To prepare crust: Roll out pastry dough. Fit half of dough into bottom of pie plate and trim off excess. Chill in refrigerator. (For detailed instructions, see "To make a double-crust pie," steps 2 and 3, page 306.)

3. To make filling: Dry blueberries thoroughly on baking sheet lined with 2 thicknesses of paper towels.

Green glazed pottery bowl with blueberries, early 1900s

4. Combine blueberries, sugar, flour, salt, lemon zest, and lemon juice in bowl.

5. Add blueberry mixture to pie shell. Dot with butter. Add top crust, seal and crimp edges, and cut decorative slits. Brush top crust and edges with beaten egg. (For detailed instructions, see "To make a double-crust pie," step 4, page 306.)

6. Place pie on baking sheet. Bake 20 minutes and check crust for browning. If crust is browning too quickly, cover loosely with foil. Bake another 25 to 30 minutes, or until top crust is evenly browned and juices begin to bubble. Cool pie on rack at least 2 hours before serving. Store loosely covered with wax paper at room temperature.

➤➤ TIPS ON BAKING PIES ◄◄

Although there has been some debate about whether or not to bake pies on the bottom rack of the oven, we have found that using the middle rack didn't affect the quality of the pies we tested, and it was easier to take pies in and out of the oven.

To solve the problem of pie edges that brown more quickly than the centers, we cover our pies loosely with a piece of foil halfway through the baking process. Placing a ring of foil to fit around the edges of the pie as it bakes can be helpful, too. Commercial edge protectors are also available. For a shiny top crust, brush on an egg wash before baking. For an opaque brown color, brush on cream.

Strawberry Rhubarb Pie

{ 1 9 5 0 s }

FOR CRUST

Pastry for double-crust pie,
  divided in half and chilled
  (see Sheila's Sweet Pie Crust
  on page 306)

1 egg, beaten

FOR FILLING

4 to 5 stalks rhubarb, trimmed
  and cut into ½-inch pieces
  (about 4 cups)

1½ cups sugar

¼ cup flour

¼ teaspoon nutmeg

Pinch of salt

1 pint strawberries, washed,
  hulled, sliced, and drained on
  paper towels

2 tablespoons cold butter, cut into
  large dice

WE FOUND THIS RECIPE HANDWRITTEN ON AN *index card with no directions, so we tested and tested and tested. It's a very delicate pie that should be made only when strawberries and rhubarb are in season. This pie is best served the day it is made. Although strawberry rhubarb pies are often baked with a lattice crust, we like the double-crust version.*

1. Set oven rack in middle position. Preheat oven to 400°F. Coat 9-inch ovenproof glass pie plate with vegetable spray. Cover 14-inch by 16-inch baking pan with foil, shiny side up. Coat foil with vegetable spray, or use silicone liner.

2. To make crust: Roll out pastry dough. Fit half of dough into bottom of pie plate and trim off excess. Chill in refrigerator. (For detailed instructions, see "To make a double-crust pie," steps 2 and 3, page 306.)

3. To make filling: Mix rhubarb, sugar, and flour in large bowl. Set aside 1 hour.

4. Put rhubarb in strainer. Collect drained juice, pour into saucepan, and add nutmeg and salt. Cook over medium heat, stirring with wooden spoon, until juice thickens. Cool 10 minutes. Place rhubarb, strawberries, and juice in large bowl and toss to combine.

5. Add rhubarb mixture to pie shell. Dot with butter. Add top crust, seal and crimp edges, and cut decorative slits. Brush top crust and edges with beaten egg. (For detailed instructions, see "To make a double-crust pie," step 4, page 306.)

6. Place pie on baking sheet. Bake 30 minutes and check crust for browning. If crust is browning too quickly, cover loosely with foil. Bake another 15 to 20 minutes, or until top crust is evenly browned. Bottom crust should be light brown when completely baked. Cool pie on rack at least 2 hours before serving. Store pie loosely covered with wax paper at room temperature.

Green Tomato Pie

{ *1940s* }

TOMATOES ARE ACTUALLY A FRUIT, EVEN THOUGH *we think of them as a vegetable, so it's not unusual to use tomatoes in the filling for this fruit pie, with its subtle flavor of allspice. This recipe comes from The Pie Lady, in North Carolina. This is a seasonal pie best made when summer slides into fall and there are green tomatoes on the vine, a week away from turning ripe. Choose medium-size green tomatoes. The larger ones will be tough and seedy.*

1. To make crust: For detailed instructions, see Sheila's Savory Pie Crust on page 306. Coat 9-inch ovenproof glass pie pan with vegetable spray. Roll out pastry dough. Fit half of dough into bottom of pie plate and trim off excess. Chill in refrigerator.

2. Place oven rack in middle position. Preheat oven to 450°F.

3. Place tomato slices in large bowl. Sprinkle with vinegar and lemon zest. Mix sugar, flour, salt, allspice, cinnamon, and ginger in another bowl. Add to tomatoes and mix thoroughly to coat.

4. Place tomato filling in prepared pie shell and dot with butter. Brush edges of shell with beaten egg. Add top crust, seal and crimp edges, and cut decorative slits. Brush top crust and edges with beaten egg. Place pie on pan covered with foil, shiny side up, to catch drips.

5. Bake 20 minutes and check crust for browning. If crust browns too quickly, cover pie loosely with foil. Reduce oven temperature to 350°F and bake another 25 minutes, or until crust is golden brown and filling is bubbling. Remove foil, if using, for last 5 minutes of baking.

6. Cool pie on rack. Serve slightly warm or at room temperature. Store pie loosely covered with paper towel and wax paper in refrigerator. Let pie come to room temperature before serving.

Pastry for double-crust pie, divided in half and chilled (see Sheila's Savory Pie Crust on page 306; leave out optional herbs)

4 cups peeled, cored, and sliced green tomatoes (5 to 6 tomatoes) (see Tips & Touches)

1 tablespoon apple cider vinegar

Grated zest of 1/2 lemon

1 1/4 cups sugar

6 tablespoons flour

1/2 teaspoon salt

1/2 teaspoon allspice

1/4 teaspoon cinnamon

1/4 teaspoon ginger

2 tablespoons cold butter, cut into 1/4-inch dice

1 egg, beaten

TIPS & TOUCHES

- Green tomatoes do not react in the same way as ripe tomatoes to a hot and then a cold water bath for removing skins. We had to peel the green tomatoes with a vegetable peeler.

- Place a piece of wax paper under pie plate when brushing crust with egg wash.

- Wipe any egg wash that drips under the rim of the pie plate with a paper towel.

Coconut Pie from North Carolina

{ 1 9 5 0 s }

MAKES 8 SERVINGS

¼ cup butter, softened to room temperature

1 cup sugar

⅓ cup buttermilk

2 eggs

¼ teaspoon salt

1 teaspoon vanilla

½ package (3½ to 4 ounces) shredded, sweetened coconut

Unbaked 9-inch pie shell (see Sheila's Sweet Pie Crust on page 306)

THIS RECIPE CAME FROM THE PIE LADY *from North Carolina, who was active in her church and who specialized in truly Southern cakes and pies. This is one of the simplest recipes for a delicious dessert we've tried. We will not judge you if you choose to use a premade pie crust, but you may find that you have a bit of filling left over.*

1. Place oven rack in middle position. Preheat oven to 350°F.
2. Cream butter and sugar in bowl of standing mixer fitted with paddle attachment. Add buttermilk. Add eggs one at a time. Add salt and vanilla. Fold in coconut. Pour filling into pie shell. Bake about 40 minutes, or until top is firm and crust is golden brown. Cool completely on rack. Store loosely wrapped in wax paper in refrigerator.

TIPS & TOUCHES

- Whipped cream can be piped in a crisscross pattern on top of pie just before serving. This is a very sweet pie, and a little goes a long way.

Miniature enamelware funnel and flour holder, German, late 19th–early 20th century

Holiday Apple Custard Pie

MAKES 12 SLICES

WE FOUND THIS RECIPE WRITTEN ON THE *back of a private outpatient admitting notification form from Salem Hospital. The recipe was credited to someone named S. Lake. Although it was titled German Apple Pie, we found similar recipes for Swiss Apple Pie and French Apple Pie. We decided to refer to it as Holiday Apple Pie because it's not only simple to make and bakes in less than an hour, but it also presents well. No holiday is complete without a good apple pie.*

1. Set oven rack in middle position. Preheat oven to 450°F. Coat 9-inch ovenproof glass pie plate with vegetable spray.

2. Arrange approximately half of apple slices on bottom of pie crust in an overlapping pattern. Sift together sugar, cinnamon, and salt. Sprinkle half of cinnamon sugar over apples.

3. Pour heavy cream into 2-cup glass measuring cup. Add eggs and vanilla and beat with fork or small whisk to combine. Pour half of egg mixture over top of pie. Layer remaining apples in pie and sprinkle with remaining cinnamon sugar. Pour remaining cream mixture over top of pie. Dot with butter.

4. Bake 10 minutes, reduce oven temperature to 350°F, and bake 45 minutes more, or until filling bubbles rapidly and edges of crust are nicely browned. Check pie during baking; if crust is browning too quickly, cover loosely with foil. Cool pie on rack at least 2 hours before serving. This pie is best served the day it is baked. Store covered with paper towels and plastic wrap in refrigerator.

4 medium apples, peeled, cored, and cut into thin wedges (enough for 2 layers)

1 unbaked 9-inch pie shell (see Sheila's Sweet Pie Crust on page 306)

1 cup sugar

1 teaspoon cinnamon

$\frac{1}{2}$ teaspoon salt

1 cup heavy cream

2 eggs

1 teaspoon vanilla

2 tablespoons butter, cut into small dice

Lannie's Lord Have Mercy Sweet Potato Pie

{ 1 9 2 0 }

MAKES 2 PIES (8 TO 10 SLICES PER PIE)

2½ pounds raw sweet potatoes, baked and flesh removed (see "How to Prepare Sweet Potatoes for Pie")

¾ cup butter

1 cup brown sugar

2 cups sugar

3 eggs

½ cup heavy cream

2 teaspoons vanilla

2 teaspoons cinnamon

½ teaspoon cloves

½ teaspoon ginger

1 teaspoon salt

2 unbaked pie shells (see Sheila's Sweet Pie Crust on page 306)

THE RECIPE FOR THIS OUTSTANDING SWEET POTATO *Pie was given to us by Yvette Gooding. It is the pie her maternal grandmother, Lannie Waters Edmondson, made for special family gatherings. Mrs. Edmondson, a native of Kinston, North Carolina, taught Yvette how to bake when she was just 7 years old. The late Mrs. Edmondson is remembered for having a saying for every occasion and a wonderful sense of humor, too.*

1. Set oven rack in middle position. Preheat oven to 375°F.
2. Place prepared sweet potatoes in bowl of standing mixer fitted with paddle attachment. With mixer running on low, add butter. Add brown sugar and sugar. Add eggs one at a time. Add heavy cream and vanilla. Do not overbeat. Add cinnamon, cloves, ginger, and salt.
3. Pour batter into pie shells. Bake about 1 hour, or until tester inserted into pie comes out clean. The center of pie should wiggle a bit. Cool 2 to 3 hours on rack. Serve with whipped cream or vanilla ice cream. Store covered with paper towel and plastic wrap in refrigerator.

⇢⇢ HOW TO PREPARE SWEET POTATOES FOR PIE ⇠⇠

Preparing the sweet potatoes for Mrs. Edmondson's pie is worth the effort. Select large sweet pota-toes, prick them with a fork, and place them on a foil-covered (shiny side up) metal baking pan that has been coated with vegetable spray. Bake in a 400°F oven for 1 hour.

Place the baking pan on a cooling rack. Carefully cut the hot sweet potatoes in half lengthwise so that they will cool more quickly. When the potatoes are cool enough to handle, scoop out the insides (discard the skins) and place them in the bowl of a food processor fitted with the metal blade. Weigh the sweet potato pulp after scooping it, since the size and weight are hard to discern with your eyes alone. Process until the potatoes are soft and fluffy.

For 2 pies, you will need 2½ pounds or 40 ounces raw sweet potatoes to make 22 ounces of processed cooked sweet potato—approximately 4 large potatoes to start. Do not use canned sweet potatoes because freshly baked potatoes still retain some of their fiber.

ℰ TIPS & TOUCHES

- Use only orange sweet potatoes, not white ones, because the texture will be different.

Wire glass carrier, French, 1890–1910; Green Depression glass water glasses, 1930s

Pumpkin Pie with Maple Spiced Nuts

MAKES 10 SLICES

{ 1 9 3 0 s }

WE FOUND THIS RECIPE HANDWRITTEN ON A *half sheet of lined paper. The author was somewhat cryptic and left out any reference to the molasses in the directions, but we were able to translate this living recipe into a delectable pumpkin pie. We were pleasantly surprised to find this to be one of the best pumpkin pies we've ever tasted.*

1. Set oven rack in middle position. Preheat oven to 450°F.
2. Place pumpkin in large bowl. Sift brown sugar, cinnamon, ginger, and salt into pumpkin and stir with wooden spoon. Add eggs, molasses, and butter and stir to combine. Combine evaporated milk and water, add to batter, and stir until well mixed.
3. Pour batter into pie shell. Bake 15 minutes. Lower oven temperature to 350°F and bake 50 minutes. Place pie on rack and allow to cool 2 to 3 hours. Serve with vanilla ice cream and Maple Spiced Nuts. Store covered with paper towel and plastic wrap in refrigerator.

1½ cups canned pumpkin

1 cup brown sugar

1 teaspoon cinnamon

½ teaspoon ginger

½ teaspoon salt

2 eggs, beaten

1 tablespoon molasses

1 tablespoon butter, melted

1 (12-ounce) can evaporated milk

½ cup water

Unbaked pie shell, at room temperature (see Sheila's Sweet Pie Crust on page 306)

1 cup Maple Spiced Nuts

⤳ MAPLE SPICED NUTS ⤆

½ cup maple syrup

2 tablespoons butter

½ teaspoon salt

¼ teaspoon cinnamon

¼ teaspoon nutmeg

1 cup whole pecans

Heat maple syrup, butter, salt, cinnamon, nutmeg, and pecans in heavy frying pan over medium heat, stirring constantly with wooden spoon until mixture begins to boil. Boil 5 minutes, stirring constantly. Spread nut mixture on baking sheet. Place baking sheet on rack to cool. When completely cool, break into shards.

Canadian Sugar Pie
(*Tarte au Sucre*)

MAKES 10 SLICES

1½ cups brown sugar

2 tablespoons flour

⅛ teaspoon salt

Unbaked 9½-inch tart shell (see Sheila's Sweet Pie Crust on page 306)

1 teaspoon vanilla

⅓ cup heavy cream

WE FOUND THIS RECIPE HANDWRITTEN ON AN *index card filed among main dishes and salads. We believe it has ties to our neighbors to the north, with origins in France. Although it's simple and quick, this is a serious pie. We love the caramelized sugar taste of this tart, which is so representative of Canadian sweets.*

1. Set oven rack in middle position. Preheat oven to 350°F.
2. Use your hands (wear disposable gloves if desired) to combine brown sugar, flour, and salt in mixing bowl. Pick out and discard any hard particles of brown sugar. Sprinkle mixture evenly over bottom of tart shell.
3. Add vanilla to heavy cream and pour over mixture, spreading lightly with offset spatula. Bake approximately 35 minutes, or until pastry is golden brown and filling is dark and bubbling. Cool on rack. Serve either slightly warm or at room temperature with whipped cream. This tart is best when eaten the day it is baked. Store leftover pie loosely covered with paper towel and wax paper in refrigerator.

Cast-iron mold for shaping springerle cookies, American, early 1800s

Peach Streusel Pie

MAKES 8 SLICES

{ 1 9 4 0 s }

MAKING THIS PIE WAS A CHALLENGE. WE *found that using overripe peaches just didn't work. Peaches that were still a bit firm helped to control the amount of peach juice in the pie. When this pie comes out of the oven with its crown of crunchy brown sugar and almond streusel, we know it's summertime!*

1. To make streusel: Place brown sugar in medium bowl. Sift together flour, salt, and nutmeg on sheet of wax paper and add to brown sugar. Mix butter into sifted dry ingredients with your hands (wear disposable gloves if desired) until texture resembles coarse sand. Add almonds and combine. Chill streusel for 20 minutes.

2. Set oven rack in middle position. Preheat oven to 400°F. Sprinkle flour on bottom of unbaked pie crust.

3. To make pie: Sprinkle peach slices with sugar, salt, and lemon zest. Mix thoroughly and place in strainer over bowl. Let fruit drain for at least 30 minutes.

4. Remove peaches from strainer and place in medium bowl. Add nutmeg and 1/2 tablespoon of the lemon juice and toss to combine. Measure 1/2 cup of strained peach juice into small bowl. Whisk in cornstarch until dissolved. Stir in remaining 1/2 tablespoon lemon juice and vanilla. Pour cornstarch syrup over peaches and toss until slices are well coated. Gently pour fruit into pie shell. Sprinkle streusel mixture over top.

5. Bake 30 minutes. Check pie; if crust is browning too quickly, cover with foil. Continue to bake 20 to 25 minutes, or until crust is browned and fruit bubbles. Remove pie from oven and place on rack. Allow to cool 3 hours before cutting. Serve with vanilla ice cream. Store pie covered with paper towel and plastic wrap in refrigerator.

FOR STREUSEL

3/4 cup brown sugar

3 tablespoons flour

1/4 teaspoon salt

1/4 teaspoon nutmeg

3 tablespoons cold butter, cut into small dice

3/4 cup slivered almonds

FOR PIE

1 tablespoon flour

Unbaked 9-inch pie shell (see Sheila's Sweet Pie Crust on page 306)

4 cups "still-firm" peaches, sliced

1/2 cup sugar

1/4 teaspoon salt

2 teaspoons grated lemon zest

1/4 teaspoon nutmeg

1 tablespoon lemon juice, divided

3 tablespoons cornstarch

1 teaspoon vanilla

 TIPS & TOUCHES

• We have found that baking fruit pies is very subjective. Much depends on the condition of the fruit. We have always been told to use overripe peaches in pies, but we found they produced too much juice. We feel better using peaches that have a bit of firmness left in them.

One, Two, Three Open-Faced Blueberry Pie

{ 1 9 3 0 s }

MAKES 10 SLICES

FOR GLAZE

2 ounces seedless raspberry jam

FOR CRUST

Prebaked pie shell (see Sheila's Sweet Pie Crust on page 306)

FOR FILLING

4 cups blueberries, divided

$\frac{1}{2}$ cup plus 2$\frac{1}{2}$ tablespoons water

2$\frac{1}{2}$ tablespoons cornstarch

$\frac{1}{2}$ cup sugar

1 teaspoon lemon juice

2 teaspoons grated lemon zest

1 teaspoon vanilla

$\frac{1}{2}$ teaspoon cinnamon

$\frac{1}{8}$ teaspoon salt

Whipped cream

WE WISH WE COULD TELL YOU THIS *pie is as easy as 1, 2, 3. It's named as such because there are 3 stages to its construction—baking the pie shell, glazing the pie, and preparing the filling. The results are outstanding. We found the recipe handwritten in a copy of* Laboratory Recipes *owned by Rachel W. Banks.*

1. To make glaze: Cook raspberry jam in metal saucepan on low heat until bubbles form around edges, or heat jam in glass bowl in microwave for 25 seconds on low. Brush bottom and sides of cooled pie shell with glaze and let cool.

2. To make filling: Place 1 cup of the blueberries and $\frac{1}{2}$ cup of the water in metal saucepan. Bring to a boil over medium heat. Boil gently 3 to 4 minutes and remove from heat. Add cornstarch to remaining 2$\frac{1}{2}$ tablespoons water and whisk to dissolve. Add cornstarch mixture, sugar, lemon juice, lemon zest, vanilla, cinnamon, and salt to cooked blueberries. Bring to a boil over low heat and stir about 1 minute, or until blueberries have the consistency of jam.

3. Transfer cooked blueberry mixture to medium bowl. Fold in remaining 3 cups of blueberries. Add filling to pie shell and let cool at least 2 hours. Just before serving, pipe whipped cream around edge of pie. This pie is best served the day it is made, but it will still be good the next day if loosely wrapped in wax paper or placed in covered container and refrigerated.

Shoofly Pie

FOR STREUSEL

¼ cup sugar

1 cup flour

⅛ teaspoon salt

⅛ teaspoon cinnamon

⅛ teaspoon nutmeg

⅛ teaspoon ginger

¼ cup cold butter, cut into
  ½-inch dice

FOR PIE

Pastry for single-crust pie, chilled
  (see Sheila's Sweet Pie Crust on
  page 306)

½ cup molasses

½ teaspoon baking soda

½ cup water, heated to just
  under a boil

TIPS & TOUCHES

• Do not use hot tap water, which
  might contain mineral deposits.

MAKES 8 SLICES

THIS IS A VERY TRADITIONAL PENNSYLVANIA DUTCH *or German pie. We found it in the manuscript cookbook of The Pie Lady from North Carolina, another example of how heirloom recipes can cross state borders. Dark corn syrup can be substituted for the molasses. We suggest serving small pieces of this very rich pie.*

1. To make streusel: Place sugar in medium bowl. Sift together flour, salt, cinnamon, nutmeg, and ginger on sheet of wax paper and add to sugar. Work in butter with fingers (wear disposable gloves if desired) until texture resembles coarse sand.

2. To make crust: For detailed instructions, see Sheila's Sweet Pie Crust on page 306. Coat 9-inch ovenproof glass pie plate with vegetable spray. Roll out pastry dough. Fit into bottom of pie plate and trim off excess. Chill in refrigerator.

3. Set oven rack in middle position. Preheat oven to 400°F.

4. Place molasses in bowl. Dissolve baking soda in water and add to molasses, stirring with wooden spoon. Pour into prepared pie shell. Sprinkle streusel over surface of pie and bake 15 minutes. Reduce oven temperature to 350°F and bake another 25 minutes, or until tester inserted into pie comes out clean. Place pie on rack and cool completely before cutting. Store leftover pie loosely wrapped in wax paper in refrigerator.

Sugar bag, English,
early 20th century

Bavarian Fig Tart

MAKES 8 SLICES

{ 1 9 6 0 s }

THIS WAS THE TART OF CHOICE FOR *us in the 1960s, when we were just earning our reputations as sweet young things who baked. Made with sliced apples, sliced pears, or even blueberries, this browned-butter tart is easy to put together. It makes a lovely presentation, too.*

1. Set oven rack in middle position. Preheat oven to 375°F. Coat 8-inch or 9-inch tart pan (with removable bottom) with vegetable spray.

2. To make crust: Add flour, sugar, and salt to bowl of food processor fitted with metal blade. Pulse twice to combine. Add butter and pulse until mixture resembles coarse meal. Add 2 tablespoons ice water. Process just until mixture comes together in large clumps; add remaining 1 tablespoon water if necessary. Turn dough onto plastic wrap and gather into a ball. Wrap and chill 30 minutes or overnight.

3. To make filling: Heat butter in 9-inch or 10-inch frying pan over medium heat about 2 minutes, or until butter is bubbly and foamy. Continue to move butter around by swirling pan until butter is golden brown. Do not allow butter to darken or burn. Strain browned butter into glass bowl (there may be some brown spots left in the butter, but this will improve the flavor). Whisk together sugar, flour, eggs, and vanilla in bowl. Slowly add browned butter, whisking to combine.

4. Roll out dough on lightly floured surface to 1/8-inch thickness. Use rolling pin to carefully lift and transfer dough to tart pan. If crust breaks or tears, just press it together with your fingers. Press dough into bottom and sides of tart pan. Cut off excess dough with sharp knife or run your rolling pin over top edge.

5. Arrange figs, cut side up, in pattern on top of dough. Pour filling over figs. Bake 1 hour, or until tart filling is brown and bubbly; check for doneness after 45 minutes and in 5-minute increments thereafter. Serve warm or at room temperature. Sprinkle the top with confectioners' sugar before serving, if desired. Store loosely wrapped in wax paper on plate in refrigerator.

FOR CRUST

1 1/2 cups flour

1/3 cup sugar

1/8 teaspoon salt

1/2 cup cold butter, cut into large dice

2 to 3 tablespoons ice water

FOR FILLING

1/2 cup butter

1 cup sugar

1/4 cup flour

2 eggs

1 1/2 teaspoons vanilla

6 fresh figs, cut in half, stems removed

Confectioners' sugar (optional)

Frozen Citrus Pie

MAKES 8 OR 9 SLICES

THE FILLING OF THIS PIE IS AN *adaptation of the filling for a banana cream pie from Mrs. Carl Winchenbach of Waldoboro, Maine. We found her recipe in a manuscript cookbook rescued from the town dump. The crust is a living recipe from the collection of Fran Kelly DaCosta, a well-traveled sophisticate from Watertown, Massachusetts.*

1. Set oven rack in middle position. Preheat oven to 375°F. Coat 9-inch ovenproof glass pie plate with vegetable spray. Set aside medium metal bowl for custard and larger bowl for ice bath. Have ice cubes handy in the freezer.

2. To make crust: Place graham crackers in bowl of food processor fitted with metal blade. Pulse to make crumbs the size of cornmeal (about 1½ cups). Add butter and confectioners' sugar and pulse to combine. Press crumbs on bottom and sides of pie plate. Bake 8 minutes. Set on rack to cool.

3. To make filling: Combine 1¼ cups of the milk and corn syrup in heavy saucepan. Cook over medium-low heat, stirring constantly with wooden spoon until bubbles start to form around edges, up to 7 minutes. Remove from heat.

4. Whisk cornstarch into remaining ¼ cup milk. Add sugar, salt, and lemon zest and mix thoroughly. Add egg yolks, one at a time, to cornstarch mixture and whisk until well blended. Add a little of the hot milk mixture to egg mixture to temper it and whisk briskly to blend. Whisk remaining hot milk mixture into eggs.

5. Return mixture to saucepan and bring to a simmer over medium heat. Cook about 30 seconds, stirring continuously until mixture begins to thicken. Remove from heat and whisk. Add lemon juice and whisk again. Place custard in metal bowl and set bowl in ice bath. Stir occasionally until custard is chilled.

6. Pour heavy cream into bowl of standing mixer fitted with whisk attachment. Beat until thick. Gradually add confectioners' sugar. Fold 1½ cups of the whipped cream into custard and turn into cooled pie shell. Pipe remaining whipped cream around edge. Place pie in freezer several hours. Remove pie from freezer 10 minutes before serving. Store leftover pie in freezer.

FOR CRUST

12 graham crackers, 2½ inches by 5 inches each (1 sleeve from a 3-sleeve box)

¼ cup butter, melted

½ cup confectioners' sugar

FOR FILLING

1½ cups milk, divided

¼ cup light corn syrup

¼ cup cornstarch

1 cup sugar

¼ teaspoon salt

2 teaspoons grated lemon zest

6 egg yolks

½ cup lemon juice, or ¼ cup lemon juice and ¼ cup lime juice

2 cups heavy cream, chilled

¼ cup confectioners' sugar

Nectarine Betty

{ 1 9 4 0 s }

BETTIES DIFFER FROM CRUMBLES AND COBBLERS BECAUSE *they are usually made with buttered cubes of bread or bread crumbs. This betty appealed to us because it was different from all the others we found in our collection—it is made with buttered, spiced graham cracker crumbs. The layers of fruit and crumbs are further enhanced by a crispy topping of brown sugar and yet more butter.*

1. Set oven rack in middle position. Preheat oven to 375°F. Coat 9-inch by 9-inch baking pan with vegetable spray. Line 14-inch by 16-inch baking sheet with foil.

2. To make betty: Place nectarines in large bowl and sprinkle with lemon juice.

3. Place lemon zest and graham cracker crumbs in another bowl. Add butter and mix thoroughly with your hands (wear disposable gloves if desired) until texture is sandy. Add sugar, brown sugar, cinnamon, ginger, nutmeg, cloves, and salt and mix in.

4. To add topping: Layer half of crumbs on bottom of pan. Layer sliced nectarines on top of crumbs. Sprinkle remaining crumbs over fruit. Distribute brown sugar evenly over crumb topping and dot with butter.

5. Place on baking sheet in oven. Bake 30 to 35 minutes, or until topping is browned. If topping appears to be browning too quickly, cover loosely with foil. Let cool on rack until pleasantly warm. Serve warm with whipped cream or vanilla ice cream. Store covered with wax paper in refrigerator. Leftover betty may be reheated in 300°F oven for 10 minutes.

FOR BETTY

6 ripe, but still a bit firm, nectarines, cut into slices (5 to 6 cups)

3 tablespoons lemon juice

2 teaspoons grated lemon zest

1½ cups graham cracker crumbs

4 tablespoons butter, melted

¼ cup sugar

1 cup brown sugar

½ teaspoon cinnamon

¼ teaspoon ginger

¼ teaspoon nutmeg

Pinch of cloves

⅛ teaspoon salt

FOR TOPPING

½ cup brown sugar

3 tablespoons butter

 TIPS & TOUCHES

- A betty is different from a crisp because of the layer of crumbs on the bottom. Don't be surprised if these bottom crumbs are a little juicy—the fruit just melts into them.
- Sometimes the betty falls in a bit if it sits around waiting to be served, but don't fret—the dessert loses none of its flavor or appeal.

Classic Bread Pudding

{ 1 8 9 0 }

MAKES 20 SERVINGS

FOR BREAD LAYERS

½ cup plus 2 tablespoons butter, melted

14 to 16 (½-inch-thick) slices brioche, trimmed of crusts and cut in half

FOR CUSTARD

2 cups milk

2 cups heavy cream

1 cup sugar

1 teaspoon vanilla

½ teaspoon cinnamon

½ teaspoon nutmeg

¼ teaspoon salt

4 eggs, beaten

2 cups raisins, soaked in ½ cup brandy

FOR TOPPING

1 cup brown sugar

4 tablespoons butter, melted

WHEN WE READ THROUGH OUR MANY MANUSCRIPT *cookbooks, we found countless recipes for bread puddings that sounded good. It seems that the quintessential bread pudding should include elements from all of them. Although some use only stale bread, milk instead of cream, and a token egg, all of them stay with the original concept of bread, dried fruit, and custard.*

1. Set oven rack in middle position. Preheat oven to 350°F. Coat 9-inch by 13-inch ovenproof glass baking dish with vegetable spray. Set aside larger metal baking pan and rack for water bath.

2. To prepare bread: Brush melted butter on both sides of each brioche slice.

3. To make custard: Combine milk, heavy cream, sugar, vanilla, cinnamon, nutmeg, and salt in bowl. Add eggs to custard mixture and combine.

4. Pour small amount of custard in bottom of baking dish. Tilt and swirl dish until bottom is covered. Layer 6 slices of brioche on top of custard. Fill in spaces with extra brioche. Pour half of remaining custard over brioche. Drain brandy from raisins. Sprinkle half of raisins on top of custard. Add remaining brioche to dish. Pour rest of custard over brioche and sprinkle with remaining raisins.

5. To add topping: Use knife to cut 8 slits through layered pudding. Cover top of pudding with plastic wrap and press down firmly with your palm until custard rises to top. (Raisins will sink into pudding.) Let stand 10 minutes, pushing down gently on top of pudding 2 more times. Remove plastic wrap and cover entire top of pudding with brown sugar. Pour melted butter over brown sugar.

6. Place baking dish on rack in large metal pan. Pour hot water from glass measuring cup into outer pan until water level rises halfway up sides of glass dish. Place carefully in oven. Bake approximately 1 hour and 15 minutes, or until topping puffs up and begins to bubble and tester inserted into middle comes out

clean. *Do not let water bath evaporate.* Check pudding periodically during baking to be sure topping is not burning; cover loosely with foil if topping seems to be drying out.

7. Remove baking dish carefully from oven and water bath. Allow to cool on rack 30 minutes to 1 hour. Serve slightly warm or at room temperature with unsweetened whipped cream. Store covered with paper towel and plastic wrap in refrigerator.

Marion Carter's Blueberry Lemon Bread Pudding

{ *1 9 0 0* }

MAKES 16 SERVINGS

FOR BLUEBERRY LAYERS

3 cups blueberries

2 tablespoons flour

FOR BREAD LAYERS

14 to 16 (½-inch-thick) slices brioche, trimmed of crusts and cut in half

½ cup plus 2 tablespoons butter, melted

FOR CUSTARD

2 cups milk

1 cup heavy cream

¼ teaspoon salt

1 teaspoon nutmeg

1⅓ cups sugar

2 teaspoons grated lemon zest

¾ teaspoon lemon extract

1 teaspoon vanilla

6 eggs, beaten

FOR TOPPING

2 tablespoons butter, melted

⅓ cup sugar

FROM THE MANUSCRIPT COOKBOOK OF MARION A. CARTER, *this is just one of the many desserts this lady from Maine baked and recorded. We've updated it with brioche and heavy cream, but essentially it is the same recipe Marion made around the turn of the 20th century.*

1. Set oven rack in middle position. Preheat oven to 350°F. Coat 9-inch by 13-inch ovenproof glass baking dish with vegetable spray. Set aside larger metal pan and rack for water bath.

2. To prepare blueberries: Toss blueberries with flour and shake in sieve to remove excess flour.

3. To prepare bread: Brush brioche slices with melted butter.

4. To make custard: Combine 1 cup of the milk, heavy cream, salt, nutmeg, sugar, lemon zest, lemon extract, and vanilla in large bowl. Add eggs and beat to combine.

5. Layer 6 slices of buttered brioche in baking dish. Fill in spaces with extra brioche. Pour half of custard over brioche and sprinkle with half of blueberries. Add remaining brioche, custard, and blueberries in layers.

6. To add topping: Use knife to cut 8 slits through pudding. Cover top of pudding with plastic wrap and press down gently. Let stand 15 minutes, or until custard has moistened brioche layers. Remove plastic wrap. Brush with melted butter and sprinkle with sugar.

7. Place baking dish on rack in large metal pan. Pour hot water from glass measuring cup into outer pan until water level rises halfway up sides of baking dish. Cover with foil. Place carefully in oven. Bake 30 minutes, checking water level periodically and replenishing if needed. *Do not let water bath evaporate.* Remove foil and bake another 45 minutes, or until pudding is bubbling, topping has caramelized, and tester inserted into pudding comes out clean.

8. Carefully remove baking dish from water bath and oven. Allow to cool on rack 1 hour. Serve warm or at room temperature. Store covered with paper towel and plastic wrap in refrigerator.

TIPS & TOUCHES

* We used brioche, but you can use a firm bread such as *pain de mie,* challah, or even croissants.

Caramelized Apple Bread Pudding

{ 1 9 2 0 s }

FOR CARAMELIZED APPLES

½ cup butter

8 Granny Smith apples, peeled, cored, and cut into wedges (8 per apple)

3 tablespoons lemon juice

2 teaspoons grated lemon zest

¼ cup plus 2 tablespoons sugar

1½ teaspoons cinnamon

1½ teaspoons nutmeg

¼ teaspoon salt

FOR BREAD LAYERS

14 to 16 (½-inch-thick) slices brioche or firm white bread, trimmed of crusts and cut in half

½ cup plus 2 tablespoons butter, melted

FOR CUSTARD

2 cups milk

2 cups heavy cream

1 cup plus 2 tablespoons sugar

1 teaspoon vanilla

½ teaspoon cinnamon

½ teaspoon nutmeg

½ teaspoon salt

4 eggs, beaten

WE FOUND A RECIPE FOR BREAD PUDDING *in almost every manuscript cookbook we read. Because these puddings use not only bits and pieces of leftover bread and fruit but also the staples of the larder—eggs, sugar, butter, and milk—they could be put together on the spur of the moment. This dessert can be served with Soft Caramel Sauce.*

1. Set oven rack in middle position. Preheat oven to 350°F. Coat 3-quart ovenproof glass baking dish with vegetable spray. Set aside larger metal baking pan and rack for water bath.

2. To make caramelized apples: Melt butter in large heavy frying pan. Fry apples in 2 batches, turning several times with a wooden spoon, until light golden in color. Return all apples to pan. Add lemon juice, lemon zest, and sugar and continue cooking, turning occasionally, until apples are cooked but still a little firm, 7 to 10 minutes. Add cinnamon, nutmeg, and salt. Bring apples to a boil and cook until liquid starts to thicken and caramelize, 1 to 2 minutes. Remove from heat.

3. To prepare bread: Brush brioche slices on both sides with butter.

4. To make custard: Combine milk, heavy cream, 1 cup of the sugar, vanilla, cinnamon, nutmeg, and salt in large bowl. Add eggs and whisk to combine.

5. Place ½ cup of the custard on bottom of baking dish. Tilt and swirl dish until bottom is completely covered with thin layer of custard. Layer 6 slices of brioche on top of custard. Fill in spaces with extra brioche. Layer on half of caramelized apples. Pour half of remaining custard over apples. Add remaining brioche, apples, and custard in layers.

6. Use knife to cut 8 slits through layered pudding. Cover top of pudding with plastic wrap and press down gently with your palm. Let stand 10 minutes. Remove plastic wrap and sprinkle remaining 2 tablespoons sugar over top.

7. Place baking dish on rack in large metal pan. Pour hot water from glass measuring cup into outer pan until water level rises halfway

SOFT CARAMEL SAUCE

This caramel sauce is light, intensely sweet, and incredibly smooth. It's a thick caramel you could easily stand a spoon in, and it enhances everything it is paired with. Try it over vanilla ice cream or homemade chocolate pudding.

1 cup sugar	¼ cup butter
¼ cup water	1 cup heavy cream
1 tablespoon light corn syrup	⅛ teaspoon salt

1. Combine sugar, water, and light corn syrup in heavy saucepan over high heat. Bring to a boil, stirring with wooden spoon.

2. Dip brush in water and wash down insides of pan. Reduce heat to medium high. *Do not stir.* Continue boiling until mixture turns golden brown (not dark brown), about 6 minutes.

3. Remove pan from heat. Swirl sauce gently in pan twice. Add butter and stir slowly until melted. Add cream (sauce may foam up) and stir again. (If caramel seizes—doesn't join with cream—place pan on medium heat and stir with wooden spoon until smooth, about 1 minute.) Add salt. Pour caramel sauce into glass containers. Cool to room temperature and store in refrigerator for up to 2 weeks. Sauce will thicken on standing. **Makes approximately 2 cups**

up sides of baking dish. Place carefully in oven. Bake approximately 1 hour and 15 minutes, or until top is nicely browned and batter and apples have risen to top. Check pudding occasionally during baking and cover loosely with foil if topping seems to be drying out. *Do not let water bath evaporate.*

8. Carefully remove baking dish from oven and warm water bath. Allow to cool on rack 1 hour. Serve pudding warm or cold with unsweetened whipped cream or vanilla ice cream. Store covered with paper towel and plastic wrap in refrigerator.

TIPS & TOUCHES

- Each apple should be cut into at least eight wedges.
- It is easier to fry apples in two batches. You can also use two pans to fry apples; just be sure to divide the other ingredients equally between the two pans.
- Caramelized apples can be made the day before and refrigerated.
- Challah or good-quality sourdough or white bread can be used instead of brioche.

Grandma's Secret Warm Banana Meringue Pudding

{ 1 9 4 0 s }

MAKES 16 GENEROUS SERVINGS

FOR CUSTARD

1¼ cups sugar

1 cup flour

¼ teaspoon salt

4 cups milk

1 cup heavy cream

8 egg yolks

2 teaspoons vanilla

10 ounces vanilla wafers

6 to 8 ripe bananas, sliced
    crosswise

FOR MERINGUE

8 egg whites

¼ teaspoon cream of tartar

½ cup plus 1 tablespoon sugar

YVETTE GOODING LEARNED TO MAKE THIS PUDDING *when baking in the kitchen with her grandmother Lannie Waters Edmondson, a magnificent home cook. When we tried this pudding, we doubled the recipe and were rewarded with a dessert that tastes—and looks—spectacular. Guess the secret is out!*

1. Set oven rack in middle position. Preheat oven to 350°F. Coat 9-inch by 13-inch ovenproof glass baking dish with vegetable spray.

2. To make custard: Sift sugar, flour, and salt into large heavy pan. Add milk and heavy cream and mix thoroughly. Add egg yolks one at a time, blending well after each. Cook mixture over medium to medium-high heat, stirring constantly with wooden spoon, about 10 minutes, or until thickened. Remove from heat and strain through sieve. Add vanilla to cooked custard.

3. Spread small amount of custard on bottom of baking dish. Swirl to cover evenly. Cover with half of vanilla wafers. Cover wafers with half of bananas and press down gently with your palm.

4. Pour generous layer of custard on top of wafers. Add remaining wafers and bananas in 2 layers. Pour remaining custard on top, smoothing with spatula so that all wafers and bananas are covered. Press down again gently with palm of your hand. Bake pudding for 10 minutes.

5. To make meringue: Add egg whites and cream of tartar to bowl of standing mixer fitted with whisk attachment. Whip on low speed. Gradually increase speed to medium and whip until soft peaks form. Add sugar in thirds while increasing speed of mixer to high. Beat until stiff peaks are formed. Meringue should not be dry.

6. Remove pudding from oven and mound meringue on top, spreading until entire surface is covered. (Be sure to seal edges.) Return pudding to oven and bake about 20 minutes, checking every 5 minutes to be sure it does not burn. Remove from oven and place on rack to cool. Serve when slightly warm. Store leftover pudding in refrigerator.

Sweet Potato Pudding

{ 1 9 3 0 s }

WE FOUND SEVERAL RECIPES FOR THIS PUDDING *in our collection of manuscript cookbooks, but this is the version we decided to try. It's another recipe Yvette Gooding learned from her late grandmother Lannie. Yvette makes this pudding frequently for her 2 sons, Patrick and Andrew. This pudding calls for grated raw sweet potatoes, so it has a bit of texture to it. This is a very good choice for a holiday dessert.*

4 large sweet potatoes

½ cup butter, softened to room temperature

1 cup firmly packed brown sugar, divided

½ cup sugar

3 eggs

2 teaspoons vanilla

½ teaspoon cinnamon

½ teaspoon nutmeg

¼ teaspoon salt

¾ cup milk

¼ cup heavy cream

1. Set oven rack in middle position. Preheat oven to 350°F. Coat 9-inch by 13-inch ovenproof glass baking dish with vegetable spray.

2. Peel and quarter sweet potatoes. Grate in food processor fitted with metal grating blade or by hand. Process grated sweet potato in bowl of food processor fitted with metal blade or chop hand-grated potatoes with a knife. (You should have about 11 cups.) Sweet potatoes should be smooth.

3. Cream butter, ½ cup of the brown sugar, and sugar in bowl of standing mixer fitted with paddle attachment. Add eggs and vanilla. Add cinnamon, nutmeg, salt, milk, and heavy cream and combine. Fold in grated, chopped sweet potato. Place in prepared dish. Sprinkle remaining ½ cup brown sugar over top of pudding.

4. Bake 1 hour, or until top of pudding is caramelized and tester inserted into middle comes out clean. Cover with foil if pudding browns too quickly. Serve pudding hot or cold with whipped cream. Store leftover pudding in dish covered with wax paper in refrigerator.

China custard cups; wire holder, American, 1930s

Elinor's Persimmon Pudding

MAKES 12 SLICES

{ *1940s* }

This was the signature dessert of Elinor *Inman Jennings. We waited more than 30 years to try it because we had never baked with persimmons before. It was a revelation! The result is a rich pudding with a firm crumb. Raisins and nuts add to the texture. This extrasweet dessert does well with a touch of whipped cream.*

1. Set oven rack in middle position. Preheat oven to 350°F. Coat bottom and sides of 1½-quart ovenproof glass baking dish with butter or vegetable spray. Cut parchment paper liner to fit bottom of pan and coat it with vegetable spray. Set aside larger metal pan and rack for water bath.

2. Place persimmons in bowl of food processor fitted with metal blade. Pulse until creamy. Measure 1 cup of persimmon pulp and place in bowl.

3. Sift together flour, sugar, baking soda, cinnamon, and salt in medium bowl. Add milk to sifted dry ingredients and mix. Fold in persimmon pulp. Fold in raisins and walnuts. Fold in butter.

4. Place mixture into baking dish. Cover with foil. Place dish on rack in large pan. Pour hot water from glass measuring cup into outer pan until water level rises halfway up sides of baking dish. Place carefully in oven. Bake 1 hour to 1 hour and 15 minutes. Check water bath occasionally and add more water if needed. *Do not let the water bath evaporate.* Remove foil after 30 minutes. Pudding is done when tester inserted in center comes out clean.

5. Carefully remove baking dish from oven and water bath. Allow to cool on rack 30 minutes. Serve warm or at room temperature with fruit sauce or whipped cream flavored with brandy. Store leftover pudding loosely covered with wax paper in refrigerator.

2 ripe persimmons, quartered and skins removed

1 cup flour

1 cup sugar

1 teaspoon baking soda

1 teaspoon cinnamon

1 teaspoon salt

½ cup milk

1 cup golden raisins

1 cup chopped walnuts

1 tablespoon butter, melted

Brandied whipped cream (optional)

 Tips & Touches

- After the pudding cools, you can poke holes in the top with a skewer and pour brandy over it, instead of adding brandy to the whipped cream. Although Elinor did not believe in drinking alcoholic beverages herself, we don't think she would have objected if your whipped cream were slightly enhanced with a touch of brandy. We also like to brush the top of the pudding with warmed apricot jam and decorate it with candied fruit, almonds, and pecans. We suggest that you brush the decorative fruit and nuts with more of the warm apricot jam.

Cheese Blintzes

{1940s}

FOR BLINTZES

2 eggs, beaten

¾ cup water

½ cup flour

4 tablespoons butter, melted, plus extra for frying

1 teaspoon sugar

Pinch of salt

1 teaspoon vanilla

FOR FILLING

6 ounces farmer's cheese or pot cheese

4 ounces (½ package) cream cheese

1 egg, lightly beaten

2 teaspoons sugar

½ teaspoon vanilla

Pinch of salt

TIPS & TOUCHES

- You can also fill your blintzes with fresh blueberries mixed with sugar and a little cinnamon.

WE REMEMBER OUR MOTHER MAKING BLINTZES IN *the early summer. The ritual was always the same—the clean white bed sheet on the kitchen table, the battered little frying pan, and the crumpled piece of wax paper dipped in melted butter for greasing it. After each blintz was fried, she'd flip the pan onto the covered table, lining them up on the sheet. We'd rush to eat the filled blintzes with sour cream and applesauce.*

1. Coat 8-inch frying pan with vegetable spray. Set aside sheets of wax paper or parchment paper to place between blintzes.

2. To make blintzes: Combine eggs and water in bowl. Add flour, butter, sugar, salt, and vanilla and whisk until smooth. Strain batter to remove any lumps.

3. Heat pan on medium-high heat. Pour ¼ cup of batter into pan, swirl to cover bottom of pan lightly, and pour excess batter back into bowl. Fry until blintz comes away from pan and is opaque in color. Loosen edges of blintz with butter knife and flip with spatula onto wax paper or parchment paper. Place each cooled blintz between sheets of wax or parchment paper. Continue to fry blintzes, spraying pan before each one, until batter is used up.

4. To make filling: Combine farmer's or pot cheese, cream cheese, egg, sugar, vanilla, and salt in bowl. Beat with wooden spoon until combined.

5. Place blintz on work surface and spoon some filling onto center. Fold in 2 opposite edges, overlapping in middle, and then fold in ends to make a neat package. Repeat for each blintz, dividing the filling evenly among them.

6. Melt 1 tablespoon butter in frying pan or on greased griddle and add blintzes. Fry until golden brown on both sides, turning once. Serve at once with sour cream and applesauce. Store leftover or unfried blintzes on plate, loosely wrapped in wax paper in refrigerator.

Pineapple Raisin Dessert Kugel

MAKES 16 SERVINGS

{ *1930s* }

WE LOVE KUGEL, ESPECIALLY SWEET DAIRY KUGEL *made with but-*
ter, cheese, sugar, eggs, and sour cream. Some argue that kugel is meant to be
served as an accompaniment to a main dish. We disagree. We think kugel can be
eaten for breakfast, lunch, and dinner, in between meals, and even as a dessert!

1. Set oven rack in middle position. Preheat oven to 350°F. Coat
   9-inch by 13-inch ovenproof glass baking dish with vegetable spray.
2. To make kugel: Cook noodles according to package directions
   and drain thoroughly.
3. Place noodles in large bowl. Mix in cottage cheese, brown sugar,
   and sour cream. Add eggs, butter, salt, nutmeg, cinnamon, and
   vanilla and mix to combine.
4. Roll pineapple in paper towels to remove excess moisture. Chop
   coarsely and fold into noodle mixture. Fold in raisins.
5. To add topping: Turn noodle mixture into baking dish. Pour
   melted butter over top and sprinkle with brown sugar. Bake 50 to
   55 minutes, or until kugel bubbles and noodles on top turn
   golden brown. Place on rack to cool. Serve hot or cold with sour
   cream. Store covered with wax paper in refrigerator.

FOR KUGEL

1 (12-ounce) package wide
   egg noodles

2 cups cottage cheese

1/2 cup brown sugar

1 cup sour cream

4 eggs, beaten

1/2 cup butter, melted

1/4 teaspoon salt

1/4 teaspoon nutmeg

1/2 teaspoon cinnamon

1 teaspoon vanilla

1 cup canned pineapple
   chunks, drained

1 cup raisins

FOR TOPPING

3 tablespoons butter, melted

4 tablespoons brown sugar

Frosted Pan Hermits

{ 1 9 2 0 s }

MAKES 24 BARS

FOR HERMITS

1½ cups plus 2 tablespoons flour, divided

2 teaspoons baking powder

½ teaspoon salt

¼ teaspoon cloves

½ teaspoon nutmeg

½ teaspoon cinnamon

¼ cup plus 2 tablespoons butter

1 cup brown sugar

1 egg

½ cup milk

1 cup raisins

1 cup chopped walnuts

FOR FROSTING

⅔ cup confectioners' sugar

⅛ teaspoon salt

1½ teaspoons butter

1 teaspoon vanilla

2 to 3 teaspoons milk, as needed

As children, when anyone mentioned hermits, we always pictured thin, elderly, white-bearded men living in caves. As adults, we can't forget the delicious hermits we ate as children; they were crunchy, with a light confectioners' sugar frosting on top and a hint of clove. We found more than a dozen recipes for hermits, but most of them were drop cookies. This one is simple to make and a little unusual because it is baked in one layer in a shallow pan.

1. Set oven rack in middle position. Preheat oven to 350°F. Line 9-inch by 13-inch by 1-inch jelly roll pan with foil, shiny side up. Coat foil with butter or vegetable spray.

2. To make hermits: Sift together 1½ cups of the flour, baking powder, salt, cloves, nutmeg, and cinnamon.

3. Cream butter and brown sugar in bowl of standing mixer fitted with paddle attachment. Add egg. Add sifted dry ingredients alternately with milk. Mix remaining 2 tablespoons flour with raisins and walnuts and fold into batter.

4. Pour batter into jelly roll pan and spread with offset spatula until even. Bake 25 to 30 minutes, or until tester inserted into middle comes out clean. Turn once during baking. Place pan on rack. Frost while warm.

5. To make frosting: Sift confectioners' sugar and salt into bowl. Add butter and whisk until combined. Add vanilla and enough milk to form thin frosting. Pour frosting gently over warm pan and spread evenly. Allow to set. When completely cool, cut into squares. Store hermits in single layers between sheets of wax paper in covered tin.

TIPS & TOUCHES

- If the frosting seems lumpy, it will melt when it is applied to the warm hermits. The frosting may crackle on top, too.

Edinburgh Tea Squares

{ *1 9 2 0 s — 1 9 3 0 s* }   MAKES 48 SQUARES

FOR FILLING

1 cup dried apricots

1 cup sugar

1 tablespoon lemon juice

FOR SQUARES

2 cups sifted flour

1 teaspoon salt

2 cups rolled oats

1 cup fine bread crumbs (see "How
   to Make Fine Bread Crumbs" on
   page 204)

1½ cups butter, softened to room
   temperature

2 cups firmly packed brown sugar

1 cup toasted pecans,
   coarsely chopped

TIPS & TOUCHES

* Do not use instant oatmeal for
the dough.

THIS IS ANOTHER ONE OF THOSE FOUND *treasures, a living recipe handwritten in pencil on a sheet of paper like the ones we used for our arithmetic homework. The original called for dates. We tried it with both dates and apricots, and the slightly sour taste of the apricots won because it balanced the sweetness of the squares. This is a simple recipe that looks inviting when served in frilled white paper cups.*

1. Set oven rack in middle position. Preheat oven to 350°F. Line bottom and sides of 9-inch by 13-inch metal pan with foil, shiny side up. Coat with butter or vegetable spray.

2. To make filling: Place apricots and sugar in large saucepan. Cover with water and bring to a boil. Reduce heat and simmer until apricots are soft, about 15 minutes. Drain and place in bowl to cool. Place apricots in bowl of food processor fitted with metal blade. Add lemon juice. Pulse until soft paste forms. Set aside.

3. To make squares: Combine flour, salt, oats, and bread crumbs in large mixing bowl and set aside.

4. Cream butter and brown sugar in bowl of standing mixer fitted with paddle attachment. Add dry ingredients and combine. Fold in pecans with spatula.

5. Spread half of oat and nut mixture over bottom of prepared pan, smoothing with offset spatula. Add apricot filling in even layer and smooth top. Cover with remaining oat and nut mixture and smooth with spatula. Bake about 45 minutes, or until top is light golden brown. Cool in pan on rack to room temperature and then refrigerate 3 hours. Cake will firm up as it cools. Cut into squares with wide-blade knife and serve. Store between sheets of wax paper in covered tin.

Libby's Coconut Linzer Bars

MAKES 16 2-INCH BARS

WRITTEN ON A LINED INDEX CARD, THIS *recipe for a bar cookie made with raspberry jam and coconut is an easy way to enjoy the linzer experience. We, like so many other home cooks, have baked traditional linzer cookie sandwiches, cut from a dough made with ground hazelnuts and filled with raspberry jam.*

1 (8-ounce) package unsweetened shredded coconut

1¼ cups flour

½ teaspoon salt

½ cup cold butter, cut into ½-inch dice

2 tablespoons cold water

2 eggs

½ cup sugar

¾ cup seedless raspberry jam or apricot jam

1. Set oven rack in middle position. Preheat oven to 425°F. Line bottom and 4 sides of 8-inch by 8-inch pan with foil, shiny side up. Coat foil with butter or vegetable spray.
2. Place coconut in bowl of food processor fitted with metal blade. Pulse 2 or 3 times until coconut flakes are reduced in length. Set coconut aside. (Be careful not to reduce coconut flakes to coconut dust.)
3. Place flour, salt, and butter in bowl of food processor fitted with metal blade. Process until butter is size of small peas. Add cold water, 1 tablespoon at a time. Pulse 2 more times. Particles should cling together. Remove dough from bowl of food processor and form into ball. Pat dough into bottom of pan with fingers until bottom is evenly covered. Bake 20 minutes, or until lightly browned. Place pan on rack and cool. Reduce oven temperature to 375°F.
4. Beat eggs in bowl of standing mixer fitted with paddle attachment. Gradually add sugar and continue beating until mixture is thick and light in color. Fold in coconut.
5. Spread jam over cooled pastry to within ¼ inch of edges. Carefully spread coconut mixture over jam. Return pan to oven and bake 25 minutes, or until coconut is golden brown. Place pan on rack and cool completely. Cut into bars. Store between sheets of wax paper in covered tin.

Hungarian Crisscross Cookies

{ *1930s* }

FOR COOKIES

2½ cups flour

⅓ cup sugar

1 teaspoon baking powder

½ teaspoon salt

¼ teaspoon cloves

½ teaspoon cinnamon

1 cup cold butter, cut into
    ½-inch pieces

1 teaspoon grated lemon zest

4 teaspoons lemon juice

2 tablespoons ice water

¼ cup confectioners' sugar

FOR FILLING

1 cup to 1¾ cups apricot,
    raspberry, or plum jam, at room
    temperature

Tips & Touches

- We used a half jelly roll pan. We found that one of our shallow pans had ¾-inch sides and one had 1-inch sides. Both pans are suitable for this recipe.
- We used an 18-inch ruler with a metal edge to measure and cut the strips of dough. You can also use a sharp knife.

THIS IS OUR SECOND ENCOUNTER WITH HUNGARIAN *Crisscross Cookies. The first ones we tasted and baked in the 1970s were adapted from a handwritten recipe from the Midwest, which we later misplaced. We were over-joyed to find this second recipe, which was written on a lined index card. The jewel-like jam filling peeking from the geometrically consistent pastry strips makes a great presentation.*

1. Set oven rack in middle position. Preheat oven to 350°F. Line bottom and sides of 9-inch by 13-inch by 1-inch jelly roll pan with foil, shiny side up. Coat foil with butter or vegetable spray.

2. To make cookies: Place flour, sugar, baking powder, salt, cloves, and cinnamon in bowl of food processor fitted with metal blade. Pulse 2 or 3 times until combined. Add butter and combine until mixture is crumbly. Add lemon zest, lemon juice, and ice water. Process just until dough comes together. Gather dough and scraps, form into ball, and wrap in sheet of wax paper. Chill dough 1 hour, or until firm.

3. To add filling: Divide dough into thirds. Return one third to refrigerator. Pat two thirds into pan, making sure dough reaches into edges and corners. Spread jam evenly over dough with offset spatula.

4. Turn out remaining dough onto floured wax paper. Pat to make rectangle ¼-inch thick. Cut into ½-inch-wide strips along length of rectangle. Carefully lift strips and place them diagonally over layer of jam. Place additional strips in the opposite direction, for a lattice effect. You may have to patch strips of dough. Use remaining strips to form borders around edges of pan.

5. Bake 35 to 40 minutes, or until crust is golden brown and jam is bubbling slightly. Remove from oven and place on rack to cool. Lightly sprinkle confectioners' sugar over top while still warm. Sugar will be absorbed by filling but will remain on crust. When completely cool, remove pastry from foil and cut into squares. Store between sheets of wax paper in covered tin.

Butterscotch Bars with Brown Sugar Meringue Topping

MAKES 40 BARS

{ 1 9 3 0 s }

THIS IS A DELICIOUS SWEET BAR. It's *like 2 cookies in 1, a bar cookie and a brown sugar meringue. This Butterscotch Bar was very popular with Midwestern ladies and their bridge clubs during the 1930s and 1940s. Variations are still being exchanged at 21st-century bridge parties.*

1. Set oven rack in middle position. Preheat oven to 350°F. Line bottom and sides of 9-inch by 13-inch pan with foil, shiny side up, and coat with vegetable spray. Line 14-inch by 16-inch baking sheet with foil.

2. To make bars: Place pecan pieces on baking sheet. Toast in oven 7 to 10 minutes, stirring a few times for even browning. Do not allow pecan pieces to burn. Cool to room temperature.

3. Combine flour, baking powder, salt, and brown sugar in bowl of food processor fitted with metal blade. Add butter. Process until butter is size of small peas. Add egg yolks and vanilla and pulse 3 or 4 times until mixture has consistency of sandy clumps.

4. Pat mixture into pan and level off by pressing with small offset spatula. Press pecans into mixture.

5. To make topping: Place egg whites in bowl of standing mixer fitted with whisk attachment. Beat until whites hold a peak when whisk is lifted. Add brown sugar and beat at highest speed about 4 minutes. Spread meringue over pecan layer. Bake 25 minutes, or until tester inserted into bars comes out clean. The meringue will crack slightly, but this will not significantly affect appearance. Let cool on rack completely and cut into squares. Store between sheets of wax paper in covered tin.

FOR BARS

2 cups pecan pieces

1½ cups flour

1½ teaspoons baking powder

⅛ teaspoon salt

1 cup brown sugar

½ cup cold butter, cut into dice

2 egg yolks

1 teaspoon vanilla

FOR TOPPING

2 egg whites

1 cup brown sugar

Mama's Apricot Strudel with Cream Cheese Crust

MAKES 40 SLICES

{ *1940s* }

THIS WAS ONE OF THE RECIPES WE *loved baking with our mother. It was a tradition to bake this when summer was just a memory, and we were turning to winter's offerings of dried, candied, and preserved fruit.*

1. Set oven rack in middle position. Preheat oven to 400°F. Cover 14-inch by 16-inch baking sheet with foil, shiny side up. Coat foil with vegetable spray or use silicone liner.

2. To make filling: Place apricots in saucepan, cover with water, and bring to a boil over medium heat. Cover and simmer about 15 minutes, or until apricots form soft paste. Check on fruit periodically to see that it does not burn, especially toward end of cooking time. Transfer apricot paste to bowl and add lemon juice and sugar. Allow to cool.

3. To make dough: Place butter and cream cheese in bowl of standing mixer fitted with paddle attachment. Cream until soft and fluffy. Add flour and salt and mix to combine. Add milk to form soft dough. Wrap dough in plastic wrap and chill in refrigerator until firm enough to roll out.

4. Remove dough from refrigerator and divide into 4 sections. Roll out 1 section of dough on floured wax paper or parchment paper to 1/16-inch-thick rectangle. Brush surface with melted butter. Place one-fourth of apricot filling at top of dough, leaving 1-inch edge. Sprinkle one-fourth of nuts and soda cracker crumbs on top of filling. Roll strudel lengthwise from top to bottom, like jelly roll, using paper as an aid. Place strudel on baking sheet, seam side down. Repeat with remaining dough and filling.

5. Brush each strudel with melted butter. Bake 20 minutes at 400°F. Turn oven temperature down to 350°F and bake 10 to 12 minutes more. Brush once during baking with melted butter. Remove pan from oven and place on rack. Cool 10 minutes. While still on pan, cut strudel diagonally into 1-inch slices. Continue to cool. Store between sheets of wax paper in covered tin.

FOR APRICOT FILLING

8 ounces dried apricots

1 tablespoon lemon juice

1/3 cup sugar

1 cup pistachio nuts, toasted

15 soda crackers, broken into crumbs

FOR DOUGH

1/2 cup butter

4 ounces cream cheese

1 2/3 cups flour

1/4 teaspoon salt

1/4 cup cold milk

1/4 cup butter, melted

 TIPS & TOUCHES

- Serve this strudel dusted with confectioners' sugar. It is best when eaten within 2 days.

The Samels-Carbarnes Family Adventures

MAKES 72 COOKIES

1 cup butter, softened to room temperature

1½ cups sugar

2 cups chopped, pitted dates

2 tablespoons milk

2 eggs, beaten

½ teaspoon salt

1 teaspoon vanilla

1 cup toasted walnuts, chopped

4 cups crispy rice cereal

1 (7-ounce) package shredded, sweetened coconut

DEBRA SAMELS FIRST TASTED THESE COOKIES WHEN *her mother, Mary Bohen Carbarnes, made them for the Platteville Free Methodist Church Christmas Bazaar in Wisconsin. Mrs. Carbarnes, who was the chairman of the bazaar, grew up near an Amish community and was a talented home baker. She put together a family cookbook for her 5 daughters. Zoe and Jack Samels, her grandchildren, both love to make Adventures.*

1. Line baking sheet with parchment paper.
2. Place butter and sugar in heavy-bottomed 2-quart saucepan and whisk to combine. Add dates and place pan over medium heat. Bring to a boil, stirring with wooden spoon, and remove from heat.
3. Combine milk and eggs in small bowl. Add ⅓ cup of hot date mixture and whisk quickly to temper eggs. Return egg mixture to saucepan and stir briskly. Bring to a boil over medium heat, stirring with wooden spoon. Boil 2 minutes. Remove mixture from heat. Add salt and vanilla.
4. Place walnuts and crispy rice cereal in large bowl. Add date mixture and stir to combine. Allow to cool. When cool enough to handle, scoop dough by the tablespoonful and roll into balls. Roll balls in coconut and place on prepared baking sheet. Adventures will firm up while standing. Place in fluted paper cups and serve. Store between sheets of wax paper in covered tin.

Aunt Liz O'Neill's Shortbread

MAKES 32 1-INCH BY 2-INCH PIECES

{ *1 9 3 0 s* }

Liz O'Neill was a great-aunt to Danese *and Barbara Carey.
A native of Glasgow and a superb shortbread maker, Aunt Liz immigrated to the
United States as a young woman. The Carey sisters would sit at Aunt Liz's table
taking notes while watching her bake. Although shortbread is traditionally made
by hand, we have interpreted this recipe using a standing mixer.*

1. Set oven rack in middle position. Preheat oven to 350°F. Line
   bottom and sides of 9-inch by 9-inch by 2-inch pan with foil.
   Grease foil with butter or coat with vegetable spray.

2. Cream butter, sugar, and salt in bowl of standing mixer fitted
   with paddle attachment. Add flour ½ cup at a time, beating just
   until flour is completely absorbed and dough comes together. Do
   not overbeat or shortbread will be tough.

3. Gently pat dough into pan. Do not press too hard or shortbread
   will be tough, not crumbly, after baking. Press down edges of
   dough with tines of fork. Prick top of dough evenly about
   25 times.

4. Bake 35 minutes, or until shortbread is light brown. Cover
   loosely with foil if surface browns too quickly. Cool on rack 20 to
   25 minutes, or until slightly warm. Score shortbread with a knife
   into 1-inch by 2-inch pieces, but do not cut through entirely.
   When completely cool, cut into pieces along scored lines. The
   texture should be sandy and crumbly.

1 cup butter

½ cup sugar

⅛ teaspoon salt

2⅓ cups sifted flour

TIPS & TOUCHES

* If you don't use all the flour in
  the shortbread, save it; it can
  be reused.

The Five Isabelles' Orange Drop Cakes

{ 1 9 2 0 s }

MAKES APPROXIMATELY 6 DOZEN 2-INCH COOKIES

FOR DROP CAKES

4½ cups flour

3 teaspoons baking powder

1 teaspoon baking soda

½ teaspoon salt

1 cup butter, softened to room temperature

2 cups sugar

2 eggs

3 tablespoons grated orange zest

½ cup orange juice

1 cup buttermilk

Coarse sanding sugar (optional)

FOR ICING (OPTIONAL)

1 pound confectioners' sugar

2 tablespoons grated orange zest

3 tablespoons orange juice

Pinch of salt

TIPS & TOUCHES

* Cookies can be finished with either sanding sugar or icing, not both.

WE RECEIVED THIS RECIPE FOR BUTTERY ORANGE *Drop Cakes from Mandy Timney Finizio. She found it handwritten on the inside back cover of her Grandmother Porter's 1922 copy of* Good Housekeeping's Book of Menus, Recipes, and Household Discoveries. *When Mandy's mother, also an Isabelle, was a child, Mrs. Porter taught her how to bake these legendary treats. There has been an Isabelle in each of the last 5 generations of Mandy's family, and all of them know how to make these cookies.*

1. To make drop cakes: Set oven rack in middle position. Preheat oven to 375°F. Line 14-inch by 16-inch baking sheet with foil, shiny side up, and coat with vegetable spray, or use silicone liner. Prepare 2 trays, if desired.

2. Sift flour, baking powder, baking soda, and salt in large bowl and set aside. Cream butter and sugar in bowl of standing mixer fitted with paddle attachment until fluffy. Add eggs, one at a time, beating after each addition. Add orange zest. Add one-third of dry ingredients and the orange juice and beat to combine. Add remaining dry ingredients, one-third at a time, alternating with buttermilk. Beat until smooth.

3. Drop dough by tablespoon on prepared baking sheet, or use disposable plastic piping bag for more uniform results. Do not pipe or drop more than 25 cookies per baking sheet (5 rows of 5 cookies). Flatten any peaks on cookies with finger dipped in cold water. Sprinkle with sanding sugar, if using. Bake 12 to 13 minutes, or until cookies are golden, with lightly browned edges. Place baking sheet on rack and let cool 2 minutes. Transfer cookies to rack with metal spatula and cool completely.

4. To make icing, if using: Sift confectioners' sugar into large bowl. Add orange zest, orange juice, and salt and whisk briskly to combine. Icing should be soft enough to drizzle over cakes; thicken with confectioners' sugar or thin with orange juice, as needed. Drizzle icing over cakes and let stand on racks until icing is completely dry. Store between sheets of wax paper in covered tin.

Lacy Oatmeal Cookies

MAKES 36 COOKIES

{1930s}

THESE DAINTY COOKIES ARE DELICIOUS AND NOT *nearly as heavy as the substantial oatmeal cookies we usually bake. Melted butter makes them light and lacy. We found this recipe typed and pasted at the end of the cookie chapter in a well-worn 1928 copy of* The Rumford Complete Cook Book *by Lily Haxworth Wallace. This book was produced by the department of home economics of the Rumford Company, which distributed Rumford Baking Powder.*

1. Set oven rack in middle position. Preheat oven to 350°F. Cover 14-inch by 16-inch baking sheet with foil, shiny side up. Coat foil with vegetable spray, or use silicone liner.
2. Combine sugar and butter in bowl of standing mixer fitted with paddle attachment. Beat in egg and vanilla. Add oats, flour, salt, and baking powder and mix well. Fold in chocolate chips and pecans.
3. Drop by teaspoons onto baking sheet at least 1½ to 2 inches apart. Bake 13 minutes, or until edges are lightly browned. Place baking sheet on rack to cool. (Do not remove cookies from baking sheet until they are completely cool.) Store cookies between sheets of parchment paper or wax paper in covered tin.

1 cup sugar

½ cup butter, melted

1 egg

½ teaspoon vanilla

1 cup quick-cooking oats

¼ cup flour

¼ teaspoon salt

¼ teaspoon baking powder

½ cup mini chocolate chips

½ cup finely chopped pecans or other nuts

⇥ BAKING WITH OATMEAL ⇤

Be sure to choose the right type of oats for baking. The size, shape, and texture of the oat grain may vary because of the amount of processing or rolling. As a rule of thumb, use old-fashioned or quick-cooking oats, not instant oatmeal, for oatmeal cookies. Pinhead oats, also known as Irish, Scottish, or steel-cut oats, should be used for cooked cereals or hearty coarse-grained breads.

Oats may be added to toppings for crisps and crumbles. Their nutty taste enhances the flavor of baked fruit. The coarse texture of oats prevents a topping from soaking up fruit juices and becoming soggy.

Nathalie's Ginger Whale Cookies

MAKES APPROXIMATELY 7 DOZEN 3½-INCH COOKIES

4 cups flour

½ teaspoon salt

1 teaspoon cinnamon

½ teaspoon nutmeg

½ teaspoon ginger

⅛ teaspoon cloves

½ cup butter, softened to room temperature

¼ cup sugar

1 egg

1 cup molasses

2 teaspoons baking soda

2 tablespoons hot water

¼ cup small raisins or chocolate dots

Tips & Touches

- Scraps of dough can be put together and rerolled. These cookies may be a little crisper.
- Various cookie cutters can be used, but a pod of whales is very nice.

WE'VE HAD THIS RECIPE FOR ALMOST 50 *years. Printed on a small piece of light blue paper, it came with a handmade cookie cutter in the shape of a whale. Designed and sold by Nathalie Woods, from Marblehead, Massachusetts, this crisp ginger cookie sports a raisin for an eye, and its tail can be placed at any angle. Sheila bought the cookie cutter while visiting her friend, Ruth Hadley, in Marblehead. This recipe is also similar to 1 we found in a manuscript cookbook, credited to "Edna."*

1. Sift flour, salt, cinnamon, nutmeg, ginger, and cloves into large mixing bowl and set aside.

2. Cream butter and sugar in bowl of standing mixer fitted with paddle attachment until fluffy. Add egg. Add molasses and combine. Dissolve baking soda in hot water and add to creamed ingredients. Add sifted dry ingredients in thirds and mix thoroughly. Scoop cookie dough onto sheet of wax paper or plastic wrap, form into disk, and chill in refrigerator at least 2 hours or overnight.

3. Set oven rack in middle position. Preheat oven to 375°F. Line 14-inch by 16-inch baking sheet with foil, shiny side up, and coat with vegetable spray, or use silicone liner. Prepare 2 trays, if desired.

4. Divide chilled dough in 4 parts. On floured piece of wax paper, roll dough ¼-inch thick. Cut out cookies with fish- or whale-shaped cutters. Place 2 inches apart on prepared baking sheet, putting no more than 16 cookies on sheet. Add raisin or chocolate dot to each cookie for an eye. Bake 10 to 12 minutes. Cool on rack until firm. Store between sheets of wax paper in covered tin.

Pistachio Crescents

MAKES 70 COOKIES

VARIATIONS OF THIS RECIPE KEEP POPPING UP, *and we've seen versions using chopped almonds and chopped walnuts, too. We prefer chopped pistachios because we love the slight green color of the nuts and their very Middle Eastern flavor. The veil of confectioners' sugar adds a bit of glamour to the crescents appearance.*

1. Set oven rack in middle position. Preheat oven to 350°F. Cover 14-inch by 16-inch baking sheet with foil, shiny side up. Coat foil with vegetable spray, or use silicone liner.

2. To make dough: Sift together flour and salt. Cream butter and sugar in bowl of standing mixer fitted with paddle attachment. Add vanilla and pistachios and combine. Add sifted dry ingredients gradually until dough begins to form. Gather up dough from bowl and knead gently to combine. Continue if dough is workable; if it is too soft to handle, chill in refrigerator until it is manageable.

3. With floured hands or wearing disposable gloves, break off about 1 teaspoon of dough. Roll dough between your hands to form 1½-inch-long rope. Shape rope into crescent and place on baking sheet. Repeat with remaining dough, spacing crescents 1½ inches apart and allowing 30 per sheet (crescents do not spread). Bake 17 minutes, or until lightly brown. Place baking sheet on rack and cool 2 to 3 minutes.

4. To add topping: Remove cookies from baking sheet (they may still be hot), dredge in confectioners' sugar, and set on rack until completely cool. Slip sheet of wax paper under rack. Sift confectioners' sugar generously over cookies. Allow 10 minutes for sugar to set. Store between sheets of wax paper in covered tin.

FOR DOUGH

2½ cups flour

¼ teaspoon salt

1 cup butter

¾ cup sugar

1½ teaspoons vanilla

1 cup pistachios, toasted and ground

FOR TOPPING

1½ cups confectioners' sugar, sifted

TIPS & TOUCHES

- Use the same dough to make Pistachio Thumbprint Cookies. Roll the dough into a ball, place it on the baking sheet, and make a thumbprint impression in the center of the cookie. Place a toasted pistachio in the depression. Each baking sheet will hold 24 cookies. Bake as for crescents, let cool 3 minutes, and transfer to a rack. Sift confectioners' sugar over the top. Store as for Pistachio Crescents.

Chinese Almond Cookies

MAKES 48 COOKIES

FOR COOKIES

3 cups flour

1 cup sugar

1 teaspoon baking powder

$\frac{1}{2}$ teaspoon salt

1 cup cold lard, cut into
    small chunks

1 teaspoon almond extract

1 egg, beaten

FOR TOPPING

1 egg, beaten

48 blanched whole almonds,
    untoasted

TIPS & TOUCHES

* This cookie can be made with
  butter, but the original lard produces a cookie with a more substantial texture and flavor.

WE SEARCHED AND SEARCHED FOR THIS RECIPE *among the many boxes of loose recipes we've been saving for the past 40 years. We found it unexpectedly, a small slip of paper with a few handwritten lines, and the yellowed scrap proved as reliable as when we first tried this recipe many years ago. This is representative of the flaky cookies served as dessert at many of the restaurants in U.S. Chinatowns during the 1950s and 1960s.*

1. Set oven rack in middle position. Preheat oven to 375°F. Cover 14-inch by 16-inch baking sheet with foil, shiny side up. Coat foil with vegetable spray, or use silicone liner.

2. To make cookies: Mix flour, sugar, baking powder, and salt in bowl of food processor fitted with metal blade. Add lard and combine. Sprinkle almond extract over mixture. Add egg and process briefly until all ingredients are blended and dough starts to form. Pull together dough and chill in refrigerator 1 hour, or until firm enough to handle.

3. To add topping: With floured hands or wearing disposable gloves, roll dough into balls $1\frac{1}{4}$ inches in diameter. Place balls on baking sheet and flatten with palm of your hand. Brush tops with beaten egg and place almond in center. Bake 12 minutes, turning baking sheet once after 6 minutes if your oven tends to overbrown. Cool on rack. Store cookies between sheets of parchment paper or wax paper in covered tin.

Bessie's Taglich (Bubbe's Cookies)

{ *1 9 0 8* }

MAKES 55 COOKIES

FOR COOKIES

4 cups flour

2 teaspoons baking powder

1 teaspoon salt

²⁄₃ cup vegetable oil

1 cup sugar

4 eggs

FOR FILLING

½ cup golden raisins

½ cup plum jam

½ cup walnut crumbs

½ cup sweetened
   shredded coconut

FOR HONEY DIP

½ cup honey

THIS IS THE RECIPE FOR BESSIE ROTHBLOTT'S *taglich, a Canadian cookie by way of Poland. These were Bessie's signature cookies. They are a substantial rolled confection filled with golden raisins, plum jam, walnut crumbs, and coconut, baked to a warm brown and then boiled in honey. The slightly sour plum jam balances the sweetness of the coconut and honey.*

1. Set oven rack in middle position. Preheat oven to 375°F. Cover 14-inch by 16-inch baking sheet with foil, shiny side up. Coat foil with vegetable spray, or use silicone liner.

2. To make cookies: Sift together flour, baking powder, and salt.

3. Place oil and sugar in bowl of standing mixer fitted with paddle attachment. Combine until smooth. Add eggs, one at a time, and mix thoroughly. Add sifted dry ingredients in thirds. Batter will begin to form dough. Chill dough in refrigerator 1 hour, or until firm enough to roll out.

4. To make filling: Combine raisins, jam, walnut crumbs, and coconut in bowl. Chill in refrigerator until ready to use.

5. Roll out chilled dough on floured wax paper or parchment paper to thickness slightly less than ³⁄₁₆ inch. Cut 2³⁄₄-inch circles using cookie cutter or biscuit cutter.

⇥ HOW LONG TO CHILL DOUGH ⇤

You may notice that we advise you to chill your dough before rolling out or forming the cookies in this chapter. We've found that several of the doughs we've been using need at least 1 hour in the refrigerator before we can work with them. This doesn't mean that you can't chill the dough for longer than 1 hour or overnight if you don't have time to finish the recipe. Some doughs, like the yeast dough for Dorothy Katziff Brass's Refrigerator Coffee Rolls (page 34), need to be refrigerated overnight.

➤➤ KNOW YOUR OVEN ◄◄

After reading the handwritten recipes in our collection of manuscript cookbooks, we found that there was no mention of how to cope with differing oven temperatures or baking times. The recipe would simply ask for a hot or quick or slow oven. Some very old sources even suggested that you place flour or a piece of paper in your stove to judge the level of heat by how quickly the flour or paper browned. Some brave souls even mentioned placing a hand into the oven and quickly removing it to judge the temperature. We don't recommend doing any of these!

Instead, we ask you to get to know your oven. In order to remove the guesswork from your oven, we suggest you invest in an accurate oven thermometer. If you find that it takes a longer or shorter time for a cookie or pie or cake to brown or to test done when you bake in your own oven, go by your own guidelines. If you need to turn a sheet of cookies or brownies halfway through the baking process to be sure of even browning, do so. If you find the temperature that we suggest is too high or too low to produce the desired finished result in your oven, adjust the recipe accordingly. Remember, you and your stove have an intimate relationship, and no one knows it better than you do.

6. Place $\frac{1}{2}$ teaspoon filling horizontally in center of each dough circle. With floured hands, roll up dough circles toward you, making neat little packages. Using palm of your hand, roll each package toward you 2 or 3 times until it resembles something between rugelach and mini egg roll. Place on baking sheet. Bake 23 to 25 minutes, or until warm brown in color. Place baking sheet on rack to cool.

7. To make honey dip: Coat cooling rack with vegetable spray and set it on top of foil-covered baking sheet. Place honey in heavy metal saucepan, bring to a boil over medium heat, and reduce heat so honey is at a low boil. Dip taglich, two at a time, into honey. Lift out with long-handled tongs and place on cooling rack. Allow to cool. Store loosely covered with wax paper in covered tin.

Nell's Wonderful Peanut Butter Cookies

MAKES 42 COOKIES

{ 1930s }

THIS IS A GREAT SIMPLE RECIPE. THAT'S *all we can say about it. We used tasty salted oil-roasted peanuts. We found that the salt and the oil were essential to this full-flavored treat. We found this recipe jotted on the back of a bridge tally. Dare we say it's a winner?*

1. Set oven rack in middle position. Preheat oven to 350°F. Cover 14-inch by 16-inch baking sheet with foil, shiny side up. Coat foil with vegetable spray, or use silicone liner.
2. Sift together flour, baking soda, and baking powder.
3. Cream butter, brown sugar, sugar, and peanut butter in bowl of standing mixer fitted with paddle attachment. Add egg and mix thoroughly. Add sifted dry ingredients. Fold in peanuts and mini chocolate chips.
4. Chill dough in refrigerator 1 hour, or until it is firm enough to handle. With floured hands or wearing disposable gloves, roll dough into balls about 1 inch in diameter. Place balls on baking sheet 2 inches apart and flatten with bottom of glass dipped in flour. Bake 12 minutes, or until golden brown. Cool on rack. Store between sheets of parchment paper or wax paper in covered tin.

1¼ cups flour

½ teaspoon baking soda

½ teaspoon baking powder

½ cup butter

½ cup brown sugar

½ cup sugar

½ cup smooth peanut butter

1 egg

½ cup broken salted peanuts (not dry-roasted)

½ cup mini chocolate chips

TIPS & TOUCHES

- We've found that using salted and oiled peanuts lends a richness to these cookies that dry-roasted peanuts do not. If you have to use unsalted dry-roasted peanuts, be sure to add ¼ teaspoon salt to the recipe.

Aunt Ida's Poppy Seed Cookies

MAKES 60 COOKIES

3 cups flour

2 teaspoons baking powder

½ cup poppy seeds

1 cup peanut oil

1 cup sugar

3 eggs

1 teaspoon vanilla

THIS WAS OUR AUNT IDA TUCKER KATZIFF's *signature cookie. She baked this cookie for more than 60 years to the delight of 4 generations of our family, transporting the treats to parties in covered tins. We baked these cookies and served them at Aunt Ida's memorial gathering after her funeral since this recipe is a part of her legacy. She always stored her poppy seeds in the freezer to keep them fresh.*

1. Set oven rack in middle position. Preheat oven to 350°F. Cover 14-inch by 16-inch baking sheet with foil, shiny side up. Coat foil with vegetable spray, or use silicone liner.

2. Sift together flour and baking powder and add poppy seeds.

3. Whisk peanut oil, sugar, eggs, and vanilla in medium bowl. Add sifted dry ingredients and mix to combine. Chill dough in refrigerator 1 hour, or until firm enough to handle.

4. With floured hands or wearing disposable gloves, break off teaspoon-size pieces of dough and roll into small balls. Place dough balls on baking sheet about 2 inches apart, or 12 cookies per sheet. Pat into circles with your fingers (rather than rolling or stamping). Bake 10 to 12 minutes, or until lightly browned around edges. Let cookies cool 1 minute on baking sheet on rack and then transfer cookies to rack. Cookies will become crisp as they cool. Store between sheets of wax paper in covered tin or freeze in tightly sealed plastic bag or container.

Green Depression glass and tin measuring cup beater, 1930s

Donna's Ginger Snaps

MAKES 48 COOKIES

{ *1940s* }

THESE CRISPY COOKIES ARE THE BEST GINGER *snaps we've tasted in a long time. We found this cookie recipe handwritten in a copy of* Laboratory Recipes *owned by Rachel W. Banks. This edition also contained the handwritten recipe for One, Two, Three Open-Faced Blueberry Pie (page 322). Thank you, Donna. You should be proud.*

1. Set oven rack in middle position. Preheat oven to 350°F. Cover 14-inch by 16-inch baking sheet with foil, shiny side up. Coat foil with vegetable spray, or use silicone liner.

2. Sift together flour, ginger, nutmeg, cinnamon, baking soda, and salt.

3. Cream butter and sugar in bowl of standing mixer fitted with paddle attachment. Add egg. Beat in molasses and jam or marmalade. Add sifted dry ingredients gradually until well blended.

4. Wrap dough in plastic wrap and chill in refrigerator for 1 hour, or until firm enough to handle. With floured hands or wearing disposable gloves, break off 1½ teaspoons of dough and roll into ball. Continue until all dough is rolled. Roll balls in sugar and place on baking sheet, spaced at least 1½ inches apart, or 12 cookies per sheet, to allow for spreading during baking. Bake 14 minutes, or until golden brown. Cool on baking sheet on rack. Cookies will firm up when cool. Store between sheets of parchment paper or wax paper in covered tin.

2 cups flour

2 teaspoons ginger

1 teaspoon nutmeg

1 teaspoon cinnamon

2 teaspoons baking soda

½ teaspoon salt

¾ cup butter

1 cup sugar

1 egg

¼ cup molasses

¼ cup ginger jam or bitter orange marmalade

¾ cup sugar (for rolling cookies)

 TIPS & TOUCHES

- We confess. We added the ginger jam or the marmalade because we wanted to add a little more texture and depth to the cookies. If you don't have ginger jam or marmalade in your pantry, the grated zest of an orange will add extra zing.

Maple Syrup Cookie Sandwiches with Lemon Cream Filling

MAKES 60 COOKIES OR 30 FILLED SANDWICHES

FOR COOKIES

2 cups flour

½ teaspoon salt

½ teaspoon baking soda

1 cup maple syrup or cane syrup

½ cup butter

1 egg

2 teaspoons maple extract (optional)

FOR LEMON CREAM FILLING

2 cups confectioners' sugar

⅛ teaspoon salt

½ cup butter

3 teaspoons grated lemon zest

4 teaspoons lemon juice

TIPS & TOUCHES

• When we first tested this recipe, the cookies had a very subtle maple taste. The maple syrup gives these cookies their delicate texture. We decided they really needed to taste more "maple-y," so we added the maple extract.

WE WERE THRILLED TO FIND THIS HANDWRITTEN *recipe for cookies made with maple syrup. We liked them so much, we decided to pair them with a lemon cream filling, creating the gustatory opportunity to take them apart, lick the lemon cream, and eat the cookies slowly to make them last. We found that it is easier to use a pastry bag to pipe and fill these cookies to ensure that they are uniform in size and shape.*

1. Set oven rack in middle position. Preheat oven to 350°F. Cover 14-inch by 16-inch baking sheet with foil, shiny side up. Coat foil with vegetable spray, or use silicone liner.

2. To make cookies: Sift together flour, salt, and baking soda.

3. Mix maple or cane syrup and butter in bowl of standing mixer fitted with paddle attachment. Add egg and mix to combine. Gradually beat in sifted dry ingredients until batter becomes smooth. Add maple extract, if desired.

4. Chill batter in refrigerator until firm enough to pipe with pastry bag. Fit pastry bag with plain Ateco #804 metal tip and fill bag with batter. Pipe cookies onto baking sheet, making each cookie about 1½ inches in diameter and allowing no more than 20 cookies per sheet. Bake 18 minutes, or until golden brown. Place baking sheet on rack. Let rest 2 minutes, then carefully transfer cookies from baking sheet to rack. Cookies will crisp upon standing.

5. To make lemon cream filling: Sift confectioners' sugar and salt into small bowl. Add butter and combine. Whisk in lemon zest and lemon juice. Fit pastry bag with Ateco #806 metal tip and fill with lemon cream. Pipe generous squiggle of filling on half of cookies. Place remaining cookies on top of filling and press together gently, sandwiching the cream in between. Store cookies between sheets of wax paper in covered tin in refrigerator. Remove from refrigerator no more than 10 minutes before serving. This buttery filling will melt at room temperature.

Brown Sugar Macaroons

{ 1 9 3 0 s }

MAKES 45 MACAROONS

2 egg whites

2 cups brown sugar

2 cups chopped salted pecans

⅛ teaspoon salt (optional; use if
   pecans are unsalted)

TIPS & TOUCHES

- We left the batter for the macaroons in the refrigerator overnight
  and found that the next day it
  produced cookies that were
  just as good. This is a real help
  if you're too busy to make the
  whole recipe the day you put
  them together.

THIS RECIPE IS ONE WE HOLD DEAR *because it was the first living recipe we ever tried. We found it handwritten in a 1926 copy of* Laboratory Recipes *by Harriet Folger, prepared for the School of Domestic Science of the Boston YWCA. This copy of the book is the source of several wonderful recipes we've used over the years.*

1. Set oven rack in middle position. Preheat oven to 350°F. Cover 14-inch by 16-inch baking sheet with foil, shiny side up. Coat foil with vegetable spray, or use silicone liner.

2. Place egg whites in bowl of standing mixer fitted with whisk attachment. Beat to form stiff peaks. Slowly fold in brown sugar and pecans. The egg whites will deflate, causing the mixture to become pastelike. Add salt if needed.

3. Drop walnut-sized pieces of mixture from teaspoon onto baking sheet, spaced 1 inch apart. Bake 20 minutes, or until pale brown. Cool on rack. When completely cool, remove from rack. Store between sheets of parchment paper or wax paper in covered tin.

Tin cookie cutters in multiple shapes, 1920s; in shape of numbers, 1950s

Marmalade Cookies

{ 1 9 0 0 s }

THIS RECIPE WAS PRINTED ON A PIECE *of yellowed newspaper found in a manuscript cookbook that spanned the early 1900s to the 1960s. The recipe called for orange marmalade, but you can use any flavor of good commercial marmalade. The cookies have an almost meringuelike taste. They are more like teacakes than cookies because they are soft and delicate and never become crisp. These cookies do not disappoint.*

1. Set oven rack in middle position. Preheat oven to 350°F. Cover 14-inch by 16-inch baking sheet with foil, shiny side up. Coat foil with vegetable spray, or use silicone liner.

2. Sift together flour, salt, and baking soda.

3. Cream butter and sugar in bowl of standing mixer fitted with paddle attachment. Add eggs and vanilla. Add sifted dry ingredients and combine. Add marmalade. Let dough rest 5 to 10 minutes in refrigerator.

4. Drop dough by teaspoons on baking sheet, about 2 inches apart. (These cookies do not spread.) Bake 15 minutes, turning baking sheet once after 7 minutes, until cookies are lightly browned.

5. Place baking sheet on rack and let cool 2 minutes. Transfer cookies to another rack and cool completely. Cookies will become firmer as they cool. Store between sheets of wax paper in covered tin.

3 cups cake flour

½ teaspoon salt

½ teaspoon baking soda

½ cup butter

1 cup sugar

2 eggs, beaten

1 teaspoon vanilla

¾ cup marmalade

TIPS & TOUCHES

- This dough will handle more easily if you keep it chilled until ready to bake. Also, keep sheets of unbaked cookies in the refrigerator until they are ready to go into the oven.

Libby's Coconut Washboards

MAKES 78 COOKIES

THIS RECIPE WAS GIVEN TO US AS *part of a collection of handwritten recipes belonging to Elizabeth Corkery, of Groton, Massachusetts. Her recipes span the 1920s through the 1970s. Be sure to use a dinner fork, not a salad fork, to make the washboards because the tines of the salad fork are too short to do a good job.*

1. Set oven rack in middle position. Preheat oven to 375°F. Cover 14-inch by 16-inch baking sheet with foil, shiny side up. Coat foil with vegetable spray, or use silicone liner.

2. Place coconut in bowl of food processor fitted with metal blade. Pulse 2 or 3 times until coconut flakes are reduced in length. (Be careful not to reduce coconut flakes to coconut dust.)

3. Sift together flour, baking powder, nutmeg, and salt.

4. Place butter and brown sugar in bowl of standing mixer fitted with paddle attachment. Cream gradually until light and fluffy. Add egg, vanilla, and almond extract. Add sifted dry ingredients, blending well. Fold in coconut.

5. Divide dough in half, cover with plastic wrap, and chill in refrigerator 1 hour, or until firm enough to handle. Place dough on floured pastry board or floured parchment paper. Spread or pat each piece into rectangle 8 inches by 12 inches by $\frac{3}{16}$ inch thick. Cut each piece lengthwise into quarters. Cut these sections into 1-inch pieces.

6. Press floured dinner fork onto each piece of dough to form washboard. (Dough will become even thinner when made into washboards.) Place washboards on baking sheet. Bake 8 minutes, or until golden brown. Cool on baking sheet on rack. Store between sheets of parchment paper or wax paper in covered tin.

1 (17-ounce) package (1⅓ cups) sweetened shredded coconut

2 cups flour

¾ teaspoon baking powder

¼ teaspoon nutmeg

⅛ teaspoon salt

¾ cup butter

1 cup brown sugar

1 egg

1 teaspoon vanilla

½ teaspoon almond extract

TIPS & TOUCHES

- It's really important to shorten the shreds of the coconut in a food processor. It's much harder to cut the cookie dough when the flakes are longer.

Sources

INGREDIENTS AND EQUIPMENT

The Baker's Catalogue (King Arthur Flour)
800-827-6836
bakerscatalogue.com
Grains, ingredients, equipment

Bob's Red Mill Natural Foods
800-349-2173
bobsredmill.com
Flours, grains

Christina's Homemade Ice Cream
Spice & Specialty Foods
1255 Cambridge Street
Cambridge, MA 02139
617-492-7021
Spices, extracts, flours, chocolate

Formaggio Kitchen
244 Huron Avenue
Cambridge, MA 02138
888-212-3224
formaggiokitchen.com
info@formaggiokitchen.com
Specialty foods, baking supplies

Nordic Ware
877-466-7342
nordicware.com
Cooking and baking equipment

Penzey's Spices
800-741-7787
penzeys.com
Spices, extracts

Sparrow Enterprises, Ltd.
855-532-5552
chocolatebysparrow.com
info@sparrowfoods.com
Chocolate, sanding sugar

Sur la Table
800-243-0852
surlatable.com
Cooking and baking supplies, equipment

The Vermont Country Store
vermontcountrystore.com
888-298-8162
Common Crackers

Williams-Sonoma
877-812-6235
williams-sonoma.com
Cooking and baking supplies, equipment

Zabar's
2245 Broadway
(at 80th Street)
New York, NY 10024
212-496-1234
zabars.com
info@zabars.com
Kosher cheese

BOOK DEALERS SPECIALIZING IN COOKBOOKS AND MANUSCRIPT COOKBOOKS

B. & S. Gventer Books & Ephemera
Bruce Gventer
P.O. Box 298
South Egremont, MA 02158-0298
413-528-2327
bgventer@bookfairs.com

Bonnie Slotnick Cookbooks
163 West Tenth Street
New York, NY 10014-3116
212-989-8962
bonnieslotnickcookbooks.com

Cooks Books
T. & M. McKirdy
34 Marine Drive
Rottingdean
Sussex BN2 7HQ UK
01273 302707

Kitchen Arts & Letters
Nach Waxman
1435 Lexington Avenue
New York, NY 10128
212-876-5550
kitchenartsandletters.com

The Reynolds
352 Front Street
Bath, ME 04530-2749
203-443-8812
oldeport@TTLC.net

Bibliography

Carlisle, Mrs. John G. *Kentucky Cookbook.* Chicago: F. Tennyson Neely, Publisher, 1893.

Editors of *Cook's Illustrated* Magazine. *The Best Recipe.* Brookline: Boston Common Press, 1999.

King, Caroline. *Victorian Cakes.* Berkeley: Harris Publishing Company, Inc., 1986.

Malgieri, Nick. *Chocolate.* New York: HarperCollins Publishers, Inc., 1998.

Malgieri, Nick. *Cookies Unlimited.* New York: HarperCollins Publishers, Inc., 2000.

Nathan, Joan. *Jewish Cooking in America.* New York: Alfred A. Knopf, 1994.

Oliver, Sandra. *Saltwater Foodways: New Englanders and Their Food, at Sea and Ashore, in the Nineteenth Century.* Mystic: Mystic Seaport Museum, Inc., 1995.

Patten, Marguerite. *We'll Eat Again: A Collection of Recipes from the War Years.* London: Hamlyn Food & Drink Series, 2004.

Rodgers, Rick. *Kaffeehaus.* New York: Clarkson Potter, 2002.

Rombauer, Irma S., and Marion Rombauer Becker. *Joy of Cooking.* Indianapolis: The Bobbs-Merrill Company, Inc., 1967.

Rombauer, Irma S., Marion Rombauer Becker, and Ethan Becker. *The All New All Purpose Joy of Cooking.* New York: Scribner, 1997.

Sax, Richard. *Classic Home Desserts: A Treasury of Heirloom and Contemporary Recipes from around the World.* Chapters Publishing Ltd., 1994.

Tighe, Eileen, editor. *Woman's Day Encyclopedia of Cookery.* New York: Fawcett Publications, Inc., 1966.

Williams, Richard L. *Foods of the World.* New York: Time-Life Books, 1971.

Conversion Chart

WEIGHT

I ounce	28 grams
1/4 pound	114 grams
I pound	454 grams
2.2 pounds	I kilogram

VOLUME

I teaspoon	5 milliliters
I tablespoon	15 milliliters
1/8 cup	30 milliliters
1/4 cup	60 milliliters
1/2 cup	120 milliliters
I cup	240 milliliters (1/4 liter)
I pint	480 milliliters
I quart	I liter
I gallon	3 3/4 liters

LENGTH

I inch	2 1/2 centimeters (25 millimeters)
12 inches	30 centimeters

OVEN TEMPERATURE

FAHRENHEIT	CENTIGRADE
212°F	100°C
225°F	107°C
250°F	121°C
275°F	135°C
300°F	149°C
325°F	163°C
350°F	177°C
375°F	191°C
400°F	204°C
425°F	218°C
450°F	232°C
475°F	246°C
500°F	260°C
525°F	274°C
550°F	288°C

SELECTED CONVERSIONS

BUTTER

I teaspoon	5 grams
I tablespoon	15 grams
1/2 cup (I stick)	115 grams
I cup (2 sticks)	230 grams
2 cups (4 sticks)	454 grams

FLOUR

I teaspoon	3 grams
I tablespoon	9 grams
I cup	120 grams

NUTS (CHOPPED)

I cup	155 grams

SUGAR (REGULAR GRANULATED)

I teaspoon	5 grams
I tablespoon	15 grams
I cup	185 grams

CONFECTIONERS' SUGAR

I teaspoon	4 grams
I tablespoon	9 grams
I cup	100 grams

Index

Boldface page numbers indicate photographs. <u>Underscored</u> references indicate boxed text.

Pickles.
cork tightly and
green tomatoes whole
small cucumbers whole
piece
to makes

Swedish Meat Balls.

1½ lbs. Veal - ground (Times)
3/4 Lb. Pork "
1 Onion chopped Very fine
3/4 Cup light Cream   ¾ Cup Cracker
2 Tablespoons flour
Crumbs savory 3/4 teaspoon Salt, pepper, pinch summer
Nutmeg. Mix all
ingredients together. form into small
Balls. Should make 40 or more. Brown
When all Meat Balls
Cup white Wine
Rinse out

MOUSSE   Serves
gelatin
lemon juice
on
chp'd
ing water
seconds)
mayonaise
Salmon
paprika
cayenne pepper
+ ½ tbs dill weed
or 2 tbs fresh

Here's what's cookin':
German Stollen
Serves
3/4 cup raisins
½ cup chopped mixed fruit & peel
cup currants
cup rum
3¾ cups flour
dry yeast
milk)
butter or margarine
sugar
grated o

kissin' wears out
cookin' don't
Recipe from the
kitchen of

From

My Recipes

Welsh Rarebit
2 tables butter
2 " cornstar...
2 teas dry musta...
1 teas salt.
a little red pepp...
2 c milk hea...
grated o...
...every thin...
is m...

...quash Pie
...and lifted squash, ...
...alt, 1 cup ...
...ffe each, 1 cup boiling milk 2...
each, 1 cupful... cinnam...

Sauerbraten
...round round steak
...vinegar
...water
...eaves
...whole clo...
...whole al...
...salt
...pepper...
...sli...

1 kernel o...

...Paté
NE ULRICH SUTT...
Tel. BO 9-4800
TE 8-8448
Date_____

...hicken livers in
...butter.
...in coarse pulp
...til no longer pink
...p chopped onion +
...cook 1 minute
...t fire +
...chopped sweet pickle
...butter

stock (?)
...up sugar
...tter to the
...he cloves,
...ot, the 1/2 teas...
...meal o...
...t salt. C...
...dd 1 yeast. +
Let raise over...

Strama...
Pint of flo...
2 tsp. yea...
1 cup of m...
Roll ou...
Quarter...
squa...